Robert Lacey was educated at Bristol Grammar School and Selwyn College, Cambridge. He began his writing career with acclaimed biographies of the Elizabethan heroes Robert, Earl of Essex, and Sir Walter Ralegh. At that time he was also a journalist and editor on the *Sunday Times*. With the success of *Majesty* in 1977, he became a full-time writer, producing a string of international bestsellers: *The Kingdom: Arabia and the House of Saud*, *Ford: The Men and the Machine*, *Grace* and, most recently, his co-authored account of life in England at the turn of the first millennium, *The Year 1000*. A father of three, Robert lives in London with his wife Sandi and younger son Bruno.

D1166215

Sotheby's — Bidding for Class

ROBERT LACEY

sphere

SPHERE

First published in Great Britain in 1998
by Little, Brown and Company
This edition published in 1999 by Warner Books
Reprinted 2000, 2002
Reprinted by Sphere in 2009, 2010

A CIP catalogue record for this book
is available from the British Library.

ISBN 978-0-7515-2362-1

Book design by Julia Sedykh
Map by Fred van Deelen

Sphere
An imprint of
Little, Brown Book Group
100 Victoria Embankment
London EC4Y 0DY

An Hachette UK Company
www.hachette.co.uk

www.littlebrown.co.uk

FOR BILL PHILLIPS

Editor in Chief

CONTENTS

CONTENTS

Sotheby's — Bidding for Class

PROLOGUE: PROPERTY OF A LADY

IT IS A JOB REQUIREMENT of auction house experts to keep a dinner jacket and black tie on the back of their office door. Private views and cocktail parties come straight after work — so at 6:00 P.M. one brisk April evening in 1996, every lavatory and spare corner of Sotheby's, New York, was alive with staff slithering into their smart evening outfits.

It was still light outside, and the auction house had decked the sidewalks around its Manhattan headquarters with canvas. To judge from the throngs of elegantly suited people milling around the tents with invitations in their hands, there could be a wedding in the offing.

In fact, it was that other ritual of spring, the rummage sale. Sotheby's, Inc., "Founded 1744," was preparing to auction the effects of Mrs. Jacqueline Kennedy Onassis — 5,914 items ranging from her cigarette lighter to her BMW. The selling would start tomorrow, but first came the "Private View," the chance to view the goods and be tempted into folly.

The successful art auction house presents itself as a temple of civilised style and judgement, but its essential function is to uncivilise the judgement of at least two normally balanced people and entice them to bid and counter-bid for any given object as far as possible above the price it would command in a shop. The appeal is to cupidity and recklessness. The trick is to persuade people who already possess more than their fair share of worldly goods that their happiness depends on acquiring even more, and the heirs of Jacqueline Kennedy Onassis had called in Sotheby's as masters of this game. The auction house has spent a profitable 250 years cultivating the paradox that rich people, at heart, are the neediest people of all.

Voyeurism battled with reverence as the guests filed past the relics, desperate to touch the sacred objects, but knowing there were niceties to observe. These were tokens of America's royalty, after all — the President's golf clubs, the desk where he signed the test-ban treaty, the children's high chair and rocking horse, and the massive diamond which Aristotle Onassis gave the widow for that troubling but defining second marriage. Auctioneers are like undertakers. They offer rituals to help us through life's less happy practicalities — and the two trades frequently operate in tandem: bury the body, then lay out the goods for sale.

"Were those pillows all together like that in the apartment?" asked one visitor anxiously, pointing at two cushions stuffed together on quite a narrow chair.

The Sotheby's expert said he thought he could recall them sitting originally at either end of a longish sofa.

"Oh, good," said the woman, relieved, "then I don't have to go home and try squeezing two pillows into all my single chairs."

These browsers were in search of magic — if those pillows were part of the widow's appeal, then perhaps that appeal might rub off on she who bought — so the various lifestyles of Jackie had been laid out and labelled: Manhattanite Jackie; country, horse-riding Jackie; book-loving Jackie; Jackie, Queen of the White House; and Jackie, Greek trophy wife — a section characterised by chunky gold bangles and fiercely gemmed monsters from the sea.

At a routine, house-clearing auction, all these things would have been thrown together in a jumble. But this is Sotheby's, so the experts had been set to work. Now standing at their stations, learned and loquacious, and just a little oily, they had a salesman's story to tell about each of the lots that fell within their particular expertise: Old Master Paintings, Porcelain, Fashion Jewelry, Contemporary Art.

Experts of still more perfumed oiliness were gliding among the crowds — the staff of Sotheby's Client Advisory Services, high-gloss and lissome young creatures, mainly female, and unfailingly silver-tongued. Client Advisory is an ancient department that was greatly expanded following the takeover of Sotheby's by Alfred Taubman, the Michigan shopping mall magnate. It was part of his revamping of the venerable London auction house, and under his aegis Client Advisory has developed into a smooth and faintly sinister organisation, whose job is to hook new bidders and reel them in. For months before the Kennedy sale, its salespeople had been working the phones, winnowing out the cranks and encouraging the buyers who sounded as if they might be serious.

"What level were you thinking of bidding to? . . . Well, there *has* been a big demand for tickets, but let me see what I can do."

Having carried out their credit checks, Client Advisory were using this preview evening to prep the big spenders they had enticed from every corner of North America. Courting potential art buyers has a long and dishonourable history. Lord Duveen, the great dealer of the twenties and thirties, would rummage through clients' wastepaper baskets, bribe servants for tip-offs, and, on one occasion, even supplied two orphaned little Japanese boys to satisfy the sexual whim of a buyer.

Sotheby's Client Advisory is quite tame by these standards, only managing some bed-and-breakfast payola: if newcomers happen to ask where they can stay in New York, Client Advisory mentions the Carlyle — and the Carlyle returns the compliment with an automatic dial button on every room telephone that gets you straight through to Sotheby's.

Dr. Ruth Westheimer, the sex guru of talk radio, was being shepherded round by someone from Client Advisory who was evidently doing a good job.

"Thank you, my dear," said the minuscule doctor, smiling up at her youthful mentor. "I can tell that you are going to enjoy a long and active sex life."

The question everyone seemed to be asking was what the Kennedy children had *not* offered for sale. If these were the things they were getting rid of, what treasures and keepsakes could possibly have remained? But this was a subject on which the normally informative Sotheby's staff would fall silent, for though an auction house cultivates the impression that it is the buyer's best friend, its contract is actually with the seller, and it was one of the conditions of the Kennedy contract that Sotheby's allow no leaks as to what the children chose to keep for themselves.

"For our mother," wrote John and Caroline in their foreword to the catalogue, "history came alive through objects and paintings, as well as books. . . . As they go out into the world, we hope that they bring with them not only their own beauty and spirit, but some of hers as well."

What these objects would bring to the Kennedys, of course, was money. That is the American way. The Egyptians took their goods to their graves with them. The great dynasties of Britain and Europe try to keep things in the family so long as there is something in the bank. But Americans prefer to turn it into cash and start anew. They are less sentimental about these things.

*   *   *

The sentiment was all on the buying side, it became clear, when the auction opened the following night, on the evening of Tuesday, April 23, 1996. It is an almost physical sensation, the hiss through the air of other people's money being spent. A busy auction room smells of cash, greed, and folly in roughly similar proportions. Part Wall Street, the opening session of the great Jackie sale was also part Night at the Opera, since, once again, the entire Sotheby's work force had decamped to the lavatories, to reappear in evening dress. The long-legged ladies of Client Advisory looked particularly succulent as they welcomed arrivals at the head of the stairs.

"Are you one of the lots?" asked an older gentleman, frail on his wife's arm, but obviously delighted finally to be meeting his Client Advisor in person.

"No, she's not," snapped his wife. "And if she is, she's not for you."

Bidders collected their paddles from the registration desk. Normally these are just what they sound — plastic bats that bear a three digit bidding number — but with over two thousand bidders already registered, Sotheby's had had to break out another digit, and the numbers had been printed on white cardboard strips like car registration plates.

"Thirteen sixty-eight!" exclaimed Joan Rivers, picking up her paddle with delight. "The year I was born!"

Lee Iacocca was in the room, but there were few other celebrities on display. The truly rich and famous preferred to bid by phone. "It's just hell getting hold of Arnie!" gasped the Old Masters expert who had been designated to relay the Schwarzenegger bids from Los Angeles, where the action hero was shooting his latest movie.

The phone bids were taken by the tuxedoed Sotheby's staff, boxed together like two juries of penguins on either side of the auctioneer, and on this night the auction box was filled by the resplendent figure of Sotheby's president and chief executive officer, Mrs. Diana D. Brooks, brash and blonde, and very much in charge. For the last few days Mrs. Brooks had been appearing in a succession of bright, almost fluorescent outfits, evidently designed to look good on television.

"Rather like the queen," remarked one visitor brightly.

"Humph," sniffed one of her loyal staff. "Try Mrs. Thatcher."

Mrs. Brooks rose to the top through the finance and corporate side of Sotheby's. She has never worked on the expert side and had still to master the deceptively simple technique of being an auctioneer. She was to lose her footing several times in the course of the Kennedy sale, yet no one could suppress the excitement of this crowd.

Lot 10 was a small, stained, wooden footstool which Sotheby's furniture department had estimated to be American, nineteenth century, of marginal value in ordinary circumstances; $100 and $150 were the figures printed in the catalogue as the auction house's low and high estimates on the item, but the little stool happened to bear on its underside a label in Jackie's own handwriting which read "Footstool JBK bedroom in White House for Caroline to climb onto window seat," and Mrs. Brooks announced that the house had already received more than two hundred absentee, or "Commission," bids on the stool.

When an auctioneer stands in his pulpit, the bible from which he takes his text is the auctioneer's "book" — once upon a time a leather-bound ledger, now, more usually, a loose-leaf ring-binder in which the details of each lot are set down. Written beside the catalogue entry is the "reserve," the secret price which auctioneer and seller have fixed as the minimum they will accept, and because it is secret, the reserve is usually entered in the book in a private, house code — DOJUSTICE, for example, representing the numerals 1–9, with X added to represent 0: thus a price of $550 would be entered in the book as SSX.

Also inscribed is an indication of the commission bids that have been sent in by bidders who cannot attend the sale, and

Sotheby's had received so many on baby Caroline's footstool that Mrs. Brooks ignored the catalogue estimates and plucked from her book a commission bid of $5,000, inviting someone in the room to do better.

There was no shortage of takers: $5,000, $5,500, $6,000, $6,500 — the bidding was up to $10,000 in no time, at which point the increments widened to $1,000 per bid. One of the Sotheby's jury box penguins was waving hard on behalf of a bidder on the telephone, and Mrs. Brooks played him off against the gestures of a serious-looking matron in one of the front rows. The lady could have been Caroline's nanny from the intensity with which she obviously wanted that stool.

There comes a point in the finest bidding contests when money ceases to be the main issue. The battle becomes a matter of appetite and ego — sheer desire — the moment for which the auction house lives. Reason is suspended. The adrenalin pumps. The entire room is caught up in the nakedness of need and nerve — and this point was reached when the nanny in the front row bid $20,000 for baby Caroline's $150 stool.

Now the rival bids were a mantra, with Mrs. Brooks the high priestess maintaining the chant. Could the nanny even hear the figures to which she was nodding her assent? $22,000, $24,000, $26,000 — the anonymous telephone bidder kept up their own pace to $29,000, when suddenly the nanny stepped out of the spell.

"Do I have $30,000?" coaxed Mrs. Brooks, leaning over the rostrum in an inviting fashion.

But $30,000 was clearly, suddenly, much too much. Reason had returned, and it was the telephone bidder who won the day — though the final bid of $29,000 grew to a total purchase price of $33,500, after the addition of the 15 percent buyer's premium, Sotheby's direct cut on the deal.

"Provenance," the technical art world expression for the origins and details of an object's previous ownership, was the catch phrase onto which reporters latched to explain the gap between $150 and $33,350 — the intrinsic worth of an object, and the price to which it can be stretched when garnished with nostalgia, glamour, and a generous helping of auction fever.

Publicity was the other P-word. The designer who bought Jackie's silver tape measure immediately made sure that his name was known to the press, as did the purchaser of the cigar humidor: "To J.F.K. — Good Health — Good Smoking — Milton Berle — 1/20/61."

Valued at $2,000 to $2,500, this small walnut box was the last lot of evening one, and after a bitter battle it was won by Marvin Schanken, the publisher of *Cigar Aficionado* magazine; $574,500 the poorer, Mr. Schanken jumped up from his seat, lit up a cigar, and was besieged by cameras, lights, and microphones as he delivered an instant press conference — though the value of this frenzied attention was somewhat mitigated by the interviewers who reported the title of his paper as *Cigar and Fishing* magazine.

The best part of 6,000 objects cannot be sold in a single Tuesday evening, even when they are grouped in 1,301 lots, so through the rest of the week, Sotheby's had scheduled eight further sales. The sessions ran through, with scarcely a break, at ten A.M., two P.M., and six P.M. every day, with the auctioneers working in shifts, and on the morning of Wednesday, April 24, it fell to Henry Wyndham, chairman of Sotheby's, London, to climb into the auction box to find out whether the hysteria of the opening night was a flash in the pan.

Wyndham learned his trade at the rival auction house of Christie's, a name mentioned at Sotheby's as infrequently as possible (and vice versa). His dry, brisk style goes back to the roots of English high-society auctioneering. Immensely tall and mildly unctuous, Wyndham peered out anxiously from the rostrum like a country curate in a Jane Austen novel, but with this congregation he had nothing to fear. The opening lot, a collection of breakfast cups and saucers, "some repairs and imperfections," sold for $8,050, while fourteen dusty old baskets brought $9,200.

"Your last chance of a cocktail," chortled Wyndham, as he knocked down a $200 plated cocktail shaker for $20,000.

Next morning the prices were still more extraordinary, as a $100 necklace of fake pearls went for $211,500. If one revelation of this sale was that Mrs. Onassis was a secret smoker, another was that much of her jewelry was fake. The catalogue described how she actually got Kenneth Jay Lane to make a paste copy of a Van Cleef & Arpels necklace, and wore the replica, considering this a huge joke.

"She was a woman who added style to jewels," explained John Block, Sotheby's jewelry king, "rather than wearing jewels to add style to her."

This is the auction house rationalization of offering fake jewelry for sale. You could draw the moral that you do not need to spend money to demonstrate class, but this was not the lesson drawn by Mrs. Kennedy's disciples at Sotheby's. They made furious bids on the plastic facsimiles, and the Kenneth Jay Lane imitation necklace — a glass concoction available on the TV shopping channel for a few hundred dollars — went for $90,500.

By Thursday night, when the golf clubs came up for sale, even the auction house was allowing itself discreet merriment at the folly it had engendered. "These will definitely improve your game," announced William Stahl, Executive Vice President, Americana, unsuccessfully trying to keep a straight face as he presided over bidding that took the dead President's irons to $387,500 and his woods to $772,500, including the 15 percent buyer's premium.

It takes two bidders to make a crazy price, and since no one was yet aware that the winner of the woods was Arnold Schwarzenegger, who had been bidding over the phone via the Old Masters expert, the cameras and lights converged on the man in the room who had bid over $700,000 before he dropped out. This underbidder turned out to be a Long Island businessman, just hitting his fifties, who remembered being in high school when Kennedy was shot, and who was clearly still moved by those memories of hope, and of hope frustrated.

"We were young. He was young. He was *our* president."

Next morning he came into the ten o'clock sale with his wife and paid $123,500 to secure Lot 818, the very first of the day, a book of inaugural presidential addresses, from Washington to JFK, inscribed by Jacqueline Kennedy to her mother and step-father a few days after her husband's death: "for Mummy and Uncle Hugh. Jack was going to give you this for Christmas — Please accept it now from me — With all my love, Jackie, December 1963."

The psychoanalytical explanation of compulsive collecting is that it goes back to childhood. Babies reach out for objects — a blanket, a beloved doll, or perhaps a teddy bear — according to the American psychologist Dr. Werner Muensterberger, "to undo the trauma of loneliness when the infant discovers mother's absence." Collecting grows from this to become "a more or less perpetual attempt to surround oneself with magically potent objects," these objects helping to shape the collector's sense of identity and self-esteem.

This made very good sense of the bidders gathered at Sotheby's in almost religious compulsion. Fiftyish to a man, with just a few women, they clearly wanted to recapture something they felt they had lost. They all said it more or less explicitly when the cameras encircled them. They were revelling in the purchasing power which gave them the ability to snap up these talismen of their youth — and to be children once again. As Dr. Muensterberger put it: "What else are collectibles but toys that grown-ups take seriously?"

*   *   *

At 6:28 P.M. on the evening of Friday, April 26, Mrs. Brooks took the final bid on the final lot — $70,000 for the 1992 BMW 325i (book price $18,000–$22,000) — and the room went flat, collapsing in mutual exhaustion. The end had come as a sort of exorcism, and people lingered round their seats, unwilling to admit it was all over and to walk outside into the rain.

Mrs. Brooks picked up the microphone to trot out the statistics in weary triumph. A total of 104,611 catalogues were sold for $5.82 million (profits to charity), and all 1,301 lots sold for a total of $34.5 million, which, the saleroom correspondents calculated, probably yielded an operating profit to Sotheby's of around $4 million. The highest price was commanded by Ari's massive engagement diamond ($2.59 million), the lowest by six books about Asia ($1,250). The news that it was Arnie who paid three quarters of a million dollars for the golf clubs was greeted with a ragged cheer. There were 566 successful buyers, which meant that many people bought more than one thing — and 518 of those buyers were American.

But the most promising statistic from Sotheby's point of view was that no less than 415 of the buyers had never bought at Sotheby's before. Client Advisory had done a good job. John Block's jewelry department now had the names, addresses, and bank details of nearly one hundred people who had laid down $20,000 or more on fake gems. These buyers could certainly count on receiving the catalogue of the next jewelry sale — and if they bid on Jackie's things with any seriousness, they would probably get a call wondering if they would not, perhaps, care to come in one day to the boardroom and view the contents of some future sale over lunch.

Auctions are all about loot and hope. They are fundamentally larcenous rituals, with buyers hoping to steal a bargain, while sellers hope to extort a ridiculous price. It is the auctioneers' job to glide between these two irreconcilable illusions, extracting their own commission through the creation of magic and their ability to suspend disbelief. Encouraging both sides in their contradictory expectations, the auctioneer must be all things to all men — part confidant, part confidence trickster — and it is small wonder that suspicions of guile and sharp practice wreath auction house reputations to this day. Auctioneers are the high-end hucksters of the consumer culture, wizards who can turn the remnants of death into a celebration, and can even shape the bitterness of divorce and financial disaster into a profitable fête.

It is their particular skill to conjure money out of aspiration. Kennedy memorabilia was bought and sold long before Sotheby's staged the great Jackie sale. The Heritage Collectors' Gallery of Bucks County, Pennsylvania, has been dealing in investment-quality historical documents for many years, and had a signed, typewritten copy of a JFK speech on sale at the time of Sotheby's auction. One month later the speech was still for sale at $7,500 — though it would have sold in a minute for $25,000 or more if Sotheby's had put it on the block in New York.

After the sale, people spoke of the "Jackie factor." The difference between $7,500 (still for sale) and $25,000 (sold) reflected the "Sotheby's factor"— the stage management that added value in its own right. Searching through Mrs. Onassis's jewel boxes, a Sotheby's expert unearthed eleven minuscule diamonds, small, light, and undistinguished, worth no more than $50 each. They might have fallen off a larger piece. Perhaps they were intended as trimming to a necklace or bracelet clasp — and certainly nobody knew if the lady herself ever touched them or even knew of their existence.

But Sotheby's took the eleven little stones, arranged them in the shape of a "J" on black velvet, and offered them as Lot 441, sandwiched between Lot 440, a Van Cleef & Arpels ruby and diamond ring, and Lot 442, a classic and lavish Van Cleef necklace, both gifts to the new bride from her admiring Greek. The little "J" of $50 diamonds went for $17,250.

All's fair in love and auctioneering. Rearranging eleven

anonymous diamonds into the shape of a "J" might strike some people as sharp practice, but its artfulness is the essence of the auction biz — the conversion of debris into dreams. When the heirs of a modern American goddess wanted the best price for her bric-à-brac, where else should they turn but to Sotheby's?

It is the assumption of most people today that they can be defined by their material possessions. Fine things display a fine person. Well-chosen goods have become the badges of modern accomplishment, and what was once the hallmark of a small ruling elite has become the preoccupation of a growing multitude. As wealth has spread, so has the need to display it. Purchasing power has been directed towards the acquisition of paintings, furniture, old books, jewelry, and the other objects which society decrees to be tokens of taste and style, and it is the purpose of this book to describe how one English auction house first cottoned on to this business, then exploited it and developed it wider. *By their bids ye shall know them. . . .*

When people buy at Sotheby's, they are seeking to satisfy a variety of needs. They may explain their motives in terms of taste, or history or sentiment, but they are laying out their money fundamentally in hopes of acquiring something that can bring a new dimension to their lives. They are bidding for class. The ostentatious and insecure are seeking to validate themselves in the eyes of others. The passionate collector is driven by the quasi-spiritual impulse to possess beauty. But all are making their purchase in pursuit of some extra validation for themselves.

It is the newly rich who tend to crave this validation more urgently than others. They want the tokens which say they have arrived — and which ideally give the impression that they have been at their destination for some time. For centuries the British have excelled in the cunning of this transformation, from the bestowing of ancient-sounding titles to the stitching of Savile Row suits, and the art auction houses have laboured in the same tradition, prospering through their ability to identify new money and to provide what it needs to seem old. That is why their story begins in eighteenth-century London, in the heady days when a King George was on the throne, and when new wealth was being created on a scale that the world had never seen before.

PART ONE

Founder — Samuel Baker

1

IT WAS IN EIGHTEENTH-CENTURY England that, for the first time in human history, a nation took to industrial manufacturing and started to become seriously rich. The steam engine that Thomas Newcomen devised in 1705 to drain the tin mines of Cornwall heralded new ways of working and new sources of wealth. Thanks to machinery, a single unit of labour could produce miraculously more than it had produced before, and so could a unit of money. It was the beginning of the modern, affluent society. By 1750, Britain was the first country to have more of its inhabitants earning their living from urban pursuits like trade and industry than from farming.

Twenty percent of these town-dwellers lived in London, a glittering exhalation of the new prosperity. Visitors to the fast-expanding capital were amazed by the tall, glass windows in shopping streets like the Strand, with their oil-lit displays of manufactured wares. A grand new residential quarter, the "West End," was being developed to house the swelling new class of entrepreneurs for whom Jeremy Bentham, the philosopher

of the new materialism, was shortly to invent a new word —
"capitalist." London, wrote Joseph Addison in *The Spectator* in
1711, was "a kind of emporium to the whole earth," and it was
in the bustling alleys and courtyards of eighteenth-century London that a quick-witted young book dealer named Samuel
Baker founded the business that would come to be known as
Sotheby's.

Baker was a "chancer," from what we can tell, a spry, young
book dealer's book dealer, sniffing out the precious books which
were growth items in King George II's England, and selling
them on to the trade. When he got his hands on a collection that
was too big to hawk from door to door, he would take a room
in a pub or coffeehouse and invite the booksellers to come to
him. Samuel Baker's first catalogue, dated February 1734, invited
purchasers to the Angel and Crown in Russell Street, Covent
Garden. Baker promised that his books would "be sold Cheap,"
as priced in his catalogue, and that he would remain at the tav-
ern "every Day till all are sold."

Samuel Baker was just twenty-one when he issued this catalogue, and in the course of the next ten years he issued a dozen
or so more. Books were crucial accoutrements to the increasingly complex lifestyle of the eighteenth-century English gentleman. Books were art. Books were science and technology. In
an age of comparatively low-tech pleasures, they were the data
banks from which the literate could extract drama, music, erotica — almost any kind of diversion. The library was the entertainment centre of every Georgian vicarage and country house.

The token of a gentleman's knowledge, books were also a token of his style. Mass-produced in one sense, they could be considered works of art when their spines had been stitched and
enclosed in their fine leather and gilt bindings. They could be
enjoyed at so many levels. Enrichments for the sensitive spirit,
they could also serve as items of social display for the crass and
worldly — and their prices reflected this. With every year,

Samuel Baker's catalogues grew thicker and his turnover increased. A typical Baker catalogue of the late 1730s listed history, theology, medicine, and law, along with a selection of the latest popular romances and novels.

But selling at the fixed prices in his catalogue set a ceiling on Sam Baker's income, and in the mid-1740s the portly and plausible young dealer got his hands on a collection which tempted him to venture a step beyond. The practice of selling books by auction had come to England from Holland about seventy years earlier. The classic "Dutch auction" was a back-to-front process whereby the auctioneer would invite bids at a price way beyond what he hoped to receive, and then slip downwards with grudging drama until he could tempt someone to rise to the bait. But this time-consuming procedure was only suitable for individual lots of high value. When it came to books, the Dutch auctioned from the lowest bid up, and this was the system set out in the earliest known English book auction catalogue, dated 1676. Samuel Baker worked out his own conditions of sale, but the basic principle was the same: "He who bids most is the Buyer."

Baker had secured the library of the Rt. Hon. Sir John Stanley, Bart., "containing several Hundred scarce and valuable Books in all branches of Polite Literature," and he invited customers to a large entertaining room which he had leased at the top of the Exeter Exchange, an arcade cum shopping mall that occupied a prominent position in the Strand. Here, over the course of ten March evenings in the mid-1740s, the rotund and jovial Samuel Baker held his first recorded auctions — and the sales went well. He secured good prices, and it was not long before other libraries of note were consigned for him to auction — the books of Henry Fielding, author of *Tom Jones,* the collection of John Wilkes, renegade supporter of American independence, and the library of Dr. Richard Mead, physician to Queen Anne and London's most fashionable doctor. Mead's treasures had filled a private museum in the garden of his house at Great Ormond Street, and Baker raised more than £5,508 from the sale of his books.

Samuel Baker did well enough from his auctions to stop renting premises. By the early 1750s his advertisements were inviting clients to his own establishment in York Street, Covent Garden, and as he rose in the world, he built himself a house in the country. It was three hours by horse and carriage from central London, on the fringes of Epping Forest, and as Sam grew older he spent more and more time there in the company of his wife, Rebecca. The couple had no children, but Sam had his business — and his books.

In another rite of social progress, Sam commissioned Charles Grignion, a fashionable painter, to execute his portrait, which now hangs outside the boardroom of Sotheby's offices in London — "Fundator Noster. b. 1713." A solid, parrot-nosed gentleman wearing a wig, the venerable Samuel looks out at the world with all the gravitas of a judge or a cabinet minister, no longer the young chancer, but, at sixty years of age, the doyen of London's book auctioneers. When the British Museum wanted to dispose of its duplicate books and manuscripts, Samuel Baker was the man to whom they turned. If the Duke of Bedford's library needed cataloguing, it was Sam who went out to stay at Woburn Abbey — though he had so many books to get through, he complained, that he had no time to stroll in the park.

Needing someone to share the burden, he took on George Leigh, a vicar's son who knew about books, and in 1767 the firm of Samuel Baker became known as Baker and Leigh. The partnership flourished, and with Sam having no children, it might have made sense for George Leigh to buy out his partner and take over the business entirely. But Sam had a nephew, John Sotheby, his sister's son, an ingratiating young fellow with an attractive wife, Betsy. Sam's own wife, Rebecca, had died in 1768 and the old man was looking for company. So the young Sothe-

bys became his surrogate family, moving in on his life to help
him organize dinner parties out at Epping — and also keep an
eye on the business as he spent more of his time out of town.
Would Betsy look in at York Street, asks old Sam in several of
his surviving letters, and get George Leigh to write and let him
know what is going on?

By the time Sam Baker died in April 1778 at the age of sixty-
six, it had been decided that nephew John Sotheby would inherit. The stock in the business was carefully valued and divided
between George Leigh and his new, thirty-eight-year-old partner, and in July 1778, after just a few weeks when the firm
operated under the name of George Leigh, a new firm of
auctioneers presented itself to the London book trade —
Messrs. Leigh and Sotheby.

It has always been a source of mild embarrassment to the
modern Sotheby's that the family-sounding business was not actually started by a Sotheby, for their claim to be the world's old-
est auction house rests on the date of Samuel Baker's first
auction in the Strand. "Founded in 1744," read the company's
catalogues and stationery.

But this is doubly misleading, for nothing was actually
founded in that year. If Sam Baker's freelance book dealing was
ever formally "founded" as a business, it was in 1734, the date of
his earliest surviving catalogue — and 1744 is a modern mis-
reading of the old Gregorian calendar, which was reformed in
Britain in 1752. Until then, the first three months of any year
were known by the number of the year that had just ended, as
well as by the number of the year that had just begun, and following this confusing custom, Baker recorded the date on the title page of his first auction catalogue as March 11, 1744–5. Since
1744 had already ended the previous December 31, however,
March 11 actually fell in 1745 by the modern reckoning —
which leaves Sotheby's claimed date of foundation floating in a
vacuum of non-existent time. This is only a detail in the con-

text of two and a half centuries of busy trading, but it provides an appropriately mirage-like starting point for a business where nothing is ever quite what it seems.

"Started trading under the name of Sotheby in 1778" would be the more correct statement for the modern company letter-head, but that certainly would not do. By the time Sotheby's actually became Sotheby's in 1778, the rival house of Christie's had already been in business for a dozen years.

James Christie was a boy from humble origins. His father was said to be a feather-bed beater. Christie Senior beat the fluff back into the mattresses of the insomniac rich, and his son was to make his name and fortune from knowing how the rich wanted things, and from making sure they were not disappointed.

James Christie *liked* the rich. He was at ease in their company. He had charm, an easy polish, and the ability to give the impression he belonged — which, as he prospered, he did. By 1778, James Christie was already established as England's premier auctioneer. Aged forty-eight in that year, Christie had his portrait painted by his friend and occasional art consultant Thomas Gainsborough, who depicted the auctioneer leaning casually on a painting from his stockroom and holding some sort of list in his hand. Elegantly bewigged and tailored, James Christie looked established and confident, unmistakably at the top of the heap.

Fixing on art, the most spiritually uplifting ingredient of his merchandise, was what made James Christie a new sort of auctioneer. If people thought to classify him at all, they did not associate him with grocers or butchers or other practitioners of "trade." They set him among London's actors and artists and that sprinkling of creative folk that lend spice to high society. Dr. Johnson, David Garrick, Oliver Goldsmith, Gainsborough, and

Sir Joshua Reynolds — there was no shortage of such figures in the prosperous and exciting ferment of Georgian London, and James Christie rubbed shoulders with them all. He was one of "us," not one of "them," and through his purloining of social and intellectual distinction, he stole for the auction a status it had never enjoyed before.

Auctioneering is an ancient and less than reputable profession which can trace its history back to earliest times. Classical sources describe the selling at auction of women, slaves, and the possessions of the battlefield dead, and in England it was associated with the "Great Dispersal" that followed the 1649 beheading of King Charles I. The dead monarch's art collection, the finest in the western world, was auctioned off by Parliament to foreign bargain-hunters in an unseemly scramble that dispersed the treasures around Europe, and until the advent of James Christie a century later, the auction process was generally associated with the sad and seedy redistribution of used personal belongings — a connotation which car and bankruptcy auctions retain to this day.

As an economic mechanism, the auction is the quickest and most direct method of establishing a market price and of getting money on the nail. Meat markets, fish markets, stock markets, bond markets — all work on the auction principle, and in the Middle Ages, such trade auctions were usually closed affairs, organised within the regulated system of the mercantile guilds.

Sam Baker first set himself up in York Street because Covent Garden lay outside the City of London and its onerous guild regulations. He could hold public auctions there. Covent Garden was the free port of Georgian commerce. Strategically situated between the old cities of London and Westminster, it was an "anything goes" zone where the famous flower and vegetable market operated by its own rules, surrounded by a saucy and disorderly melee of theatres, coffee shops, brothels, and bars.

The movements of Sotheby's London headquarters — from the firm's beginnings in the 1730s and 1740s in Covent Garden, where Samuel Baker sold books in several locations. In 1818 the business moved down to Wellington Street beside Waterloo Bridge. This was the firm's home for a century, until 1917, when it transplanted to its present London base at 34–35 New Bond Street and set up as a full-scale art auction house. Christie's has always operated in London's West End, firstly in Pall Mall, where James Christie started holding his art auctions in 1766, and from 1823 in nearby King Street, St. James's, Christie's modern headquarters.

James Christie deliberately turned his back on this louche ambience when he founded his own auction rooms in 1766. He opened his doors in Pall Mall, in the heart of the increasingly fashionable "West End," and he restricted admission to invitation only. Coaches with postilions and liveried footmen crammed the street on the evenings of his private views. People vied for invitation cards, and they were checked by a lofty doorman brought over from the Opera House, who knew every society figure by sight and made sure that no one of unimportance was admitted.

The auction as practiced by James Christie was much more than banal redistribution. It was a source of excitement and fun. Diverting attention from the usually sad process of death or financial misfortune which had brought the object to his rooms, Christie concentrated on the glamour and *importance* which it could bring to some new person's life. He was famous for his eloquence in the auction box. When he started into his patter, according to one contemporary witness, "the ladies would say he was irresistible." James Christie was rated one of London's most attractive men, and under his aegis, the auction process took on a novel quality: for the first time in history, going to the saleroom was chic.

The demands of fashionability were exercising an increasing hold on the soul of eighteenth-century England. Fashionable display had always been the essence of life at court, but as the Industrial Revolution spread wealth in new directions, so the preoccupation with what was fashionable spread down and across the social chain. Jeremy Bentham's new capitalists were people who had time to think and time to preen. The growing number of newspapers wrote about fashion. The advertisements which supported these new publications promoted the latest "this" or the smartest "that" — and the event which demonstrated this repercussion of affluence was the arrival in London each year of the French Doll.

The French Fashion Doll was a life-size mannequin created and clothed by the couturier of the moment in Paris, and it had been coming to England for many years. Originally a gift from the French court to their compeers in London, the Doll had become by the mid-eighteenth century a commercial export of the French fashion industry, providing a tempting advertisement of the latest Paris fashions. Battles had been known to break off so that the French Doll could pass on its way, the generals on both sides gallantly doffing their hats in an act of courtesy to the ladies.

As the years went by, the mannequins became more elaborate — models not just for clothing, but for hairstyles, makeup, jewelry, and even underwear — and the mannequin became a source of interest to people outside the court. Tastes and aspirations once confined to an elite were becoming less exclusive.

Traditionalists like Joseph Addison denounced this expanding homage to what he called the "wooden mademoiselle," fuming at the foreign subversion of simple, traditional British tastes. But the simple British seemed very happy to be subverted. After arriving at St. James's, to be studied by the queen's dressmakers and her ladies, the Doll was shifted to King Street, where Covent Garden seamstresses dashed off copies for their aspiring clients — and the Doll then moved on to a final, even more distant, destination. On July 12, 1733, the *New England Weekly Journal* reported the arrival in Massachusetts of the mannequin "brought from London by Captain White," so that the ladies of the colonies could also be apprised of the trends.

Fashion is a function of money, and by the time George III came to the throne in 1760, England had more than enough money to indulge its fads. "Mad King George" is popularly associated with the loss of the American colonies, but the loss proved tolerable as he presided at home over an age of spreading luxury such as Britain had never known. The nation was awash with the wealth created by the beginnings of mass production, and the new rich spent happily to acquire houses appropriate to their new prestige: St. James's Square, Hanover Square, Berkeley and Grosvenor Squares, Cavendish, Portman, and Manchester — these grand new piazzas provided a new size and style of unit to accommodate the swelling numbers of the moneyed middle classes, while out in the countryside, development intensified in an older tradition.

Between the years of 1710 and 1740, by one estimate, 148 country houses were built or rebuilt in England, and the construction intensified to reach a climax in the third quarter of the century. You can stumble across a few Tudor or medieval country homes in Britain today, and their occasional, awkward Victorian equivalents — but the classic English country place is Georgian, for this was the golden age of the English country house.

These private palaces of the newly wealthy were the buildings that needed books to fill up their libraries and paintings to cover their walls — but their owners knew enough to know they wanted more than standard merchandise, for the ironmaster or merchant who built himself a house in the country had passed beyond simple display. He was in pursuit of a more elusive ideal, the historic model of the leisured and cultivated knight of the shires, the heart of old England that stood for history, tradition, true pedigree, and class.

James Christie offered exactly what this aspiring client wanted. His opening sale in December 1766 presented "the Property of a Noble PERSONAGE (deceas'd) — Household furniture, Fire-arms, china . . . And a large quantity of Madeira and high Flavour'd Claret." Lifestyle for sale. Old oil paintings, classic sculptures, historic bronzes — Christie's new sort of auction house provided the channel by which the badges of social status could be passed from the old elite to the new.

For centuries, the royal court had been the unique source of social advancement. Items of prestige like jewels, paintings, and even clothes were discreetly transferred by agents who hung around the royal circle. But the Industrial Revolution brought systematic production to this commerce as well, and James Christie was the first of its entrepreneurs, employing publicity and modern advertising techniques to market his unusual category of merchandise. The noble personage whose effects he auctioned in December 1766 was unnamed, but in the following year Christie was able to advertise pictures from the collection of the Duke of Leeds himself, and as the sales went by, fewer sellers opted for the anonymity of "Property of a Gentleman." The identity of the owner, Christie discovered, could be a major factor in stretching the bids of buyers who, fundamentally, were in the market for identity themselves.

Christie's nose for such intangibles was the essence of his success. When he auctioned horses, they were pedigreed, and the
Dutch tulip bulbs that he offered were invariably "finely bred."
He would even deal in farm land if it carried particular status.
On one famous occasion he invited bids on a complete village
in Surrey, the borough of Gatton, whose hammer price of
£39,000 reflected the fact that it carried the automatic right to
represent the borough in the House of Commons.

Modern economists have a technical term for items that
command such emotion-led prices and reach levels uncon-
nected with any objective calculation of their labour content
and raw material costs. They are defined as "positional" or "ex-
pressive" goods, since people price them according to their ability to *position* their owner in society, or to *express* some view of
who or what they are. These buyers have usually acquired all the
basic, material goods they need. They are looking for something
extra, and when they came to James Christie the thing they were
looking for was taste.

"Taste" was the alibi by which eighteenth-century England
maintained that its frenzy of acquisition contained more meaning than the simple spiral of competitive display. In earlier times
it had been considered eccentric to collect things — or even sin-
ful. The church warned against the accumulation of worldly
possessions. Now, in the eighteenth century, collectors began to
call themselves "connoisseurs," and the ability to respond to
beauty became identified as a moral quality.

In 1719, the painter Jonathan Richardson published his
thoughts on the qualifications that entitled a man to be called a
connoisseur, and having listed them quite confidently, he concluded with a question that was almost apologetic: "Are not
these, and the exercise of them, well becoming a gentleman?"

By 1792 when Richardson's treatise was republished, the note
of apology seemed out of place, for by then few people any
longer doubted that your worth as a person could be expressed
by the skill with which you selected and handled your things.

Once upon a time people had pursued the good. Now they pursued goods — and the dealers in goods, like James Christie, were the high priests of this new religion.

It was easy to forget when James Christie took his place in the auctioneer's box — his rostrum was designed for him by none other than the maestro of mahogany, Thomas Chippendale — that there was always one basic reason for the sale. The sellers wanted money, no matter how eminent they might be, and they often wanted it in a hurry.

If you committed goods for sale with James Christie, he was willing to put down cash against part of the estimated sale price. "Money advanced on valuables" was a most convenient and discreet facility that he included in his earliest conditions of sale. It did make him more or less a pawnbroker, and it also meant that he was effectively the owner, or part owner, of the goods that he was putting up for sale. As such, Christie could hardly claim to be an independent judge of the items that he praised so eloquently from the rostrum. But he went on claiming independence, and people did not think too hard about it.

Not even the royal family were too grand to turn to James Christie when they needed cash. He had made it fashionable to buy at auction, but, equally important, he had made it sociably acceptable to sell. In 1777 he auctioned the jewelry of Frederick, Prince of Wales, and in 1787, the pictures and furniture of Princess Amelia at her residence in Cavendish Square. He handled the library of Dr. Johnson following the great man's death in 1784, and the personal collection of pictures, drawings, and prints built up by Sir Joshua Reynolds.

These were late-winter and spring sales, timed to catch society while it was still in London. By midsummer Christie was off to the country with carriages and tents, setting up the paraphernalia of country house sales. Nor was his business restricted to auctions. His most spectacular coup was as a private dealer, when he organised the sale by private treaty of Sir Robert Walpole's extraordinary collection of nearly two hundred Old Masters. Chic though the auction process had become, it did not yet have the high seriousness — the holiness, almost — to handle world-class masterpieces. Christie still held a number of mundane bankruptcy sales, so he put on another hat to tie up a confidential transfer of the entire Walpole collection to Catherine the Great of Russia.

Questions were asked in parliament as to how such a national resource could be permitted to leave the country, but — like Charles I's collection a century earlier — the collection was hardly a home-grown treasure. It had been plundered from every corner of the continent by the British dealers who scurried around Europe's distressed aristocrats, wielding the purchasing power of the mighty guinea. Christie himself auctioned European collections in London — the pictures, coins, medals, and bronzes of Prince Carafa of Naples, the pictures of Count Brühl, prime minister to the king of Saxony. Art followed money as England's young grandees, the dollar tourists of the eighteenth-century, returned from their Grand Tours of Europe, their carriages groaning under the weight of books, prints, paintings, and every imaginable portable *objet d'art*.

Britain's greatest inflow of art from Europe followed the outbreak of the French Revolution in 1789, when London became the clearing-house for the goods of the deposed French élite. Christie auctioned the pictures which Lebrun, the Paris dealer, precipitately unloaded, and organised a series of major porcelain sales from the factories of Sèvres and Chantilly. Proud of his knowledge of gems, he sold the magnificent jewels of Madame du Barry, the mistress of Louis XV, following her execution in 1793, and the payments to mysterious agents that are listed in his accounts suggest that the auctioneer employed some enterprising Scarlet Pimpernels in order to secure property from other victims of the guillotine.

The Revolution and the wars that followed delivered a mortal blow to Paris's status as the center of the European fine art market. London took over that role, and the master auctioneer of London was James Christie. He could sell anything to anyone. One autumn afternoon in 1781, he was conducting a country house auction near Marlow on the Thames, when King George III happened to pass by. Never one to miss an opportunity, Christie hastened to set out some curious ivory chairs and a couch on the lawn for His Majesty's inspection — and the furniture caught the King's fancy. Christie promptly withdrew the lots from the auction and sold them directly in a royal private treaty sale. They are in the Royal Collection to this day.

We know the details of this sale because an account of it appeared a few days later in the *Morning Chronicle* — in which James Christie had shares. He was also a shareholder in the *Chronicle's* competitor, the *Morning Post,* and he used both papers to advertise his wares. Manipulating the press, dealing with kings and empresses, advancing credit, selling by private treaty, recruiting the opinions of distinguished artists to "validate" items at his sales, James Christie was an auctioneer without parallel — in a totally different league from Messrs. Leigh and Sotheby, who went on making their decent but obscure living through these years selling books and manuscripts from Samuel Baker's old premises in York Street, Covent Garden.

Through an accident of inheritance, the name of Sotheby happens to have been present at the moment when the gloss and razzmatazz of modern fine art auctioneering was invented, and the company founded by Samuel Baker owed its growth and existence to the bubbling prosperity of a new world, new money, and new tastes. But Baker, Leigh, and Sotheby do not seem to have appreciated the opportunity offered by this heady phenomenon, and they certainly did little to define this new market or to develop it. The distinction for all that belongs to James Christie.

2

IN MAY 1835 THE GERMAN art historian Dr. Gustav Waagen arrived in London on the English leg of his vastly ambitious project to compile a catalogue of Europe's artistic treasures. France, Italy, the Netherlands, Spain, Russia, and Germany — the learned *Doktor* surveyed them all, and nowhere, he concluded, were there collectors who had acquired more than the English. It was just possible there was a greater residue of art still remaining in Italy, but that was virtually matched by the prizes which Waagen encountered in the private collections of England in the mid-1830s. No other nation, he reported, could match the taste, wealth, and sheer energy with which the English moneyed classes had devoted themselves to the acquisition of furniture and art for the last hundred years.

Waagen explained this predominance in terms of the goods thrown onto the market by the wars of the eighteenth-century, and, in particular, by the devastation of the recent Revolutionary and Napoleonic Wars.

"Scarcely was a country overrun by the French," he wrote, "when Englishmen were at hand with their guineas."

In his massive three-volume *Works of Art and Artists in England*, Waagen catalogued country house after country house whose walls were loaded with masterpieces, and he remarked on how the English liked to scatter the most fabulous treasures around their homes in apparently casual confusion, very different from the continental tradition of displaying bronzes and *objets d'art* in special galleries and museum-style display cases. The English were so flush with art, they took it for granted, and Waagen traced the growth of this superfluity back to the Grand Tour, which had made London the centre of Europe's art market. Taste had provoked demand, which had stimulated prices, and now the natural consequence "was that whoever in Europe wished to sell pictures of great value sought to dispose of them in England."

This had made London the centre of the European art business. The British dealers who had formerly pitched their tents around Europe, had come home to set up grand galleries in the West End. Now the business came to them, and they secured much of their raw material from London's auction houses, particularly Christie's, which had passed into the hands of James Christie's grandson. Two new salerooms, Bonhams and Phillips, had sprung up in the 1790s on the strength of the loot pouring across the Channel, and even the modest book-dealing partnership of Leigh and Sotheby had managed to capture their share. In 1793 they had sold the books of the great survivor Charles Maurice de Talleyrand when he fled to America to avoid the Terror, and in 1823 the firm had organised one of the last and most intriguing of the war sales — the auction of the books which Napoleon had taken with him to his exile in St. Helena.

By 1823 both Leigh and John Sotheby had died, and the business was in the hands of John's only son, Samuel Sotheby, who had shifted the saleroom to new premises at 13 Wellington Street, the approach road to Waterloo Bridge. Just off the Strand to the south of Covent Garden, this was a scruffy and bohemian area thronging with book dealers and old print shops. Open, secondhand bookstalls littered the pavement, and here Samuel took a ninety-nine-year lease on two townhouses which he knocked together.

It was Samuel Sotheby who established the connection between the Sotheby name and high-quality auctioneering. He had no particular social connections, but he was a veritable professor of rare books, a passion which he had imbibed through long hours in the company of his father's partner, George Leigh. Samuel had actually been closer to Leigh than he had been to his own father, John, and when he had a son of his own, he had asked Leigh to be the godfather, christening the boy Samuel Leigh Sotheby.

Samuel doted on his only son, bringing the boy into the business at an early age and, given the similarity of their names, it was not surprising that outsiders tended to see old Samuel Sotheby and young Samuel Leigh Sotheby as one. Both were fired by the same passions. Old Samuel was particularly enthralled by the romance of William Caxton, Gutenberg, and the days of early printing. The aesthetic of the old wood and parchment-bound volumes with their hand-carved typefaces entranced him, and his son worked with him to produce learned discourses which they edited and published together in a father-son partnership: *The Typography of the Fifteenth Century; Principia Typographica; Memoranda Relating to the Block Books Preserved in the Bibliothèque Impériale, Paris.*

The two Sothebys also had dreams to extend their family business beyond books, organising London's first auction of autograph letters in 1819. In 1829 they took a step into the art field when they organized four sales of the romantic paintings, drawings, and sketches of Richard Parkes Bonington, the Nottingham artist who had worked in France with Delacroix, and in 1835 they auctioned the beautifully preserved Egyptian mummies, tomb jewelry, and exotic statues collected by Henry Salt, the British consul general in Egypt.

"Auctioneers of Literary Property and Works Illustrative of the Fine Arts." In December 1843, the house of Sotheby started running a new and more ambitious description of its business. Nearly a hundred years had passed since Samuel Baker's first recorded book auction, and his successors were working hard to expand their vistas. But there was no sense in which Sotheby's, after a century of business, could be said to rival the stature of Christie's, which remained the aristocracy's first choice for house-clearings, and which would occasionally deign to pass libraries that it could not handle across town to Wellington Street.

Workaday, reputable, and thoroughly honest, the two Sothebys had had to work hard for a living — as one observer noted in 1842 when Samuel Sotheby died at the age of seventy. Samuel had been "strictly exemplary," wrote the *Gentleman's Magazine* in a warm obituary which dwelt on the respect that the senior Sotheby had come to command across the world of books. But the obituary writer remarked that the late Mr. Sotheby had not been "so happy as he deserved in realizing his fortune in a very arduous profession." By the mid-nineteenth century it was the dealers that were enjoying the major profits from the markets in art and in books. They cultivated customers on a one-to-one basis, and they used the auction rooms as the wholesale source of the goods which they then retailed to their clients.

Old Samuel Sotheby had run his auction room almost as an institution of learning, and his son Samuel Leigh intensified that. Never fully educated because he had joined the company at such a tender age, Samuel Leigh Sotheby made up for lost schooling by soaking his brains in his books. He posed for his portrait with a classical urn which he was depicted studying raptly, an earnest Victorian gentleman with white mutton-chop whiskers, touched with the happy madness of the self-taught. The Numismatic Society, the Society of Antiquaries, the Royal Geographical Society — Samuel Leigh was an energetic contributor to the proceedings of a variety of London's learned bodies. And when the Crystal Palace was moved from Hyde Park to be reassembled near the site of his country home at Norwood in south London, he published two learned papers on *that*.

Following the death of his father, Samuel Leigh Sotheby came to rely on John Wilkinson, the firm's senior accountant, and from 1850, the company traded under the name of S. Leigh Sotheby and John Wilkinson. Ten years later the partnership opened a purpose-built gallery further up Wellington Street to display the growing number of engravings and antiquities they were selling, and they started with an exhibition, not a sale, of Samuel Leigh Sotheby's personal collection of art — 267 exhibits, each one proudly described and catalogued by its owner, "S. Leigh Sotheby, Fellow of the Society of Arts." One particular entry was four pages long, describing the history of a classical urn.

Samuel Leigh had first spotted the urn at Colnaghi's, one of the smartest of the West End dealers, and feeling convinced that he had discovered a rare treasure, he had purchased it at once "lest it be taken out of the country." This was the urn that he was depicted holding in his portrait.

But then one of Samuel Leigh's nephews discovered an almost identical vase, with the number 954 embossed on its base, and further research embarrassingly revealed that, far from being antique, Samuel Leigh Sotheby's treasured terra-cotta urn was actually a modern reproduction in a limited edition by the firm of Wedgwood. The collector had been fooled, and he cheerfully admitted as much in his catalogue entry.

"A thought of the possibility of the vase being a modern production," he wrote, ". . . never for a moment entered my head."

The clever nephew had suggested that his discovery be kept quiet, since no one seemed to know the difference. But Samuel Leigh Sotheby would have none of this. He included the fake vase in his exhibition as a deliberate illustration of the pitfalls of collecting, and, in addition to his long catalogue entry, he had a full account of his misadventures stuffed inside the urn, so that any future owner should be aware of all the facts.

It was, on the face of it, a naive exercise. Even Sotheby's official historian describes Samuel Leigh as "slightly dotty." But Samuel Leigh's four-page ode to a fake urn illustrated what made this Sotheby a serious auctioneer, since the spurious urn had been sold at quite a high, "antique" price, by a dealer who had either known, or had failed to find out, the facts about its origins. The auctioneer had taken the trouble to find out the truth, and had not been afraid to publish it, even though it made his original enthusiasm look foolish.

This was not to say that art dealers were crooks or fools, or that all virtue resided in Samuel Leigh Sotheby. But it did show that an expert auctioneer could claim a place beside any other specialist — and could aspire to be more than just a salesman. Sotheby's might be a long way from matching the social clout of the West End dealers, and they lagged way behind Christie's in auctioneering prestige, but thanks to Samuel Leigh Sotheby, they were developing a reputation for expertise that was, in the long run, to prove equally important.

Later in 1861, Samuel Leigh Sotheby travelled down to Devon for some fishing, his one non-academic enthusiasm. He had taken a lease on Buckfastleigh Abbey, a Gothic mansion where he planned to spend much of the summer trout fishing in the river Dart. But one day in June his body was found lying face-downward in the shallow water of the river — the victim, the Coroner later decided, of a heart attack. Samuel Leigh was still in his fifties, but he had been suffering for some time, it turned out, from blackouts and fainting fits.

He left no heir to continue the business. His only surviving son was mentally handicapped and lived in Ireland in the care of a doctor. There was no possibility of the boy ever being able to assume any role in the running of the firm, so that was the end

of the saleroom Sothebys. They had come into the auction business by an accident of blood, and they departed in the same
fashion — after just three generations.

The cathedral-like Crystal Palace which had so fascinated
Samuel Leigh Sotheby was a monument to the towering preeminence of Victorian Britain. But the Great Exhibition's
panoply of wondrous devices also heralded the end of that supremacy, for among the agricultural machines was the mechanical reaper of Cyrus Hall McCormick, a spidery-looking
contraption which the inventor had brought from his factory in
Chicago. By the 1860s thousands of such mechanical reapers
were harvesting the great plains of North America, more than
halving farm labour costs, and thus halving the price of grain
sent to Europe.

Cheap bread was good news for city dwellers and factory
workers, but it was a disaster for the farmers of Europe. Worst
hit of all were the landed magnates whose way of life had been
built on the rents from their agricultural estates. Tenants could
no longer pay their rents. Land revenues and land prices fell. The
changes provoked by the cheap food that flooded into Europe in
the 1870s produced a massive change in the world's flows of
wealth — and where wealth flows, there flows art. A century
earlier London had been a magnet for Europe's disposable treasures. Now London's dealers and auction houses set to work dis-
mantling the collections they had helped to build over the
previous hundred years.

It had always been part of the ritual of the Englishman making good that once he had purchased his country estate, he
would summon his lawyer and frame his will in the form of a
trust or "entail" which would ensure that his achievement could
not be frittered away by improvident heirs. The entail would define those family heirlooms that could not be sold.

But as rents collapsed in the second half of the nineteenth century England's landed magnates were in desperate need of cash, and the Settled Lands Acts of 1882 and 1884 were passed to allow entailed estates to sell off their heirlooms. The legislation provoked a torrent of spectacular sales, starting immediately with the dispersal of the collections of the Duke of Hamilton in the summer of 1882. Publicly avowing his need for money, the 12th Duke sold off the treasures accumulated by his father and grandfather in the course of the previous century — more than six thousand works of art, furnishings, books, and manuscripts, many acquired at auction and now passing again through the auction process in the opposite direction.

The job was so huge that it was handled by Christie's and Sotheby's working together. Sotheby's sold the books and manuscripts, while Christie's sold the paintings and furniture, and this was to become a pattern in the rush of treasure-laden auctions that marked the closing decades of the nineteenth century.

Both houses had by now lost their original family connections. The last James Christie, the great-grandson of the founder, had had little involvement in the business, and he sold the final block of family shares in 1889. Over in Wellington Street, Samuel Leigh Sotheby's partner James Wilkinson had acquired the book auction house from Samuel Leigh's widow in 1861, and was operating in partnership with Edward Grose Hodge, a Cornishman who had joined the firm in the 1840s.

The names of both auction houses clearly indicated the importance of their currently active partners — Sotheby, Wilkinson and Hodge, and Christie, Manson and Woods. But these were such mouthfuls that it was in the hectic trading of the late nineteenth century that Christie's and Sotheby's, the family brand names, became permanently established — as the *Strand* magazine illustrated in an 1890 feature on the London auction business:

For sales of pictures, of fine furniture, of old china, of jewelry, and of all kinds of costly curiosities, it is "Christie's first and the rest nowhere." . . . In the department of what is called literary property, that is to say, of books, prints, and old drawings, the firm of Sotheby, Wilkinson & Hodge, in their humble, not to say pokey, quarters in Wellington Street, Strand, still hold a position as high as Christie's themselves. When a great library is dispersed . . . it is commonly Sotheby's that has the sale of it; and they, too, have a reputation for understanding the sale of engravings or Rembrandt etchings which is not surpassed by the reputation of King Street [Christie's].

This tribute to Sotheby's expertise beyond the world of books reflected the efforts of John Wilkinson and Edward Hodge to maintain Samuel Leigh Sotheby's dreams of expansion. A pair of definitely Victorian gentlemen who, through twenty years of close partnership, invariably addressed each other in their letters as "dear Mr. Wilkinson" and "dear Mr. Hodge," they organized sales of prints and paintings, as well as of ceramics, antiques, and specialty categories that ranged from autograph letters to wine. But books and precious manuscripts were their bread and butter, and as they searched for new buyers, they followed the basic rule in times of economic change — find the new source of wealth, and sell to it.

Americans had been buying books in London from the earliest days of the colonies. Tradition has it that Samuel Baker sold books to Benjamin Franklin. But this one-way trade became a flood in the decades after 1870. Henry Clay Folger, Henry E. Huntington, J. Pierpont Morgan — the names over the great libraries of modern America bear witness to the passions of its turn-of-the-century bibliophiles. If, today, a British scholar wishes to consult the most significant editions of Shakespeare or the original of almost any classic of English literature, the scholar must cross the Atlantic. This massive transfer of literary treasure was accomplished in the years around 1900 by the lavish deployment of dollars — and many of them passed through the hands of Messrs. Sotheby, Wilkinson and Hodge.

John Wilkinson retired from the firm in the mid-1880s, handing over to Edward Hodge, who liked to embellish his auctions with poetic discursions that he delivered before starting the bidding on unusually noteworthy lots. As in the days of Samuel Leigh Sotheby, there was something of the university common room about Wellington Street, as the dealers sat around the great table and listened to Hodge's learned mini-lectures. An engraving of the time shows the bearded Hodge looking down from his desk over a dozen or so solemn and top-hatted figures, the principal antiquarian book dealers of the day. The walls of the little room are lined with books, and a porter stands on a ladder pulling down the lots to be passed around the table for inspection. It is a fusty, scarcely commercial scene, with the atmosphere of a drowsy gentleman's club, very different from the smart and theatrical occasions being staged by Christie's in St. James's.

Hodge's son Tom was also working in the company, and in 1896 he graduated to the status of full partner. Tall and precise, with a handsome shock of white hair and moustache, the younger Hodge would arrive early at Wellington Street every morning to go through the mail. He gave short shrift to letters offering properties which he deemed "N.S.V."— "No Sale Value"— dispatching them straight into the wastepaper basket. Letters considered worthy of a reply were dealt with personally, in his own rapid-fire and almost illegible hand. "Young" Mr. Hodge was not a believer in newfangled office procedures. His filing system consisted of a few old envelopes kept on the window-sills, and he would have nothing to do with the typewriter.

Tom Hodge was forty-seven when his father died in 1907, and he himself was not in the best of health. He suffered from lumbago, which took him on regular visits to therapeutic spas, and he was in the mood to take things easy when his father's death suddenly made the issue critical. Inexplicably for someone who had made his living from the disposal of legacies and estates, old Edward Hodge had died without leaving a will.

The fate of Sotheby's suddenly hung upon the financial requirements of the Hodge family, for the auction house had been the old man's principal asset, and, in addition to Tom, there were two daughters and two other sons who were now looking to Sotheby's for their inheritance. Cash had to be liberated from the family shareholding, and within weeks of his father's death, Tom Hodge entered into negotiations with Hodgson's of Chancery Lane, a book dealership founded in the 1860s, to discuss the possibility of a buyout.

His asking price was reasonable — just £30,000 for the business. But Hodgson's queried Sotheby's profitability, seizing on the fact that the lease on Wellington Street was shortly to end, when the firm would have to pay for new premises; £30,000 was too much, they said, and went on haggling in negotiations which dragged out for nearly two years.

"This correspondence is harder work than business!" wrote Tom Hodge in exasperation in December 1908. He was under pressure to generate cash for his brothers and sisters, and Hodgson's were beating him down, clearly calculating that he had nowhere else to turn.

Hodge decided to call their bluff. At a shooting party that winter he had bumped into a childhood friend, Clement Anderson Montague Barlow, a vicar's son who had gone on from Repton, where he was head boy, and Cambridge, where he got a first in law, to enjoy some success as a barrister. Just embarking on a career in politics, Montague Barlow was a man of energy and considerable ambition, and he had a shrewd idea of how the slumbering old firm of Sotheby's could be transformed into a very successful business indeed.

Barlow said he thought he could find three capable partners willing to pay a proper price for the three blocks of shares that Tom Hodge was offering, and shortly afterwards he arrived at Wellington Street to present his candidates. They were bright and able young men — Felix Warre, an old Etonian who was an expert in coins and antiquities, and Geoffrey Hobson, an Harrovian who knew about books.

"Well now," Tom Hodge is said to have responded, "we have here two prospective partners. Where is the third?"

"I am the third," replied Montague Barlow.

PART TWO

Love Letters and the Vision
of Montague Barlow

3

WHEN MONTAGUE BARLOW was offered the chance to buy Sotheby's in the winter of 1908–9, he was a nearly middle-aged man whose wealth fell far short of his talents. Dwarfish and plump, with a walrus moustache and coal black, bright eyes, Barlow had something Napoleonic about him. His shiny, bald pate barely touched five feet four, and it was constantly abuzz with grand schemes and strategies.

In 1909 Montague Barlow was taking his first steps in politics. He had recently secured the Conservative candidacy for South Salford in the suburbs of Manchester, a reasonably safe seat, and he seemed destined for Westminster. The future Montague Barlow M.P. saw how the world was changing, and he had some deeply held convictions about how society might be made a fairer place. He also envisioned a grand political career for himself, moving up from the House of Commons to the Cabinet, and perhaps even to Downing Street. But in an age when M.P.s were expected to support themselves in the style of independent gentlemen, Montague Barlow was in urgent need of money, and he saw Sotheby's as the way that he could make it.

Until he came to Sotheby's Montague Barlow had been making a poor living as a barrister. His father, an unbearably upright Victorian cleric, had regarded trade or finance with disdain. The Very Reverend Dean of Peterborough had allowed his son just two career options — medicine or the law — and young Montague had chosen law in the ecclesiastical courts. For nearly twenty years he had argued disputes over charities and religious endowments, which sharpened his intellect but barely paid the rent. To supplement his meagre income, he delivered lectures at the London School of Economics and did law exam marking at London University.

Then his father died, and, at almost the same moment, Barlow bumped into Tom Hodge and his opportune proposal. The would-be M.P. had found a new way ahead for himself — and he was to find a new way ahead for Sotheby's. His arrival marked the beginning of the company's modern history, for he had identified the crucial element with which he could reinvent the old book auction business — expertise. The primary legacy of the Sotheby family years was a reputation for scholarship and integrity, and Barlow saw how this could be profitably exploited in a world whose class divisions were weakening. Professional expertise was commanding an ever greater price, and social redistribution was in the air. That meant business for an auction house like Sotheby's, and the fact that the lease on the firm's poky old rooms beside Waterloo Bridge had only a few years to run was not the drawback that it might seem. The vision of Montague Barlow set Sotheby's in altogether grander premises.

The two partners he had recruited both shared and exemplified his vision. Geoffrey Hobson, not yet thirty and the son of a successful Liverpool businessman, lived and breathed expertise. Partially deaf as a result of a middle-ear infection which would, today, have been cured by penicillin, Hobson was a natural scholar who had won a first at Oxford and had an eye for beautiful things. Show Geoffrey Hobson a Siennese painting, and he could sit in front of it for hours.

With his deafness and a certain aloofness, Hobson was underqualified in the charm department. But that deficiency was more than balanced by the smoothness of Felix Warre, the easygoing young man that Barlow brought in to make up the trio. Known as "Bear" on account of his broad oarsman's shoulders, Felix Warre was a hero of the river both at Eton and Oxford, where he won several blues. Warre's expertise lay in coins and antiquities, two profitable growth areas in the developing American market. He had the sociable charm of a dealer, and he turned out to be a natural in the auction box.

Hobson and Warre were the only new partners whose names were made public in October 1909 when the buyout of Sotheby, Wilkinson and Hodge was announced. Montague Barlow felt it unwise to complicate his relations with the Conservative party of South Salford by informing them that the ecclesiastical lawyer they had selected as their candidate had suddenly become an auctioneer. Sotheby's new owner had highly developed social antennae. He understood people's uneasy relationship with change, and he knew that, expertise or no, auctioneering lacked the professional cachet of the law. For the next two years — in the course of which he won election to Parliament — he remained a practising barrister so far as the world was concerned, going to his chambers in the Inns of Court first thing every morning, before sneaking across the Strand to Wellington Street.

Barlow was the poorest of the new partners, and he had had to borrow to raise his stake — £16,000, as compared to the £17,000 paid by Warre and the £36,000 invested by Geoffrey Hobson. But there was no doubt that Barlow was the new boss. He moved into the main office at Wellington Street, where he sat side by side at a partners' desk with Tom Hodge, who had agreed to stay on for two years to teach his successors the business.

Hodge had originally agreed to work out his two years for no pay, but the new partners soon decided he was worth more than that. Though working only four days a week, and going home at 4:30 (the other partners and staff all slaved from 9:30 A.M. to 7:00 P.M., Monday to Friday, with a long morning's work on Saturday), Tom Hodge was paid a full partner's salary — and he liked this arrangement so much that he rescinded his decision to retire.

Hodge had been dabbling in a profitable sideline — the sale of libraries, or parts of libraries, by private treaty. For exceptional properties, the auction house could use its contacts to match buyer and seller privately, working on a discreet one-to-one basis and moving into the prestigious and remunerative field of the dealer. This could yield considerably more profit than the saleroom commission of 12½ percent. In 1902, Hodge had been offered a collection of early books and manuscripts which included more than thirty fifteenth-century volumes from the press of William Caxton, and though there was no commission on the deal up to £100,000, Hodge was told he could pocket anything he fetched over that. He had managed to place the entire collection in America with J. Pierpont Morgan for £130,000 — $15.8 million today.

Even when expenses were allowed for, this single inflow of £30,000 had netted Sotheby's the equivalent of a full year's trading profit, and in the years that followed, Hodge made further private deals with a number of Americans and with the one English collector who could match transatlantic purchasing power — Dyson Perrins, the developer of Lea and Perrins' famous Worcestershire sauce. Perrins paid some handsome prices at Sotheby's, but he was more famous for what he did not pay the porter whom he regularly cajoled into shifting his heavy books and manuscripts.

"I'll give you a tip," promised the sauce manufacturer one day when he confronted this porter with a particularly weighty load, and after the last book had been shifted, the tip was duly forth-coming.

"When your bottle of sauce is half empty," he confided to the porter, "top it up with water. You won't notice the differ-ence."

Auction houses seldom publicise their sales by private treaty. It infuriates dealers, who view the practice — correctly — as poaching on dealer territory. But it was one of several areas where Montague Barlow saw potential growth for Sotheby's, and politics provided him with some valuable connections. In November 1913, he was invited up to Chatsworth, the stateliest of Britain's stately homes, where the Duke of Devonshire was embarrassed by a lack of cash.

His Grace's embarrassment was reflected in the fact that he himself did not meet with Barlow. It was the duchess and the Chatsworth librarian who got the job of showing the visi-tor around the library and explaining the essence of his mission. Which books did Sotheby's think they could sell discreetly and quickly, and how much did they think they could get for them?

Earlier Dukes of Devonshire had been formidable book col-lectors, the 6th Duke making the greatest contribution in the glory days of the early nineteenth century, when he had paid record prices at auction. It was from his trophies that Barlow se-lected twenty-five superb William Caxtons — among them *The History of Troy*, the first book printed in the English language — together with a collection of early plays and playbills which had once belonged to J. P. Kemble, the eighteenth-century Shake-spearean actor. Comprising more than 7,500 plays and playbills dating from the great years of English drama before 1640, Kem-ble's collection was distinguished by some magnificent early edi-tions of Shakespeare.

Barlow came rushing back to London. He was due to travel to America for Christmas, which was only a few weeks away, and he felt sure he could find a buyer for these treasures in New York. He had a special catalogue prepared in record time, and he got the books bundled up in twenty-seven large packing cases, ready for dispatch and inspection.

But the inspection proved unnecessary, for Barlow had started cabling even before he landed in America, piquing the interest of H. E. Huntington, the railway tycoon, and persuading Huntington to buy the entire collection, sight unseen, for $750,000 ($15.9 million today). Sotheby's new arrival had pulled off the firm's most profitable coup ever — and as a dealer, not an auctioneer.

The sale of the Chatsworth treasures was a spectacular achievement for a business which, thanks to Tom Hodge's conservatism, still had only one typewriter, and not a woman in the office. The accounts at Wellington Street were entered in copperplate handwriting in a leather-bound ledger, and it was in copperplate that most of the letters were still written. The partners would grab one of the dark-suited clerks who wielded a dip-and-scratch pen, and would dictate their correspondence to them.

Monday morning, at 9:30 sharp, was when Hodge, Barlow, Hobson, and Warre gathered to go through the correspondence and to discuss the week ahead. Having won his seat in South Salford in 1910, Barlow had gone public with his role at Sotheby's, and he was very much the busy spirit. Since etchings fell within his responsiblity, he decided he should learn about the technique, and he would bustle off to South Kensington for etching classes, encasing his roly-poly form in overalls to protect his House of Commons suit from the acid.

Felix Warre was proving a particularly relaxed and genial auctioneer, while Geoffrey Hobson was developing an interest in rare book bindings that was to make him a world authority in that field. Hobson was in charge of Sotheby's book department, and in 1913 he masterminded one of the first twentieth-century sales to capture attention beyond the art trade:

> I love your verses with all my heart, dear Miss Barrett — and this is no off-hand complimentary letter that I shall write, whatever else — no prompt matter-of-course recognition of your genius . . . I do, as I say, love these books with all my heart — and I love you too.

The famous love letters between the poet Robert Browning and Miss Elizabeth Barrett of Wimpole Street, had been published following Browning's death in 1889. But in 1912 the couple's only son "Pen" had died, having failed to will the letters, or the contents of his parents' four romantic homes in Italy, to any of nearly two dozen possible heirs and claimants. Everything had to be turned into money, and thanks to Sotheby's track record in the sale of manuscripts, it was Sotheby's who got the sale.

The supreme scholar of the auction house, Hobson immediately plunged himself into the study of Browning, and he spent a happy summer in Italy going through the different homes and arranging the packing and dispatch of their contents to London. He decided that the love letters and the poet's death mask were so precious that he should take them home personally in his luggage, but as his train crossed the frontier, he was questioned by customs officials, who wanted to know what he was carrying in the hat box on the rack over his head.

Hobson was a talented linguist. In addition to classical Latin and Greek, he had a fluent command of French, German, Italian, Spanish, Portuguese, and Dutch. But the Italian for "death mask" temporarily eluded him.

"I have up there," he said, searching slowly for words as the other passengers in the crowded compartment listened fascinated, "the face of a dead man."

The answer was good enough for the customs men, but in the course of the miles that followed, Hobson's fellow passengers seemed to find compelling reasons for leaving the compartment. The Englishman spent the rest of his journey in magnificent solitude.

The propriety of auctioning off the Barrett-Browning love letters provoked fierce debate in a society where privacy and restraint were counted primary virtues. Elizabeth Barrett's elopement with Browning was still a matter of scandal for some. But the publication of Hobson's erudite catalogue changed many minds, for, as Montague Barlow had forseen, expertise could cast a new light on previously sensitive transactions. The intelligence of Hobson's descriptions lent dignity to a rummage through some very intimate chattels. It provided the alibi that everyone needed thoroughly to relish the sale, and Barlow skillfully capitalised on the controversy to his advantage, turning the Browning auction into an event that took on national significance.

At the last moment, Sotheby's succumbed to an attack of good taste, deciding that the lovingly transported death mask was too intimate to auction. But more than 1,400 other lots went on sale in Wellington Street in May 1913. They ranged from engraved cuff links to dinner plates, and the prize item was Lot 166:

BROWNING (Robert and Elizabeth Barrett) THE LOVE LETTERS, a Series of Two Hundred and Eighty-four from Robert and Two Hundred and Eighty-seven from Elizabeth Barrett Browning, in the original cases where they were always kept until sent for publication, her letters being kept by him in a marqueterie box, and his by her in a collapsible gold tooled leather case.

The bidding was started by the dealer Frank Sabin, and battle was joined by his great rival, Alfred Quaritch. It is a rule of the auction box to concentrate on no more than two bidders at a time, only looking for other interest when one drops out — and neither dealer did. Felix Warre went from Sabin to Quaritch and back again as the two men fought their way upwards with crisp, curt nods. After two minutes they were already above £6,000, and Quaritch seemed to have won when he went to £6,500.

The two dealers were old protagonists in the Wellington Street saleroom. "Sabin, Quaritch, Sabin, Sabin, Quaritch," read consecutive entries in the clerk's annotated record of the sale. Ten minutes earlier the two men had tussled bitterly over Lot 152, the manuscripts of Elizabeth Barrett Browning's *Sonnets from the Portuguese,* and Quaritch had been the winner. But when it came to the love letters, Sabin was not prepared to yield. He went to £6,550 — more than $700,000 in modern prices — and Felix Warre turned to Quaritch for a counter bid. As the whole room waited, Quaritch slowly shook his head.

The entire sale raised nearly £28,000 — over $3 million in modern prices. Attracting headlines like "EXTRAORDINARY BID- DING AT SOTHEBY'S," it was a massive and very public triumph for the new partnership at Wellington Street. In less than four years, Barlow's syndicate had achieved some spectacular results, and Barlow set them out in a detailed report that he prepared for his partners at the end of 1913. Sales commissions, other rev- enues, and sales days had all increased dramatically, and Barlow had also been able to clip expenses by nearly 15 percent. In 1913 Sotheby's had started charging clients for the illustration of their property in catalogues, which made the catalogues dramatically more graphic, while also reducing the cost.

Precisely calculated and hard-headed business practice was one of the many innovations of the Barlow era — but the most dramatic new development seems to have happened by accident. Hurrying down an ill-lit corridor in Wellington Street one day, Montague Barlow had stumbled on a pile of pictures. Legend has it that these were awaiting delivery to Christie's, under the long-standing arrangement whereby Sotheby's stuck to books and Christie's stuck to pictures. The stumble caused Barlow to look harder at the dusty canvases, and it got his mind working. In conversations with Tom Hodge he had frequently discussed how Sotheby's could diversify beyond books, and the new partnership's vision for the future had always included a build-up of expertise, together with a move to new premises that would be suitable for the staging of full-scale picture sales.

But why wait? A few months later a portrait by the Dutch painter Frans Hals arrived at Wellington Street, and Barlow decided to put the painting in with a sale of drawings, etchings, and other minor works that had been arranged for June 20, 1913, a few weeks after the Browning sale. It was a full-blown portrait from the artist's best period, a rich portrayal of a Dutch burgher in all his glory, and, quite by chance, Christie's happened to be selling two other Frans Hals paintings on the same day.

When the bidding was over, it turned out that Sotheby's had got more for their Frans Hals than Christie's had for either of theirs. At £9,000, in fact, Sotheby's had achieved the highest price for any painting sold at auction in London that year. Coupled with the publicity and prices generated by the Browning sale, it made Sotheby's the auctioneers of the moment. Christie's would have to look to their laurels.

4

THE BUILD-UP TO WAR in the summer of 1914 put the ambitions of Montague Barlow on hold. Parliament was meeting every day, and Barlow virtually lived at the House of Commons, running Sotheby's by means of notes that shuttled to and from Wellington Street along the Thames Embankment.

Within days of hostilities being declared, Barlow was up in his constituency in Manchester, throwing his energies into the raising of one, two, and eventually five battalions of Lancashire Fusiliers. It was a task ideally suited to his prodigious appetite for work and organization.

"*Re War,*" he wrote to Tom Hodge late in September, 1914. "I have a big job on hand with the Battalion. I am now under orders from the War Office to build them a camp."

Re the auction business, Barlow felt that it would not be possible to hold any sales before the following spring.

"Our booksellers," he wrote, "have practically no market for their goods at all."

Felix Warre, the oarsman, was the only partner who was young and fit enough to serve, and he was soon in France with the King's Royal Rifle Corps, where he was to fight with distinction and win a Military Cross, coming home wounded. A number of Sotheby's porters also served in the trenches, and one of them, Bill Addison, was delighted to look up one day and see his old boss, now Captain Warre, riding a horse at the head of a column of approaching soldiers.

"Aye-aye, sir! Aye-aye, sir!" called Addison, scrambling happily from his trench and waving his arms in the air.

To the porter's chagrin, however, Captain Warre appeared quite unaware of Addison's cries, riding on impassively as if his former employee did not exist, and it was not until many years later, when the war was over and everyone was back at their appointed places in the saleroom, that the porter discovered he had not been dreaming.

"By the way, Addison," Warre remarked casually one day. "The correct thing to do in the Army when you see an officer passing at the head of a company is to stand to attention and salute — *not* to jump up and down shouting, 'Aye-aye, sir.' "

The social gradations inside the auction house curiously mirrored the ranks of the armed forces. Running the show, and greatly deferred to, were the partners and experts, while the book-keeping and administrative work was in the hands of clerks, the non-commissioned officers. The porters made up the other ranks.

Geoffrey Hobson's incisive mind was enlisted by the Foreign Office for diplomatic consultancy, so that left Tom Hodge as the only full-time manager at Wellington Street. Starting in February 1915, Hodge was able to scrape up one sale a month, building up to six in June and seven in July — most of them executors' sales of estates that had to be settled, since the administration of wills and inheritances continued in war as in peace. As a business that serviced the consequences of dying,

Sotheby's hardly had to worry about the long-term impact of war upon their turnover.

It was early in 1916 that Montague Barlow invited Emily Millicent Sowerby, a lively and bird-like spinster of thirty-three, to join Sotheby's — under certain conditions.

"His great concern," she later remembered, "was that any women employed by the firm should look as unattractive to the male as possible. He reminded me that numbers of men came into the salerooms, and it was most important that their attention should not be distracted by elegant females.

"'That dress you have on, for instance, Miss Sowerby . . .'"

Miss Sowerby promised that when she came to Wellington Street she would conceal herself beneath the most unbecoming dark blue housecoat she could find, and, thanks to the gaps left by the men called away to serve their country, Sotheby's had its first female expert. A graduate of Girton College, Cambridge, Millicent Sowerby was known and respected in the book world. She had worked as a cataloguer for the dealer Wilfred Voynich. But her arrival proved too much for Sotheby's paterfamilias.

Tom Hodge was already in a state of shock. Soon after the outbreak of war, Barlow had engaged two females to work as secretaries, and he had compounded the offence by purchasing them typewriters. Mr. Hodge had reluctantly consented to this innovation, on condition that no correspondent should be insulted by receiving a letter addressed in a typewritten envelope. All envelopes from Sotheby's continued to be addressed by hand. But the appearance of Miss Sowerby on the expert staff was the final straw. Tom Hodge was already resentful of the way that Barlow and his partners had shaken up the old Hodge family business, and he stalked off to permanent retirement in Sussex.

Sotheby's envelopes were typed from the end of 1916 onwards, and more women came to Wellington Street. Montague

Barlow brought in his sisters, Evelyn and Margaret, to help the part-time Geoffrey Hobson. A stout pair of matrons who dressed in blue housecoats, Evelyn and Margaret were supporters of the movement for women's voting rights, but Miss Sowerby did not find them congenial. When she approached Margaret Barlow on the subject of one of the new cleaning ladies who shared the women's cloakroom, but who suffered from head lice, she was briskly informed that women must expect that sort of thing when they earned their own living.

Miss Sowerby found Montague Barlow altogether more sympathetic. Putting into practice his progressive social principles, he split up the working day at Sotheby's with breaks for elevenses in the morning, and tea in the afternoon, since he was concerned that work at the close of the day should be as accurate and useful as that in the earlier hours. He employed a full-time tea lady to keep the staff refreshed and alert, and he insisted that everyone should take three full weeks of paid holiday every year.

Barlow also considered that no one should spoil a holiday by traveling on it. So after regular bank holidays, only those who lived in London were expected to be at their desks on time the following day. Miss Sowerby's family lived in Yorkshire, and she would never get into her office before lunch on the day following a holiday, since the rule was that those who had gone away were simply required to take the first possible train next morning.

Millicent Sowerby wrote an entertaining memoir of her years at Sotheby's, including a frank description of a phenomenon that was seldom discussed openly — the "knockout," or unofficial auction process which resulted when a "ring" of dealers conspired to keep auction prices low. The ring would agree in advance not to bid against each other on certain lots, thus securing these items for low prices, and would then adjourn to hold their own private auction, or "knockout," of what they had secured.

The traditional way of combating the "knockout" was for

the seller and the auction house to agree in advance on a reserve, the price below which the property would not be sold, and if the bidding failed to reach the reserve, the auctioneer would "buy in" the property, effectively withdrawing the lot on behalf of the seller.

When it came to the selling of rugs and carpets, however, the market was so dominated by one ring of Armenian dealers that Barlow decided to adopt more aggressive tactics. He extended special credit to a minute but elegant Armenian named Benlian, who would bid stoutly against the ring, to the fury of his compatriots. Once the reserve price was safely passed, Barlow would mysteriously fail to notice Benlian's bidding, and would land the sale on the member of the ring who had been bidding against him.

"I no bid! I no bid!" the buyer would angrily cry, and a cluster of fingers would point accusingly at the dapper Benlian, who would stand, smiling inscrutably, beside the rostrum.

But the Armenians still secured enough bargains for their noisy post-auction knockouts to dominate proceedings in a tea room around the corner from Wellington Street, and there was another saleroom racket, the inverse of the knockout, which actually suited the auction house very well. This occurred when a dealer was not bidding for his own stock, but was trying to secure a book on the orders of a client. In that event, the dealer wanted a high price, since it would yield him a high commission. He would make a signal to the ring, indicating that he wanted the bidding pushed up to as far as possible — and this was a practice which Sotheby's did nothing to discourage. As auctioneers, their first duty was to the seller, after all.

The appointment of Millicent Sowerby had reflected a renewed increase in the volume of books coming to Sotheby's, for business picked up as the world learned to live with the war. By 1917 sales were running at quite healthy levels, and having made his patriotic contribution to the war effort, Montague Barlow turned his energies to the cornerstone of his strategy for Sotheby's — the move from Waterloo Bridge to Christie's territory in the West End of London.

The move had been planned before the war. Aware from the start that their time in Wellington Street was limited, Barlow and his partners had always had their eyes on the West End. It was the centerpiece of their ambition to move Sotheby's up in the world. In 1912 they had discussed a possible merger with the auctioneers and estate agents Knight, Frank & Rutley for the sake of occupying part of their elegant Hanover Square offices, and when the negotiations fell through, they commissioned Sir Howard Frank to find them West End premises in any case.

Frank found them the ideal new home — a disused picture gallery in the middle of Mayfair. The building had once been an inn, so there were capacious cellars for the storage of goods. A wine merchant had constructed a drive-in loading bay — ideal for the added volume of furniture and large paintings which Barlow and his partners hoped to shift — and there was a cluster of offices to house the experts and the clerical staff. The antique clutter of Waterloo Bridge no longer harmonized with the ambitions of Barlow, but the new premises had a whiff of Wellington Street's amiable chaos, while also being situated at a most prestigious address — 34 and 35 New Bond Street.

Back in 1835, Samuel Leigh Sotheby had installed a curious black statue over the front door of Wellington Street, a bust of Sekhmet, the savage Egyptian lion goddess created by Ra from the fire of his eyes as a creature of vengeance to punish men for their sins. This intimidating mascot was an unsold lot from the sale of Henry Salt's Egyptian antiquities, one of Sotheby's early-nineteenth-century steps towards diversification, and eighty years later, the transfer of the Sekhmet's black and ravaged features to Mayfair marked another stage in the journey. The lion goddess was installed over the main entrance in New Bond

Street in the summer of 1917, and a celebration was organized around an exhibition of work by one of the major wartime charities, the Lord Roberts Workshops. This charity provided care and employment for wounded servicemen, a worthy cause which qualified the auction house for a visit from Queen Mary, and for a party which Millicent Sowerby described as a "magnificent house-warming."

Millicent and the Barlow sisters, the secretaries, the tea lady, and the cleaning ladies all took off their blue housecoats and paraded in their finery. Crowds gathered outside to cheer the arrival of Her Majesty, and the Queen was so impressed that she arranged for her daughter, Princess Mary, the future Princess Royal, to visit next day. It was the beginning of a close relationship between Sotheby's and Queen Mary, the House of Windsor's demon collector.

Sotheby's was on the map. The possibility of snaring such a royal visit was precisely why Barlow and his partners had moved their premises to the West End. Their immediate neighbours in New Bond Street were Mademoiselle Elsie, hatmaker to the Queen, and Madame M. Henry, court dressmaker. Two of London's most eminent art dealers, Agnew and Colnaghi, were only a few doors away, along with book dealers like F. S. Ellis and Frank Sabin. Christie's were in King Street, to the south of Piccadilly, so Sotheby's could stake its claim to the northern half of London's art and antiques quarter.

In the summer of 1919 Montague Barlow gathered his staff in the new premises for a grand Victory Dinner. Blue housecoats were discarded once again and wartime medals were on display. Barlow was able to show off the neckbadge and star of his own K.B.E., the knighthood he had been awarded for his work in raising the regiments in Lancashire, and the newly elevated Sir Montague announced a novel and generous bonus scheme that would give every member of staff a share in the profits of the business.

The dinner was a celebration for those who had survived and got back from the war. But it was also a celebration of the fundamental transformation that Montague Barlow and his partners had accomplished for Sotheby's — the move across town, the diversification away from books, and the gearing up for competition with Christie's as a full-service auction house. It was the beginning of a new era.

5

THE ARRIVAL OF SOTHEBY'S in the West End of London sent a clear message to the ancient and half-friendly auction house with whom they had once collaborated. Christie's and Sotheby's were no longer half-friends — or friends in any conceivable way. By starting to sell serious pictures and then moving to New Bond Street, the book auctioneers had thrown down the gauntlet — though Christie's did not give them the satisfaction of obviously picking it up. Nestling complacently in the heart of clubland, Christie's was profiting nicely from the rush of house sales provoked by the swingeing tax and death duty increases needed to pay for the war. The lords of King Street would have died rather than admit to a moment's exertion over their upstart rivals to the north of Piccadilly.

Exerting himself, however, was something of which Sir Montague Barlow was never ashamed. He had set his sights on challenging Christie's at the very essence of their supremacy, the sale of great paintings from the grand old houses of England, and to undercut the competition, he had reduced Sotheby's

commission to sellers from 12½ percent — the standard rate
charged by both auction houses — to 7½ percent on pictures,
drawings, armour, furniture, silver, jewelry, and the other categories where Sotheby's had ground to make up.

The new Mayfair auction house instituted a programme of
aggressive advertising, buying newspaper space to publicise major sales "in a bold and arresting way [as Barlow put it in one
memo] . . . plenty of space being left blank so as to draw attention to the printed matter." And Sotheby's also worked hard at
cultivating the saleroom correspondents with leaks and tip-offs
before the sales. When they got results, their gratitude verged on
the obscene.

"A word of congratulation and appreciation on your ad-
mirable article in today's paper," wrote Geoffrey Hobson in May
1917 to A.C.R. Carter of the *Daily Telegraph*. "You have taught
me to expect much from you, but I was surprised both by the
matter and the manner of your notice of the Wilton treasures.
The information about Montmorency himself and recent sales
of armour was extraordinarily interesting, and selected with
your unerring eye for the picturesque and opportune. The *Telegraph* should be proud of having such a contributor. . . ."

The Wilton treasures were a collection of paintings, tapestries, and fine suits of armour from one of the great houses of
England, the seat of the Herbert family, Earls of Pembroke since
the middle of the sixteenth century. Forced onto the market by
death duties, it was exactly the sort of property that would once
have gone to Christie's as a matter of course, and Sotheby's was
cock-a-hoop that their competitive commission cuts had secured such prestigious business so soon after their move. They
advertised the Wilton property as the high spot of their New
Bond Street opening season in June 1917, giving pride of place
in the advertisements to two suits of armour which the Pembrokes traced back to the same year as their title — 1557.

Barlow was delighted when the *Burlington Magazine* asked if

Charles ffoulkes, Keeper of the Armoury of the Tower of London, and hence Britain's foremost expert on arms and armour, could inspect the two suits of armour for a special review. But the *Burlington* dropped a bombshell only days before the sale when it published the Keeper of the Armoury's verdict that the armour, which was reputed to have belonged to de Montmorency, the Constable of France, and to Louis de Bourbon, could not possibly have been worn by these distinguished warriors, since various technical factors indicated that it was not as old as the Pembroke family — or Sotheby's catalogue — had claimed.

High reserves had been set on both lots, and Sotheby's had nursed hopes of obtaining two exceptional prices. They had advertised heavily in America, whose millionaire "robber barons" had an appropriate appetite for ancient armour and weaponry. But the last-minute doubts cast by the Keeper of the Armoury made high bids unlikely. Sotheby's had taken a full page in *The Times* to refute ffoulkes's criticisms on the morning of the sale, but when Montague Barlow climbed into the rostrum at the beginning of July 1917, he knew that he would have a struggle on his hands.

It is an ancient tradition of the saleroom for an auctioneer to take imaginary bids "off the chandelier" until the prearranged reserve price on any item has been reached. If there is only one bidder in the room, this apparently deceptive practice is the only way of discovering whether the solitary bidder is prepared to raise his bid to the price that the seller is prepared to accept. The bidding has to lead him up to the level of the reserve, and the modern art auction houses openly acknowledge the practice — though they wince at mention of the chandelier. They prefer to call it "bidding on behalf of the consignor," and in July 1917, Montague Barlow used the process to get the bidding to £14,000 for one suit of armour, and £10,000 for the other. Both these prices, however, were short of the reserve, so Barlow took a further imaginary bid of £500 on each lot — to find that no genuine bidders were prepared to follow him.

At this point a modern auctioneer, having done his best for the seller, is ethically (and in New York State, legally) required to admit failure and to "buy in" the lot. Sotheby's and Christie's auctioneers do not rejoice in the practice, but they now make it clear from the box whenever a lot has been "passed" or "bought in." When the auction house later publishes the statistics of the sale, it sets out the quantity of "bought-ins," or failures, as compared to lots sold — the ratio being generally considered the measure of the auction's efficiency and success. A bought-in proportion of below 10 percent is considered good going.

But such openness was not the norm in 1917. "Sold to Mr. Worthington!" Auctioneers had their own stock of fictitious names which they would call out to let their clerk know they had failed to get their price on an item, while the room was given to believe they had achieved a genuine sale — and this was the device Montague Barlow used to pretend that £14,500 and £10,500 were genuine and successful bids. After the auction, Sotheby's announced that they had achieved a total of £52,819 from the Wilton treasures.

But the two sales of armour totalling £25,000 were not genuine, and Barlow had also had to buy in a Rembrandt portrait which he pretended to have sold for £11,500. This meant that Sotheby's had secured a mere £16,319 in genuine bids for Pembroke — a miserable yield.

Sotheby's debut West End sale had proved a flop, and the art world came up with a sinister explanation of the devastating timing of the Keeper of the Armoury's *Burlington* review. Ffoulkes had many long-standing relationships, personal and professional, with Christie's. Christie's were a major channel through which the Tower of London had long acquired and disposed of armour, and though collusion was impossible to prove, Geoffrey Hobson went to his grave convinced that the Keeper of the Armoury had had Christie's well-being "very much at heart" when he sabotaged Sotheby's grand New Bond Street opening. Whatever Christie's might claim, it was clear they were by no means indifferent to the appearance of an aggressive rival on their doorstep.

As Montague Barlow, Geoffrey Hobson, and Felix Warre looked out at the world in the aftermath of World War I, they were surveying a society that had undergone immense transformation — and for a nimble auction house, transformation spelled opportunity. The British tax system was aggressively redistributing the wealth of the nation, estate duties were more confiscatory than ever, and grandees like the Pembrokes were on the retreat. Hardly had the British assembled a heritage, it seemed, but they were being compelled to demolish it. The palatial London mansions of the noble families were coming down one by one, their memory surviving only in the names of the hotels and apartment blocks which took their place, and what could be guessed at before 1914 was now apparent for all to see. The British aristocracy was being compelled to sell up — mostly to foreign buyers.

Sotheby's book business reflected this with some incredible sales. In 1919, Millicent Sowerby, who had been kept on the staff to cope with the post-war rush of auctions, had the thrill of seeing a 1599 edition of Shakespeare's *Venus and Adonis* go for £15,100 — inevitably, perhaps, to the acquisitive Henry Huntington. It was the highest known price paid to that date for a printed book, prompting cheers in the saleroom, the first ever heard at New Bond Street — though critics deplored the dispersal and export from Britain of such treasures in the hands, as Dr. M. R. James, the Provost of Eton, put it, of "Boches,* Jews and Transatlantics."

Christie's were enjoying similar success with the sale of pictures, while dealers like Duveen and Knoedler were making

* "Boches" — World War I slang for Germans.

their fortunes from the shipping of high-quality Old Masters to rich Americans. There had never been a tradition of selling such classic, museum-quality masterpieces at auction — at Christie's or anywhere else. On the irregular occasions such paintings came on the market, they were assumed to require the reverence and discretion of a private sale. But that left a lot of perfectly good and profitable art for Sotheby's to handle, and if the auction house wanted to carve out a place in the paintings and drawings market, they would have to make good their commitment to offer expertise.

Their first recruit came to them through the Pembroke armour débâcle. Charles Bell, a distinguished scholar who was Keeper of the Department of Fine Arts at Oxford's Ashmolean Museum, was struck by the publicity that Sotheby's had managed to generate for the Wilton sale, but had been unimpressed by the cataloguing of the drawings. Bell was in the process of trying to sell the fine collection of drawings assembled by his uncle, the distinguished Victorian painter Sir Edward Poynter, President of the Royal Academy, who had just died. Bell had composed his own learned and precise catalogue of the drawings, which he had circulated privately in America in a freelance attempt at a sale.

Having drawn a blank across the Atlantic, Bell turned for help to Montague Barlow, proposing that Sotheby's should promote and sell his uncle's collection, and should use the catalogue copy that he had already prepared. Barlow willingly agreed. The Poynter collection of drawings was successfully sold at New Bond Street, and Sotheby's landed a permanent cataloguer and well-connected expert along with the sale. Starting in the spring of 1920, Charles Bell took the train down from Oxford to Paddington every Wednesday, receiving a guinea for his traveling expenses, plus a commission on what he catalogued.

Related through his prosperous banking family to such luminaries as Stanley Baldwin, Rudyard Kipling, and Sir Edward Burne-Jones, Bell had his finger on the social and artistic pulse.

His academic reputation gave him entrée to the country's finest collections. He was in demand for the expert advice he could proffer on value, provenance, condition, and the advisability of restoration — and, naturally, if the owner was thinking of selling, Bell could recommend an auction house who would handle the sale very well.

Wednesdays at New Bond Street became Old Masters day, when the Keeper of the Ashmolean went through the stacks of drawings and paintings that had been sent in for possible sale. Hunchbacked, short-sighted, and often short-tempered, Bell would squint closely at the offerings, analyzing the brushstrokes or pencil marks, and searching for tell-tale markings on the back of the frames. His eye had been sharpened by a quarter of a century of study, and he fired out his verdicts in articulate, dispassionate prose.

The new expert's opinions were the more impressive for their stringency. In one sale of drawings Bell was offered no less than fourteen "Rembrandts," but he refused to credit any of them to the hand of the master himself. "Circle of," "studio of," "school of," "manner of"* — Bell realized that the function of an auction house was to sell, but he regarded his catalogue entries as holy writ. Sceptical and academic in his attributions, the new cataloguer erred defiantly on the side of caution.

The consequence was that Sotheby's art catalogues took on a stature they had never enjoyed before. If Bell was prepared to say that a drawing was by Dürer, it was accepted as a Dürer, and within months of him starting his Wednesday trips to London the art world took note of the change. Raeburns, Rom-

---

* "Circle of" — a work of the period of the artist, and closely related to his style; "studio of" — a work possibly executed under the supervision of the artist; "school of" — a work by a pupil or follower of the artist; "manner of" — a work in the style of the artist, possibly of a later period. These are the modern definitions used in auction house catalogues. Bell helped pioneer these distinctions, but in his day they were less precise.

neys, Reynoldses, and other eighteenth-century portraits which would once have gone to Christie's as a matter of course now started turning up at Sotheby's. In June 1920, Bell's first summer with Sotheby's, he brought in a magnificent, set-piece portrait of Queen Elizabeth I by Marcus Gheeraerts the Younger, along with three fine portraits of other Elizabethan ladies. The property of Lord Willoughby de Broke, the four portraits were extravaganzas of ruffs and wigs and pearls in the grand manner. Sotheby's had never sold such a significant batch of paintings before.

Bell's expertise enriched the auction house in other fields. Thanks to his academic connections Sotheby's were able to obtain advice from such scholars as Howard Carter, the famous Egyptologist who had discovered the tomb of Tutankhamen, and the archaeologist Sir Edgar John Forsdyke, who later became director of the British Museum. The cataloguer's most useful reference, however, proved to be the expert that he nominated to succeed himself — for only four years after his Wednesday visits had become the highlight of the New Bond Street week, Charles Bell announced his resignation.

The root of the trouble was Evelyn Barlow, who had hung on to her wartime responsibility for the print and picture department, and who suffered from her brother's bossiness, without his taste or charm. She felt the need to "organise" the scholarly cataloguer, and he rebelled. Bell was a dilettante of private means who had taken on his position at Sotheby's as much for the sake of contact with art as for the monetary reward, and he decided that Evelyn Barlow was an inconvenience he had no need to tolerate — though his courteous and even-tempered letter of resignation made no reference to that.

"Almost all the firm needs," he wrote to Barlow in 1924, "to accomplish the last stages of capturing the biggest picture business is a thoroughly first class whole-time man such as it is impossible for me to become."

The man whom Bell nominated was as foreign and eccentric as Bell had been English and old school tie. Dr. Tancred Borenius was a flamboyant Finn of part-Italian descent who mingled with the Bloomsbury set and was a lecturer in the fine arts at University College, London. Borenius had picked up his art in his childhood, when his father would take him on his business trips to St. Petersburg, and would leave his son all day in the Hermitage Museum in the company of a packet of sandwiches.

Borenius's romantic marriage to his childhood sweetheart, the granddaughter of Finland's leading poet, did not stop him indulging in troubled love affairs that embarrassed even his bohemian friends, and he was prone to dinner party diatribes on obscure aspects of Finnish politics. But his eccentricities were part of a style that won him entrée to the grandest homes in the land. Borenius spent a month in Yorkshire every summer, staying with Henry Lascelles, the future Lord Harewood, and after Lascelles's marriage to Princess Mary, the Princess Royal, he became a confidant of her mother, Queen Mary, who consulted Borenius regularly on her own collecting passions.

Borenius took over Bell's Wednesday Old Master sessions in New Bond Street, and he added his cosmopolitan spice to the proceedings. Less obviously focused than Bell, the Finn would launch into a critique of the opera he had seen the previous night — he and his wife were ardent Wagnerians — or would wrap his remarkably polished English around his problems at *Apollo,* the art magazine, of which he was the founder and first editor.

Borenius had a command of no less than nine languages, which he deployed in the cultivation of obscure aristocrats and royalties all over Europe. They rewarded him with the ribbons and insignia of exotic orders of chivalry, and with silver-framed photographs which he set out proudly on the yellow and black Finnish birchwood furniture that he collected. The Doctor's energies were multi-directional, and he threw them extravagantly into his new job with Sotheby's. A Christie's director heading north on a business-scouting expedition to a major funeral was disconcerted to meet Borenius, already on his way back.

"He must have been there," the Christie's man complained, "to attend the last rites."

Barlow and his partners had got their "thoroughly first class" man, though Borenius never worked "whole time" for Sotheby's. With his magazine and his music and his work at University College, where he became a professor, his was not a spirit to be harnessed to a single plough. On every day of the week but Wednesday, Borenius would cheerfully pocket a five-guinea valuation fee from anyone who brought him a picture. These freelance "smackers under the table," as the art historian Kenneth Clark called them, were notorious in the London art world. They compromised Borenius's status in the eyes of academics and were the reason why, in Clark's opinion, the Finn failed to attain the position he most keenly coveted — the Keeper of the King's Pictures.

Borenius was paid by Sotheby's on a commission basis, as Bell had been, and by 1928–29 he was earning nearly £3,000 a year, which was more than some of the partners were getting. But it directly reflected the Doctor's impact on sales. Sotheby's turnover from paintings and drawings grew by more than 500 percent in the four years after he joined the company in 1924 — and suddenly the competition was under attack. The rush of aristocratic house sales that followed the Great War had been a windfall for Christie's and they had enjoyed massive profits, far outdistancing those of Sotheby's, which had had to meet the costs of its relocation to New Bond Street. But by 1926–27 Sotheby's profit of £27,000 was within shooting distance of Christie's £59,000, and in the following year the comparable figures were £63,000 for Sotheby's and £70,000 for their rivals. The upstarts had almost caught up.

6

IN 1922, ANDREW BONAR LAW invited Montague Barlow to take a seat in his new government as Minister of Labour. Sitting in the Conservative cabinet alongside such political giants as Lord Curzon and Stanley Baldwin, Barlow found himself close to, though not quite at the heart of, the English establishment. Labour was a comparatively new Ministry, a necessary but not dreadfully desirable job, to be allocated to an elbowing aspirant rather than to an old-style patrician, and Barlow fitted the bill exactly.

It was comparable to the uneasy niche that Barlow was seeking to carve for Sotheby's in the English class system. A politician to the core, Barlow was to marry his secretary, one of Sotheby's blue housecoat brigade, Miss Dora Louise Reed, and many years later Dora Montague Barlow was to provide a clue to what drove her remarkable husband so hard. She related how Barlow had overheard a society friend remark disparagingly, "Oh, *he's* an auctioneer" — and it had hurt.

"He was determined to make the art auctioneering business in London a gentleman's business for gentlemen," explained his

widow. "He had the vision of putting it onto an entirely different social status." In the slang of the time, Barlow wanted to
make Sotheby's "posh."

Montague Barlow had seized upon the same truth as James
Christie. Art auctioneering was all about class. Barlow was rein-
venting Sotheby's on the basis of artistic expertise and modern
management techniques, and these had generated profit. But
profit and poshness were not the same thing. It was like being
the Minister of Labour in a Conservative cabinet. It just
missed — and the same still went for Barlow's reinvented
Sotheby's. As Christie's slyly put it: Christie's were gentlemen
trying to be auctioneers, while Sotheby's were auctioneers trying to be gentlemen.

The point of the jibe was that Sotheby's remained the new
arrivals in a world where newness was anything but a virtue.
They were trying too hard, like Barlow himself — they actually
had to work for their living. There were generations to go before meritocracy would begin to remove the shame which
British upper-class snobbery attached to profit, and Barlow's
dream of gentility for Sotheby's was doomed to disappointment
in his lifetime. But that did not stop him trying.

"It is absolutely a gentleman's business . . ." he wrote in 1920
to a promising young man that he was trying to coax into the
firm as a prospective partner. "Of course we are Auctioneers,
and it is necessary that the partners should be prepared actually
to sell in the rostrum, as I do myself. But I find the auctioneering itself of great interest, and the business which deals all the
time with fine books, fine pictures, fine prints, furniture, coins,
etc., is absorbingly attractive."

The man Barlow was trying to capture was Charles des Graz,
an old Etonian who had gone into intelligence work during the
war, following an impressive career at Cambridge. According to
Millicent Sowerby, who stayed with the firm for six years after
the war, des Graz "was related to half the dukes of England."
The young Anthony Eden had been his fag at Eton, and des

Graz had had occasion to administer beatings to the future Foreign Secretary and Prime Minister.

By the tribal codes of the world that Barlow wished to impress, these were excellent qualifications, and in his eagerness to
enlist the young man, the chairman frankly confided how
Sotheby's had facilitated his own social climbing:

> I do not know whether you have ambitions in Public life or not,
> but if you have, you will find a leading position in Sotheby's (judg-
> ing by my own experience) of distinct use. I deliberately went into
> the business with a view to secure a reasonable financial position so
> that I could take up Public life properly: no man should go into the
> House of Commons unless he has at least £2,000 or £3,000 at his
> back. But, in addition to that, work at Sotheby's brings one into
> pleasant social relation with most of the leading Statesmen of the
> day. . . . In addition one gets into pleasant social touch with most
> of the big houses in England. . . .

Des Graz did not need the social contacts, but he still liked
the sound of the position that Barlow was offering. He joined
Sotheby's on probation as a junior partner in the autumn of
1920, working as Geoffrey Hobson's assistant in charge of the
book department, and he soon started taking auctions. Millicent
Sowerby found des Graz a pleasant and unassuming boss, but
certain clients found him rather too much the gentleman. Des
Graz's manner in the box was judged to be over-languid, and he
did not dress with the formality that Montague Barlow, a boiled
shirt and knife-pressed suit man, considered appropriate.

Barlow took des Graz to task, and the young man vowed to
do better. But there were further mishaps. The three senior partners conferred again and, typically, it was Barlow who decided
that the problem should be set out on paper:

> A business like ours, which you now see running successfully, has
> only been built up in the last 100 years (and has only been devel-

oped by us to three or four times its previous turnover within the
last ten years) by persistent and unremitting attention to the small-
est details. . . .

Please do not think I want to make too much of all this, but the
issues at stake are serious. We have got a great deal of capital locked
up in the business . . . and in the years to come the safety of our
capital and the future of the business will depend very largely on
the new blood which we now take in. In the rival business of
Messrs. C., undoubtedly the business is already beginning to suffer
from the fact that the juniors they took in a year or two ago are
proving to be of very little use.

To be gentlemen alone, then, was not enough. At a first
glance, Barlow's transfer of Sotheby's to the West End and the
move into the selling of pictures could be seen as a simple imitation of Christie's. But that was only the veneer. Beneath the
surface Barlow had created a rational and thought-out business
operation — the typewriters, the defined holidays and bonus
scheme, the female staff, the talent-spotting of experts. He had
filtered des Graz through a vetting process that went back to des
Graz's housemaster at Eton, and the young partner was being recruited as part of a programme of changing stockholder patterns
that looked fifteen years into the future.

Nothing was left to chance. In response to changing tax legislation, the company was reorganized in December 1924 from
a partnership into a private unlimited company — and at the
same time the name was changed. Recognizing the abbreviation
that had long been made in the trade, Sotheby, Wilkinson and
Hodge became plain Sotheby & Co.

The simplified name was significant. Montague Barlow could be
vainglorious, but his quest for recognition did not extend to getting his name on the letterhead. It could have been argued that

"Barlow, Hobson & Warre" carried more snap than "Sotheby, Wilkinson and Hodge," and it certainly described those who deserved the credit for the company's latest success. But Sotheby was the name that carried the cachet, and like Wilkinson and Hodge fifty years earlier, the new partnership had the sense to realize that.

Barlow's political career came to an abrupt end with the sweeping Labour Party victory in the general election of December 1923. He lost his seat for South Salford and decided not to seek re-election. At the age of fifty-five, he was approaching what he considered a proper age for retirement — and he was already anticipating his retirement at Sotheby's.

Very conscious of the problems Tom Hodge had experienced getting his cash out of the business, Barlow had been laying plans for his smooth departure since the recruitment of Charles des Graz in 1920. Des Graz had been given 1928, the year of Barlow's sixtieth birthday, as the deadline by which he or his father had to pay his full investment into the firm, and after his early teething difficulties, des Graz had settled down into a respected and fully labouring partner, taking particular responsibility for book sales in America, which he visited twice a year.

In 1920 the cost of des Graz's partnership had been set at £15,000. By 1927, the price of admission had risen to £20,000. This was what Charles Vere Pilkington, a socially connected Oxford graduate with artistic tastes, was charged for a directorship and full partnership that year — and the increase reflected the growth in the fortunes of the firm. The accounts for 1927–28 showed profits almost doubling to an all-time record of £63,000. This was the year that brought Sotheby's profits to within £7,000 of Christie's — a fine and triumphant moment for Barlow to cash in his shares and depart.

He gave a farewell dinner at the New Princess restaurant in Piccadilly in the spring of 1929, an eight-course banquet washed down with a 1919 champagne and 1924 Chateau Margaux. Sotheby & Co. had fifty-five members of staff in 1929, and Barlow invited every one of them — cataloguers, clerks, lady typists, porters, and partners. Barlow also invited Tom Hodge and his wife to the celebrations, and the reading of Hodge's letter of regret brought a poignant moment:

> I wish I could come, but I really cannot. . . . It is difficult to believe that you have been twenty years in the firm, but its magnificent increase in fame, power & volume of business helps one to realise it. One now may well say that my father's & my dream of Sotheby's being the leading auctioneers of everything in the way of literature & art may materialise. We were not to see it, but he relaid the foundations for the old firm, & my friends Barlow, Hobson & Warre built on them & are building. May they raise a sky scraper that will attract all the world!

Tom Hodge claimed too much for his father and himself. Until Barlow and his partners came along in 1908, Hodge had been willing to sell Sotheby's for a few thousand pounds, and to see it folded into a lesser book dealership.

But his warmth and congratulation healed a breach that dated back to his abrupt departure during the war. Incensed by the sudden manner of Hodge's going, Barlow had placed advertisements in the newspapers saying that the former partner was no longer associated with Sotheby's, and Hodge had responded by refusing to set foot in his old firm again. On several occasions in the 1920s Felix Warre had looked out of his New Bond Street office window to see Tom Hodge on a visit to London, walking down the far side of the street, his eyes set straight ahead, resolutely refusing even to glance across in the direction of Sotheby's.

Now Barlow sent Hodge a menu with other souvenirs of the gala dinner, and the old man responded with enthusiasm:

I didn't look for any reports in the papers, so missed them, but if Roberts reported for the *Times,* I'm sure he'd do as little as possible; he's never been a real friend of Sotheby's since he worked with McKay, who was hand in glove with Christie's. . . .

It was as if Hodge and Barlow were back in Wellington Street, plotting together before the war. The old man recalled the schemes that Barlow had hatched with him then and he congratulated him on their accomplishment.

"You'll be missed, I'm afraid," he wrote, "for a keen business head is worth more than knowledge, even in such a business as this. However, I daresay they'll get on. . . ."

Montague Barlow could not have timed his retirement better. His grand farewell dinner of April 1929 was held just six months before the Wall Street crash. American collectors stopped buying almost immediately. Art and auction house prices slumped — and so did the value of auction house partnerships. Barlow had cashed in his shares at the most opportune moment.

But the coming of adversity showed what Barlow had achieved at Sotheby's. At the end of the 1929–30 auction season London's rival houses did their accounting, and, for the first time ever, Sotheby's came out ahead — at £35,000 profit for the year, compared to Christie's figure of only £29,000. After little more than a dozen years in the West End, the newcomers had overtaken their more established rivals — and Sotheby's was to keep its lead through the years of Depression, managing small but steady profits for 1930–31, '31–32, and '32–33. In each of these years Christie's recorded a loss.

It was not so much that Sotheby's made more money — rather, that thanks to the business systems of Montague Barlow, they managed to lose less. Felix Warre and Geoffrey Hobson cut staff and expenditure and struggled to pull in the money owed them by the dealers to whom, following book trade practice, they had extended credit. But they could not have anticipated the approach they received in 1933. Christie's contacted them with a proposal that the two firms should amalgamate.

Christie's had been through tough times before. They had had to struggle as hard as Sotheby's in the early years of the war. But this was the first downturn they had had to share with a full-scale competitor, and after three straight years of losses their solution was simple — absorb the competition.

The first reaction of Felix Warre, who negotiated with his equivalent, Lancelot Hannen, the chairman of Christie's, suggested that Sotheby's was very impressed to be courted. They were flattered by their gentlemanly rival's approach. Warre agreed that, in the event of an amalgamation, Sotheby's would give up their New Bond Street premises and would move into Christie's King Street headquarters, with five Christie's directors on the board of the new amalgamated company — to which no name was yet given — and four directors from Sotheby's. A date of transfer was tentatively set for October 1934.

As the accountants started to analyse the balance sheets of the two houses, however, Warre and his partners came to realise they were by no means the junior partners. The figures showed that they were in the position of strength, and that it made no sense at all for them to vacate New Bond Street. With property prices depressed, they would have to write off their saleroom at a heavy loss. There was something lopsided and almost patronising about the deal — and the division of profits that Christie's was proposing for the joint venture was equally slanted.

Felix Warre changed his tone. "The figures which I presume you now have before you," he wrote to Hannen in the spring of 1933, "make it clear that your suggested division of 58% to your side and 42% to us will not do. The average for the last 5⅓ years shews that we have exceeded your average, the ratio being 51% to us and 49% to you."

Sotheby's was even more worried, continued Warre in his

most majorly style, by "your figures for the past three years. We shall be glad to discuss the matter again with you, but, as I have said, we must get the above two points settled before we pass into other topics."

The points were not settled and the amalgamation went no further. Christie's regrouped in King Street, learning to live with the reality of their competitor, while for Sotheby's, the experience marked a coming of age. For a century and three quarters they had been the bookworms, and for the last two decades the impudent newcomers. Now they had had a chance to scrutinise the competition and to appreciate the full stature of their own achievement. Christie's had approached them with grandeur, and had had to slink off rejected. Whether or not Sotheby's were gentlemen, they had proved they were very competent auctioneers.

On January 28, 1936, Geoffrey Hobson's son, Anthony, then a schoolboy at Eton, was standing in the crowd outside Windsor Castle witnessing the funeral of King George V, when he was astonished to see his father's picture expert, Tancred Borenius, walking at the heart of the procession among the crowned heads of Europe. Proudly decked out in his exotic ribbons of chivalry, the Doctor was representing his much-cultivated foreign contacts, the obscure Hapsburgs and other deposed royalties who could not make it to the ceremony.

As a book auctioneer, Sotheby's had a tradition of European contacts. In 1936 Christie's could not have produced a picture expert who knew the difference between Baden-Baden and Baden-Durlach, let alone serve as the representative of their rulers. If a letter arrived at King Street that was in German or Italian, recalls one former director, the letter was shuffled from partner to partner until one of them quietly dropped it in the wastepaper basket. England was the focus of the grandest of the English auction houses — which left their rivals with an obvious market across the Channel.

Sotheby's already had their own representative in Germany. Colonel R. G. Birch, an ex–British army officer, had built up an impressive network of contacts in the German art market, where the local auction houses had suffered badly during the inflation of the 1920s. Sellers wanted stable foreign currency for their goods, so in the autumn of 1931, Geoffrey Hobson found himself foraging Germany in Birch's company, unearthing treasures in remote Gothic castles, and also making contact with Jewish collectors who were growing apprehensive at the rising power of the Nazi party. One of these was Jakob Goldschmidt, a wealthy banker who owned a collection of eighteenth-century porcelain which he displayed in cabinets in the enormous mansion that he had built to house his art in Berlin.

Even more remarkable was Goldschmidt's collection of the still-unfashionable Impressionist painters — Manet, Renoir, van Gogh, and Cézanne. These canvases hung gaudily, but somehow harmoniously, above Goldschmidt's neat and precise porcelain, a striking collection of images that included van Gogh's brooding depiction of lovers in the shade of a huge cedar tree, the *Jardin Public à Arles,* alongside Cézanne's portrait of a boy in a red waistcoat, the *Garçon au Gilet Rouge.*

Little more than a year after he met Hobson, Goldschmidt was to flee Germany. The Nazis came to power in 1933, and the banker's fine mansion was commandeered to become Mussolini's embassy in Berlin — Goldschmidt escaping in such danger and speed that he had to leave many of his most cherished canvases behind. But he had already managed to get much of his porcelain out of Germany, and he decided to sell this in London before he left Europe for America and a new life.

Goldschmidt came to New Bond Street, taking it for granted that his previous contact with Hobson and the quality of his china would entitle him to some reduction in Sotheby's 7½ percent commission rate. But Hobson haughtily declined to lower the already reduced rate, and Goldschmidt walked down the road to St. James's. A few months later Christie's happily raised nearly £25,000 in a briskly bid sale.

Hobson was crestfallen. "I should never have talked to him myself," he admitted to Jim Kiddell, the ceramics expert who had joined Sotheby's shortly after World War I, and henceforward it was the younger and more flexible Kiddell who was entrusted with foreign missions.

Beanpole tall, with a wobbly Adam's apple and scholarly, half-moon glasses, Kiddell came from humble origins. During the war he had served in the shadowy and rather sinister Mutiny Breaking Squad. But this proved good training for the continental projects that he now undertook, for as tensions grew in Europe, Sotheby's found themselves dealing with frightened consignors who were on the run. It was the French Revolution all over again. For one escapade that involved the smuggling of property out of Berlin, Kiddell wore dark glasses, deliberately missed his scheduled cross-Channel ferry crossing, and spoke in code on telephone lines that he presumed to be tapped.

Back in England, Kiddell was part of a cheeky initiative to capture a line of business that had been Christie's specialty since the days of its founder — the country house sale. Scanning the obituary columns, and using cars to scout the countryside for likely prospects, a team of young cataloguers under Vere Pilkington snatched a succession of juicy properties away from Christie's, working with such speed that they became known as the "Flying Squad."

The trick of a good sale-on-the-premises, Jim Kiddell liked to explain, was to avoid the derelict atmosphere of the routine estate or bankruptcy disposal, since a house seldom looks its best after a death or financial disaster. The Flying Squad would scour the servants' quarters and even the attics in search of knick-knacks that could be brought down to enliven the reception rooms, so that a house prepared for a sale by Kiddell and his colleagues would often look better on viewing day than when it had been occupied by its owners.

In the course of the 1930s Sotheby's held at least twenty of these sales on the premises, more than half of them in country houses. But the Flying Squad used similar techniques in London's vanishing noble palaces, the grandest of them being the 1937 sale of the furniture, pictures, silver, and other contents of the opulent Rothschild residence at 148 Piccadilly. One of London's most sumptuous surviving mansions, 148 Piccadilly was being vacated by a younger generation in pursuit of a simpler life, since even Rothschilds have budgets to observe.

The combination of a famous name, opulent objects, and a sense of times changing made the auction a national event. BBC microphones broadcast live coverage, and the bidders were waiting outside two hours ahead of the sale. Many had come to London for the forthcoming coronation of King George VI — who, as Duke of York, had lived with his family a few doors away at 145 Piccadilly — so the saleroom was characterized by a high proportion of maharajahs, eastern potentates, and friends of Tancred Borenius.

The younger members of the firm had to work especially hard escorting these dignitaries on private viewing sessions, and there was one recent recruit who made a particular impression. Immensely tall and pale, with a thin neck and a square, jutting jaw, Peter Cecil Wilson spoke with a slight stutter and exuded an aura of great knowledge and taste.

"I've just seen a charming young man," Geoffrey Hobson told his son, Anthony, on the night he got home from interviewing Peter Wilson. "I think he's going to come into the firm and be a great success."

PART THREE

Peter Wilson

7

IF ONE SINGLE PERSON CREATED the modern Sotheby's, it was Peter Cecil Wilson, born on March 8, 1913, to parents of impressive pedigree. His father was Sir Mathew Wilson, Baronet, of Eshton Hall, Gargrave in Craven, Yorkshire; his mother, the Honourable Barbara Lister, daughter of the Fourth Baron Ribblesdale, Master of the Royal Buckhounds, of Gisburn Park, Gisburn, nearby.

This double dose of blue blood inspired the grandeur with which Wilson took Sotheby's to international supremacy in the auction business. In contrast to Montague Barlow's earnest gropings for class, Wilson had the insider's unworried grasp of what defines superiority, along with aesthetic instincts of sheer brilliance.

But he also had the ability to stand outside the elite into which he was born, and to prey on it shamelessly. Peter Wilson had a sixth sense which told him when the ostensibly prosperous were in need of ready cash — for this was the condition in which the Wilson family lived throughout his childhood. In

1916 his father sold off the family library to keep creditors at bay, and seven years later, when Peter was ten, the Wilsons had to move out of Eshton Hall entirely.

"My parents," he remembered, "were not sufficiently well off to remain there."

The house was let for ten years to a member of the W. D. and H. O. Wills tobacco family, and the Wilsons took up a rootless existence, camping with relatives and in rented accommodations.

"I was sorry about it," Wilson later reflected, "but it wasn't a terrible blow. Life had always been divided between London and there."

The good auctioneer knows how to talk up a disappointing sale, and that is what Peter Wilson did with his youthful misfortunes.

"I think a very happy childhood," he said, "is not conducive to success in later life."

Wilson's insouciance was modelled on the brittle polish of his father, Sir Mathew, known as "Scatters." This nickname was said to come from his improvidence with money, but it may also have reflected the lavishness with which he scattered his affections in the direction of ladies who were not his wife. Scatters Wilson proudly claimed responsibility for provoking more divorces than any other man in society.

Scatters was a rake, trying to finance his expensive tastes with money won at cards. An army officer and later a Member of Parliament, he was most constantly a stockbroker, charming friends to part with their money at country house weekends, where he was renowned for his shooting, and also for his practical jokes. One dull Christmas before he left Eshton, he threw a party for every Yorkshire neighbour he could discover whose name contained the word "bottom"— Bottomley, Ramsbotham, Longbottom, and so on — then set them to work introducing themselves to each other.

The Honourable Barbara Lister fell in love with Scatters Wilson because, as she later put it, he was "the champion purveyor of larks." His high jinks echoed the superior style of her father, Lord Ribblesdale, whose ineffably aristocratic portrait by John Singer Sargent hangs today near the main entrance to the National Gallery. There are those who detect the piercing blue eyes of Peter Wilson himself staring out of his grandfather's features on the canvas. With his top hat at an angle, and his rumpled cream breeches, the Master of the Buckhounds peers down quizzically at hoi polloi, the epitome of noble disdain.

Barbara Wilson had the resources to survive very well without her husband's company once his larks ceased to involve her. She knew how to put on a good face, and having been "finished" in France, she was familiar with the syndrome of the philandering husband and the wronged but loyal wife who displays her spirit by keeping the family unit intact.

"So marriage may be unhappy," she wrote in 1929, "but the children see no degradation of their home."

Effectively separated for much of her marriage, Barbara Wilson threw herself into the upbringing of her three sons, Martin, Anthony, and Peter, instructing them through the polished but cynical fables of La Fontaine, which the little boys learned to recite in French. For personal expression of her feelings, she turned to writing, pouring out her emotions in slightly precious, but intensely felt romances and memoirs that enjoyed some success. Her books were scarcely veiled accounts of her own life, and to judge from what she once wrote about Peter, she saw her youngest son as a very delicate treasure: "still in a blue-linen tunic, playing in deep meadow-grass or pasture-land, he looked like a speedwell or periwinkle flower that had strayed there."

This medley of influences produced a child of high complexity. Shy and sensitive, with a speech hesitation that was almost a stutter, Peter Wilson's unusually developed aesthetic sense was balanced by a total lack of sentimentality where money was concerned. When he went to Eton, his only distinction was the special prize he won for the finest collection of wildflowers gathered from the water-meadows of the Thames. Allowed to choose his prize, he picked out an antiquarian book — which, he was proud to relate, he later sold when offered the right price.

Tall and gangling, with limbs like matchsticks, Peter Wilson hated the athletic pursuits of British public school life, cutting games to spend his afternoons in pursuit of old books and curios. His career was shaped in the antique shops of Eton. Taste was his refuge, the one thing on which he could rely in a lonely world, ostensibly in contact with his amusing and eccentric parents, but scarcely sustained by them. With his shyness and his aesthetic proclivities, Peter Wilson was known as "an alternative Etonian."

New College, Oxford, took a chance on him, but he was gone after a year, having repeated his Eton tactics. Peter Wilson could not pass an antique shop without wanting to go in. He failed his Preliminary exams in history, and his parents dispatched their son to Europe to polish his languages. The idea was that Peter should prepare for a diplomatic career. But he came back early, and, barely twenty years old, with a wife.

Helen Ranken was a forceful Englishwoman who had been staying in the Hamburg home of the professor to whom young Wilson was sent to learn German. A trained teacher, something of a blue-stocking and five years his senior, she fell in love with the shy beanpole with a stutter. She shared his interest in flowers and his taste for Taste. She listened seriously to him, coaxing out hopes and confidences that he had previously kept to himself, and her love gave him new purpose.

"He was nothing until his marriage," remembered Wilson's elder brother Martin, talking to the author Nicholas Faith.

Sir Mathew and Lady Wilson were horrorstruck. They had sent their son to Europe to prepare to earn his living, not to complicate his life — and Helen Ranken was middle class. Her family was prosperous, but they had no social connections. Helen herself was unsophisticated. She was indifferent to the niceties of drawing-room life, and she did not accord with her mother-in-law's notions of style.

"I felt," Helen Wilson told Nicholas Faith, "she would have preferred him to marry a dancer rather than a solid bourgeois like me."

Scatters abruptly revoked the small allowance on which his youngest son had been living, and Peter had to find a job, putting his hours in the antique shops to good use by getting a position at Spink, the venerable coin and medal dealers whose premises were in King Street, next door to Christie's.

He hated it. Spink, he said later, was "cold, snobby and beastly in atmosphere." Testing the family writing tradition with a brief stint at Reuters, the news agency, he moved on to *The Connoisseur,* the art and antiques magazine — but not as a writer. The son of Sir Mathew Wilson, Baronet, became an advertising space salesman.

"In those days it was a triumph to get a job," he later recalled. "People got degrees and were very happy to go around selling silk stockings."

At the age of twenty-three Peter Wilson was ostracized by his family and virtually penniless. His visits to antique shops were now for the purpose of wheedling advertising from their owners, and he spent long hours in newsagents, checking that his magazine was properly displayed. But he passed his weekends in grander company, and it was at a Gloucestershire house party in 1936 that Peter and Helen Wilson bumped into Vere Pilkington, who was just coming up to his tenth year with Sotheby's. Wilson offered to work for nothing if Pilkington could find him a place at the firm, and he was taken almost at his word. After searching interviews with Hobson, Warre, and des Graz, he was offered a job as porter in the furniture department.

"Here, for the first time in my life, was work that I loved doing," he later recalled. "I couldn't wait to get back to it on Monday morning. I had nightmares of getting the sack from Sotheby's. I remember one nightmare was that I went into the office, someone brought in a large object and I hadn't the faintest idea whether it was valuable or not. . . . A most terrible feeling in the dream: was it going to be valuable; was I going to get the sack?"

Peter Wilson was home. Setting recruits to work as porters was the no-cost training scheme that Hobson and Warre had devised to uncover talent. The newcomers would handle and sort goods as they came in, fetch and carry for the experts, and help hang the sales. It soon became obvious if they had the all-important "eye" and a willingness to work — and Peter Wilson had both.

In the summer of 1937 New Bond Street received an unusual consignment of more than two thousand antique rings assembled by Edouard Guilhou, a Parisian collector at the turn of the century. Ranging in their histories from ancient Egypt to the France of Napoleon, the rings were described in a catalogue produced in 1912, and Geoffrey Hobson suggested that the job of checking and updating the catalogue be handed to the new trainee in the furniture department.

Peter Wilson leapt at the chance. The summer break was coming up, when the auction house traditionally shut down for a month or more, and Wilson spent his free hours scouring the libraries for extra details of Merovingian rivalries and blood feuds. With a combination of research and writing that he had been unable to muster at Oxford, he produced a sales catalogue of elegant persuasiveness, and he worked with equal energy to publicize what became, in effect, his own sale, getting close-up photographs of the more intriguing rings placed in the art magazines.

There were sarcastic mutterings among the established staff about over-cataloguing. Wilson's text told stories and made connections that went beyond bare recital of the facts. One ring had been found in the tomb of a dramatically murdered duke, another in the bed of the river Oise above Compiègne. But the stories helped publicity, and that brought in the buyers. The four-day sale attracted private collectors as well as dealers, and the proceeds of £15,000 surpassed expectations.

The partners' hunch had paid off. Felix Warre was thinking about retirement, and after the hard years of the 1930s, he wished to cash in some of his shares. The brief flurry of pre-war sales seemed a good wave to catch — and Helen Wilson had just come into some of her bourgeois inheritance. Helen gave her husband £5,000 to purchase a portion of Warre's shareholding, and in December 1938, only two years after joining as a porter, Peter Wilson became a director and junior partner in the firm.

Sir Mathew and Lady Wilson turned up for the celebratory lunch, Lady Wilson wearing a heavy velvet Regency turban of formidable proportions. She was delighted with her son, and so was Scatters. Bygones were bygones. The boy in the periwinkle suit had managed to redeem himself. Sotheby's had saved a drifting young man who could find no use for his unconventional talents, and he was to repay the auction house with his consuming devotion for the rest of his life.

8

IN THE AUTUMN OF 1939, less than twelve months after
becoming a director and partner in Sotheby's, Peter Wilson
abruptly vanished from the auction house, together with every
other male of fighting age. Hitler's invasion of Poland had
brought war to Europe.

Charles des Graz had been preparing for months, having
maintained his connections with Imperial Censorship, the mail
vetting department where he had worked during World War I.
Des Graz held the rank of deputy head, and with the opening
of hostilities, he departed to Liverpool. The Censorship needed
headquarters for its massive task of opening and snooping
through Britain's mail, and it had commandeered the staff and
facilities of Britain's largest private mail-sorting operations, the
offices of Littlewood's and Vernon's football pools.

Nominally on the lookout for chance betrayals of strategic
information by indiscreet citizens, the Censorship was actually
searching for spies. It was serious secret service, and des Graz recruited the brightest spirits he could find at Sotheby's — Peter

Wilson, Vere Pilkington, and John Taylor, an erudite young book cataloguer who had scientific expertise. The four men went up to Liverpool in the autumn of 1939.

Felix Warre and Geoffrey Hobson were the caretakers in charge of New Bond Street, with Jim Kiddell their expert in residence. A bomb shelter had already been constructed downstairs in the original wine cellars, and at the beginning of 1940 Felix Warre wrote to Christie's suggesting that the two firms should work out ways to help each other in the event of either saleroom suffering a direct hit.

"If either of our premises were knocked out," he wrote, "it would be a good thing to show a united British front if two businesses in competition were to help each other in this way."

Christie's accepted the proposal, but as the war intensified and normal business ground to a halt, the discussions went a stage further. Amalgamation was on the table again, and, as in 1933, Christie's proposed that the two companies should merge and operate out of King Street, with Sotheby's effectively becoming the subordinate partner.

As in 1933, however, the figures told a different story. Sotheby's was in better financial shape than their rivals. Their average annual profit for the years 1935–40 was £16,477, as compared with £14,957 for Christie's. Up in Liverpool, the Censorship contingent of des Graz, Pilkington, and Wilson were fiercely opposed to the idea of a merger. Wilson was particularly vociferous, and Warre went back to Christie's to say, once again, that there was no deal.

As events turned out, it was Christie's that were hit by the bomb. Their premises were gutted on the night of April 16–17, 1941, at the end of a heavy German raid on central London. Only their front door remained standing, and though Sotheby's offered help, Christie's received a better offer. Lord Derby had vacated his grand mansion beside Oxford Street, and this became Christie's base for the remainder of the hostilities.

As the tide of the war changed, so did the fortunes of the auction business. There was something of a boom as collectors felt more confident and started looking for bargains. With victory in sight, Geoffrey Hobson was able to report a healthy financial situation to the young partners preparing to return to their civilian activities:

> We have not had an overdraft since January 29, 1942, and credit balance has sometimes been over £100,000 for some weeks at a time. . . . The ratio of profits to turnover has been improved, and in every way the firm is in a far stronger position financially than in 1939.

Hobson's only complaint was that he and Warre were both feeling tired. It was clear that Sotheby's future would lie in the hands of its returning war heroes — though down in King Street there was derision at the idea that six years in the Censorship constituted serious war service.

"That fella Wilson," sniffed a Christie's partner of Sotheby's rising star. "Spent the war reading other people's letters."

There was no other way to describe what the Censorship did. After only a few months in Liverpool, Peter Wilson had been sent down to Gibraltar to the "Special Examiners" department, which picked open the supposedly sacrosanct pouches of other countries' diplomatic bags, then was moved on to Bermuda, where the Hamilton Princess Hotel had been filled with nearly three hundred women who busily rummaged through the contents of the transatlantic mails.

All allied mail bags crossing the Atlantic were diverted via Bermuda or Trinidad, where the Censorship also had offices, and were delayed for several days in mid-ocean while their contents were examined by teams under the direction of experts like Wilson. Letters were steamed open, then heated or dampened for evidence of secret inks. Code experts scanned the pattern of writing for clues, and statistics published after the war revealed that a significant number of the foreign agents uncovered in America during World War II were first identified by these Boy Scout methods.

Towards the end of the war Peter Wilson was promoted to full-scale espionage. He joined the ranks of MI6 and was transferred to Washington, where he was invited to stay on and make spying his life.

"I was vaguely tempted," he later admitted. "It was a fascinating job and such nice people."

His MI6 code number was 007. One of his friends and colleagues was the author Ian Fleming, and in later years Wilson liked to boast that he had provided the inspiration for Fleming's famous creation, James Bond.

It was not an impossible stretch. Peter Wilson was charm and intrigue personified. The themes of his career at Sotheby's were to be the seduction of clients and the stealing of sales from the enemy. There are even those who believe that Peter Wilson never fully left the world of espionage, and that all the famous things he did for Sotheby's were just a front. Rather than 007, according to this theory, Peter Wilson was a Russian spy.

The notion would provide a satisfying twist to the story if the archives of the KGB could offer any hint it was true. Sadly, the spy writer Rupert Allason, who writes under the name of Nigel West, reports otherwise. Allason has been given total access to the recently unlocked Russian files for a history of Department 3, the KGB operation in the British sphere, and he has found nothing to suggest any involvement by Peter Wilson. Burgess, Maclean, Philby, Blunt — the famous network of betrayal is fully sketched, with some other names. But Wilson is not mentioned, though the auctioneer had been an acquaintance, at one time or another, with all the traitors, either through MI6 or, in Blunt's case, through the art world, and he could also be said to have matched their social and sexual profiles. Like the real spies, Wilson was both upper crust and a surreptitious homosexual.

Wilson's homosexuality is one guilty secret which the evidence does sustain. Growing up under a law which made homosexual practice a crime, he was not open about his orientation as a youth, and his early marriage to Helen Ranken channelled him firmly in a conventional direction. The couple had two sons, born in 1937 and 1940. But the marriage was dissolved in 1947, and thereafter he followed his inclinations.

Peter Wilson's marriage fell apart in the course of the war. In 1939 Helen had accompanied her husband to work in Liverpool at the Censorship, where she used her excellent German to decipher German letters. But then Peter went abroad. He was lazy, not to say neglectful about keeping in touch with his wife, and during the long months of separation Helen started seeing Philip Ballard, a Herefordshire farmer who had courted her before her marriage and with whom she fell in love again.

Peter Wilson seems to have borne remarkably little grudge about his wife leaving him for Ballard, and after her remarriage, the family unit was to remain intact in a curious fashion. It became a tradition for Peter Wilson to join the Ballards for their Christmas celebrations, and in the summer, grown-ups and children would all pile together in a car, and head for the south of France.

"My teachers at school thought this was the ultimate in loose living," remembers Philip Wilson, the younger son, "that one's stepfather and father should go on holidays together."

Philip Wilson remembers the trio of his mother, father, and stepfather as being on the best of terms. Helen and Peter Wilson shared many interests, particularly a love of flowers. It often surprised their friends to see the separated couple so relaxed and happy in each other's company and people wondered about Wilson's ambiguous sexuality.

"Gay" would be the modern word, but it does not seem the right description for Peter Wilson. From the early 1950s onwards, his permanent companion was Harry Wright, a bluff and common ex-military type who had a weakness for the horses, and who relied on Wilson to bail him out of his gambling scrapes. Harry lived in the elegant country retreat which Wilson acquired at Mersham, near Ashford in Kent. During the week he ran the grocer's shop that he bought in the local village. But he stayed home when Wilson came down for the weekend, so he could help with the entertaining — and also with the gardening, at which he was rather better than Wilson. As one guest put it, Harry was "the wife in the country."

But Peter Wilson did not flaunt his sexual proclivities, and it seemed an irrelevant issue to many people who knew him, particularly in an age that was more discreet about such things. To most of the staff at Sotheby's, PCW — as he was known from the initials on his energetic notes and memos — was an immensely busy figure who had once been married and was now separated for reasons of which no one was quite clear. Few knew about Harry down in Kent. It was PCW's work that defined him, and, as many who were close to Peter Wilson remarked, the marriage that really mattered to him was his life-long bonding with Sotheby's.

Nineteen forty-seven, the year of Peter and Helen Wilson's divorce, also saw some major steps forward in Wilson's auction house career. Felix Warre and Geoffrey Hobson had decided Wilson should take over responsibility for new appointments and salaries. They saw him as a future head of the firm, and they set about the transition of power they had long been planning. Warre retired in July 1947, passing his role as chairman to Hobson.

Warre held a party to celebrate his departure in the back garden of his London home. There were white china bowls of fruit punch, and people got mildly tiddly. Almost the entire staff was there — forty-one people, including porters and secretaries, for the company still had the character of an old-fashioned firm of solicitors. Everybody knew everybody in the warren of Dickensian offices where the main staircase shot straight up into the saleroom. The accounts were still kept in copperplate, and each partner's name was painted at the entrance to the main staircase in the style of the old universities, with a sliding wooden indicator to show if they were "IN" or "OUT."

Christie's had taken advantage of their wartime bombing to modernise their space in St. James, and in 1947 they approached Sotheby's with the suggestion that their updated premises presented a fresh opportunity for amalgamation — their third merger proposal in fifteen years. But their initiative stemmed from the same reasons as ever. Both houses had had a tough year, and Christie's had spent too much on rebuilding. After a day of discussions, the New Bond Street partners decided that they were happy to live with competition.

The new chairman, Geoffrey Hobson, told Christie's the news. Aged sixty-four, Hobson envisaged himself heading the business for another five or six years before retiring to the book bindings which had become his passion. But he was only to manage eighteen months, having driven himself with the same fierce perfectionism he expected of everyone else. Deaf as ever, and twice as pernickety, Geoffrey Hobson died in harness in January 1949, almost forty years from the day that he, Barlow, and Warre had first moved into Sotheby's.

More rapidly than anyone had quite anticipated, the guard had been changed. Charles des Graz, the new boy whom Montague Barlow once chastised for his casual work habits, became the new chairman, and he decided on a strategic swap. Not happy with the way in which Vere Pilkington had been handling picture sales, he switched Pilkington to works of art, the empire of knick-knacks where Jim Kiddell could be relied on to take the strain. Des Graz gave pictures to Peter Wilson.

Just thirteen years after he had joined Sotheby's, Peter Wilson was handed responsibility for the way ahead. Pictures were the category which offered the prospect of greatest profit and growth at the opposition's expense. But Wilson had already set his sights beyond the besting of Christie's. The business that he wanted was the huge mainstream of the art market. He thirsted for the retail trade dominated by dealers, buying at auction and selling on to customers, and he was still more eager to challenge the enduring dealer monopoly of the very highest-ticket paintings. Dealers were the principal customers of the auction houses, but in Wilson's eyes they were also the principal competitors.

Peter Wilson's years working in Washington for British intelligence at the end of World War II had introduced him to the wealth and aspirations of the New World. Getting a taste of the American art market gave him a vision of Sotheby's becoming a more than purely British business, and he had the first chance to develop this international dimension in December 1952, when a group of Egyptian army officers deposed King Farouk, the playboy king of Egypt.

Wilson sniffed plunder immediately. As Sotheby's director of pictures, he had no special brief for a foreign palace-clearing sale, but he knew that the fez-wearing Farouk had staked a claim to being the world's greatest collector. The sale of the ex-king's treasures would provide a much-needed fillip for Sotheby's rather depressed postwar business, still hampered by lingering currency regulations. The entire London art market had been sluggish since 1945.

Wilson took the next plane to Cairo to propose an auction to the military junta, and the royal hoard proved all he had hoped. Farouk had collected almost everything — stamps, coins, medals, gold boxes, more than two thousand gold watches, Fabergé ornaments of all varieties, glass paperweights, Gallé glass, porcelain, and furniture. There was something almost noble in the thoroughness with which the ex-King had assembled the world's definitive collections of cigarette cards and even aspirins, which went back to the first Bayer paper packets of the 1840s. The impressive royal collection of erotica and pornography had had its own curator, a servant who would pick out a fresh magazine every evening, and place it on a tray beside the King's bed.

Back in England, Wilson's fellow directors expressed qualms. What if Farouk, or some heir living in exile, chose to contest the legality of the sale? Sotheby's did not have the funds to get involved in a costly lawsuit.

"There was a very strong element in Sotheby's that absolutely did not wish to go forward," Wilson later remembered with impatience at the caution of his partners. "In life one goes forward or back. I wanted to go forward."

Wilson took counsel's opinion in London on the legality of the sale. The new Egyptian government, he was told, was internationally recognized. If the new regime were to pass a law formally confiscating the property, Farouk and his family would have no possible claim. So Peter Wilson flew back to Cairo and got the law passed. The Egyptians liked the notions dreamt up by this nimble Englishman — though it was a local official who came up with the proposal that any buyer spending £5,000 or more would be allowed free access to the erotica rooms.

Competitors arrived. Parke-Bernet, the New York auction house, made a proposal, while Maurice Rheims, the French auctioneer, headed a consortium who pushed so hard that they eventually won a cut of all sales to French buyers. But it was Sotheby's that secured the principal deal, and after sixteen months of battling, cataloguing, and tireless promotion, the house sale in the desert took place. Egypt's Royal Palace's Collections went on the block in Cairo in February and March 1954.

As a business venture, the Farouk sale was a disaster. The Egyptian government professed itself disappointed with the £750,000 which Sotheby's raised, and refused to hand over the agreed expenses and sales commission. Haggling over the unpaid balance dragged on until Egypt's seizure of the Suez Canal in 1956, when the auction house had to write off the loss.

In terms of promotion, however, the Farouk sale was a triumph. Its bizarre ingredients attracted international attention, and the adventurous London auction house that had gone out to Cairo was the focus of stories everywhere. Peter Wilson had pulled off his first international publicity coup.

9

IT IS TAKEN FOR GRANTED nowadays that the world's very finest pictures should go to public auction at Sotheby's or Christie's, their prices catching the headlines in a flurry of zeroes. It seems the way to get the best price for a truly exceptional, museum-quality work of art. But this is quite a recent phenomenon. When James Christie sold Robert Walpole's collection of Old Masters to Catherine the Great in 1779, he negotiated the transaction by private treaty, acting as a dealer, rather than as an auctioneer, and until the second half of the twentieth century the classic masterpieces were nearly always placed privately by dealers. It was as if the auction process would tarnish the holiness. Auction houses handled the poor, the average, and the good when it came to paintings. But if a truly exceptional Rubens or Rembrandt came onto the market, it was handled in a private transaction by a dealer like Joseph Duveen, who sent enough Old Masters to America in the early decades of the twentieth century to become a multi-millionaire.

Duveen and his rivals like Knoedler and Wildenstein were

the emperors of the art world, trading on their own eye and taste to fill their galleries with beauty. They had the funds to buy a Raphael or a Rembrandt for stock, confident they could find the right person to invite into their private viewing room. Art milestones were their business. In 1927, Duveen paid the astonishing sum of £620,000 — roughly equivalent to Sotheby's entire turnover that year — for the connoisseur Robert Benson's collection of Italian Renaissance masterpieces, which Duveen discreetly parceled out around museums and private collectors in Europe and America.

Discretion was part of the dealer's appeal. The rich visited his vaults to glimpse canvases the world did not guess were for sale, while sellers might not care to publicize the heirlooms they had been compelled, or had been tempted, to jettison. The dealer knew where to find a special treasure, and he knew where to "place" it. He would make use of the auction houses to pick up bargains, or to offload his mistakes. But he regarded the saleroom as a sort of warehouse, and he considered that he operated at a far grander level.

The superiority of the dealer was one of the almost theological art world orthodoxies that Peter Wilson was determined to challenge. As Montague Barlow had dared to dream that Sotheby's could be more than a book auction house beside Waterloo Bridge, so Wilson came to develop a vision of auctioning not just the good pictures, but the masterpieces as well — and he saw the chance to test his theory one day in June 1956 when Vere Pilkington brought a beautiful, but scarcely known, painting by Nicolas Poussin into New Bond Street.

Pilkington had been invited out to the Norfolk home of Commander Jocelyn Beauchamp, a retired naval officer who wanted to sell off a mixed bag of possessions he had recently inherited. Pilkington could see at once that the Poussin, a vivid depiction of the nativity, was a painting of exceptional merit. Entitled *The Adoration of the Shepherds,* it glowed with a rich, golden light. The composition was a particularly vigorous example of the French artist's intelligent, structured fantasies, and, with Beauchamp's permission, Pilkington took the canvas out of its frame, wrapped it carefully against damage, and drove it straight down to London in the back of his car.

Further research revealed that the painter Joshua Reynolds had once owned the picture, and that it had been sold for 205 guineas after his death in 1792. Since then, the art world had lost sight of it. Reappearing 160 years later, *The Adoration of the Shepherds* was like a fresh discovery, without any doubts as to authenticity. Sotheby's major summer painting sale was coming up in four weeks' time, on July 11, and Peter Wilson was expecting some significant buyers from America and Europe. He decided to make the Poussin the centerpiece of the sale.

Commander Beauchamp was delighted at the prospect of getting his money so quickly, but within a day or so he rang Sotheby's with an extraordinary tale. He had received a visit, he said, from a mysterious and unnamed lady, who told him that she was representing a London dealer who wanted the picture, and was prepared to pay £10,000 cash for an immediate sale. The dealer was also prepared to pay any commission Beauchamp might be charged by Sotheby's for withdrawing the painting from auction — and a few days later she came back with an even better offer. The dealer was now prepared to pay £15,000.

Sotheby's might have suspected the Commander of an overvivid imagination, if this strange scenario had not happened before. There had been several occasions in recent years when anonymous cash offers had been made to preempt fine paintings that were due to come up at auction, and Vere Pilkington had gone to the lengths of hiring a firm of private detectives to discover who was behind the scheme.

Sotheby's assumed it was a dealer, or group of dealers, trying to keep a lid on the salerooms, and Peter Wilson went into battle. Through Pilkington, he assured Beauchamp that Sotheby's could secure him a better price at auction than any dealer could achieve, and that the auction house was prepared to back its confidence with a guaranteed sum of more than £15,000. If the bidding went higher than the guarantee, Beauchamp would receive the full hammer price, less commission. If the bidding went lower, Sotheby's would make up the difference.

The Commander could not lose. The auction house had never made such an offer in its history, and the delighted Beauchamp sent his butler down to London with the painting's magnificent gold frame.

Then, only days before the sale, the Commander was back with another story. Someone at his club had told him he should not take a penny under £35,000, and this person knew about the art world. Blandly unscrupulous — since it was Sotheby's who had discovered the special value of his picture and had generated the interest which was prompting art dealers to approach him at his club — Beauchamp now said that he wanted a guarantee of £35,000, and that if he did not receive it, he would withdraw his painting from the sale.

The blackmail endorsed the doubts of those partners in Sotheby's who had been unhappy about the original guarantee.

"Quite apart from the financial risk," remembers Anthony Hobson, "it seemed to me not altogether how auctioneers ought to behave."

The first guarantee had told Beauchamp that Sotheby's was desperate for the sale. Now he was trying to exploit that weakness. The prudent course was to take him at his word and let him withdraw the picture. But Peter Wilson was adamant in the same fashion that he had pushed through the Farouk project.

"If we fail over this," he said, "we're done for."

The sale had been announced. It would be a damaging loss of face to withdraw the Poussin, and Wilson argued fiercely that the auction houses could never develop so long as people believed that only dealers could sell the really big pictures. It put a permanent ceiling on growth.

"We've got to accept this £35,000," he said. "I will sell it for whatever I can get, and we will have to make up the difference."

Pushing his reluctant colleagues as he had over the Farouk sale, Wilson rammed the £35,000 guarantee through a formal partners' meeting. On July 11, 1956, lot 119 at Sotheby's summer picture sale, *The Adoration of the Shepherds* by Nicolas Poussin, sold for just £29,000 — and Sotheby's did have to make up the difference. They paid the extra £6,000 to Commander Beauchamp from their own funds, and wrote down the sale in their books as a loss.

But the outside world knew nothing of the guarantee, nor of the loss that Sotheby's had taken. Twenty-nine thousand pounds was the highest price secured by any painting at auction in 1956. The sale of Poussin's classic was hailed as a commercial triumph by the art world press. It was a real coup for the auction houses, and it turned out to be an artistic triumph as well, for soon after the sale, the National Gallery, which had not had the nerve to compete in the hurly-burly of the auction, decided to purchase the painting from the dealer who had made the winning bid, paying a sum that was confidential, but which was rumored to be in the region of £35,000. *The Adoration of the Shepherds* by Nicolas Poussin — sold at auction at Sotheby's, but untarnished by the experience — hangs on the hallowed walls of London's National Gallery to this day.

Peter Wilson was no picture expert. He was a man of exquisite taste, with finely tuned commercial instincts, but, like Montague Barlow, he knew that expertise was the key to success in the fields that he wished to conquer. The Poussin had fallen into Sotheby's hands almost by accident, and it had been a struggle to hold on to it. It would require expertise to generate more paintings of similar excellence.

Tancred Borenius had retired as Sotheby's chief picture consultant at the end of World War II, to be replaced by Hans Gronau, a German Jew who was considerably less flamboyant but was an art historian of equal stature. Gronau had been teaching at Heidelberg University in the 1930s when his wife, Carmen, who was not Jewish, went to hear Hitler speak at the local stadium. She had gone as a matter of almost idle interest, and had returned transfixed by the exhilaration and horror of the spectacle.

"We leave for London tomorrow," she told Hans when he got home from work that night. "It was the most exciting day of my life — and if I can be impressed, think about the people who are not married to Jews."

The Gronaus came to England, where Hans was interned at the outbreak of World War II, but then joined the British army, assigned to intelligence, Italian division. Early Italian art was his specialty, and in 1945 he started working for Sotheby's three days a week, cataloguing Old Master paintings and drawings. The quality of his work attracted business, and his three days a week soon expanded to five.

But lugging a heavy load of canvases into New Bond Street one evening after a scouting trip to Yorkshire, Hans Gronau suffered a collapse. The diagnosis was a rare heart condition for which the doctors had no cure. All Gronau could do, they said, was try to slow the pace of his work, and his wife started coming into the office to help ease the strain.

Carmen Gronau was an art expert in her own right. A small, alert woman, she had been introduced to her husband by her tutor, the great Niklaus Pevsner, and she had a Ph.D. in architectural drawing of the Italian Renaissance. Her eye was as sharp as her husband's. She came from the same central European intelligentsia who had taste in the bloodstream, and when Peter Wilson first took charge of the picture department, the Gronaus clicked with him to form a highly effective, three-sided team.

Peter Wilson was unusual among upper-class Englishmen of

his generation for being entirely, and quite genuinely, devoid of anti-Semitism. If anything, his sympathies went in the opposite direction.

"I would much rather deal," he once said, "with a Jew than with a duke. If I tell a Jewish collector that I think I can get thousands more for a picture than he expected, he sees me as a partner. He'll cut me in on the deal. But if I tell a duke he owns a masterpiece that he never suspected, his first thought is whether he can cut down my commission on the extra money."

There is one school of thought which explains Sotheby's great leap forward in the years after World War II almost totally in these terms. When Jewish art dealers and collectors took refuge in London in the late 1930s and '40s, they received a distinctly warmer welcome at Sotheby's than at Christie's.

Many were less fortunate than Jakob Goldschmidt. They had not been able to get any of their stock or their collections out of Germany. But they were welcomed in New Bond Street for their taste and knowledge, particularly by Jim Kiddell, who saw them as colleagues in distress. Kiddell and Geoffrey Hobson would accompany them on their often harrowing trips to security and immigration interviews, standing personal surety for them on occasions. The Sotheby's directors would explain to the authorities how such-and-such a penniless waiter or factory hand who could scarcely speak English had once been a respected professional in his native land, and after the war the refugees repaid the compliment. Jewish émigrés were among the most innovative and successful dealers in post-war London.

The Gronaus gave Sotheby's picture department an unashamedly stringent tone. Carmen Gronau was quite capable of snorting "Rubbish!" and turning her back on some cherished dud brought in for her attention. She worked in the academic tradition of Geoffrey Hobson and Samuel Leigh Sotheby. So when Hans Gronau lost his battle with his heart condition and died in 1951, Peter Wilson did not hesitate. Once again overcoming the misgivings of his fellow directors, he insisted that Carmen should be given charge of the picture department under his supervision. Wilson had found the ideal colleague in this prickly but dedicated woman who, through misfortune, was essentially alone in the world, rather as he was.

The unlikely couple who were to revolutionise the selling of art at auction started talking early each morning, when Carmen Gronau arrived in her car at The Garden Lodge in Logan Place, the London base which Wilson rented just north of Earl's Court. Driving up to Mayfair together and parking in a garage near the office, they would take turns paying the daily fees — Carmen one day, Peter the next. It was a meticulous ritual which spoke well of Carmen's hold over her boss, for Wilson was notoriously royal in his failure to carry small change with him, and he often relied on others to pay for his taxis or cups of coffee.

If Christie's only knew, it was said, what was plotted in Carmen Gronau's car as it shuttled up the Cromwell Road at breakfast time. They made an incomparable pair — she short and tactless, he tall and incredibly smooth — and in 1956 their unusual teamwork led to a coup which was to pay more than one dividend.

In 1955, Jakob Goldschmidt, the German-Jewish collector with whom Geoffrey Hobson had quarreled in the 1930s over the sale of his porcelain, died in America, where he had managed to reassemble the gems of the Impressionist collection that had hung in his home in Berlin. His executors were his only son Erwin, a sharp but cantankerous insurance broker, and Jesse D. Wolff, an equally sharp but more urbane Manhattan lawyer, and Goldschmidt's will decreed that his pictures be sold "at such time and times and by such means as my executors may determine." Jakob Goldschmidt knew there were times to buy and times to sell, and his son took his cue, dividing his father's paintings into two separate batches. Reserving Jakob's Impressionist masterpieces for a later date, Erwin packed up fourteen good modern pictures and Old Masters, then headed for London, where he took a suite at the Savoy Hotel, and summoned Sotheby's to his bidding.

"Erwin has many faults," his father, Jakob, once said, "and all of them are mine."

One of these was a ferocious negotiating style that verged on nuclear annihilation, and it took every ounce of Peter Wilson's diplomacy to avoid the sort of showdown that had occurred between Jakob Goldschmidt and Geoffrey Hobson twenty years earlier. After complicated haggling over possible commission rates and reserves, it seemed that some agreement was possible, and Erwin presented Wilson and Gronau with a list of the pictures he had brought with him. He said that he would leave the pair alone for half an hour to come up with a price estimate.

When Goldschmidt returned, he was talking German to a companion in the corridor, and Carmen Gronau heard his words through the door — *"Die hier gefallen mir viel besser."*

She understood them immediately — "I like this lot much better"— and she grasped their significance. Sotheby's were not alone at the Savoy. Goldschmidt must have left the room to go and negotiate with someone else, and that could only be a delegation from Christie's.

It later transpired that Goldschmidt had booked two suites at the hotel at the same time, and that Sir Alec Martin, the bowler-hatted septuagenarian who had headed Christie's since 1940, had been stiff-necked in his negotiations. Unlike Peter Wilson, Martin had refused to countenance any suggestion of commission cutting, and Christie's lore recounts the showdown in the Savoy as a fateful turning point.

In the decade since the war the two rivals had been at roughly level pegging, with Christie's nudging ahead in six years out of ten. But Sotheby's had started to outdistance its rival in the twelve months ending in the middle of 1956 — the turnover figures were £1.68 million for Christie's, as compared with £2.27 million for Sotheby's — and the gap was to widen impossibly with the relationship that Peter Wilson and Carmen Gronau established with Erwin Goldschmidt. It was agreed, for a start, that Sotheby's would auction Goldschmidt's batch of fourteen pictures as the final lots of their late-November 1956 picture sale.

The market was still excited over the price achieved by the Poussin four months earlier. Three of the Goldschmidt lots failed to reach their reserve and were bought in, with Sotheby's, according to the still prevailing custom, falsely giving the impression that the pictures had found buyers. But the eleven which really did sell raised over £120,000 — nearly $300,000 at 1956 exchange rates.

Erwin Goldschmidt was delighted, for the flower of his father's collection was still to come. The Impressionist paintings that had been Jakob Goldschmidt's pride and joy were still in America, and his son now had no doubt who he wanted to sell them.

"Both Mrs. Gronau and Mr. Wilson, who are the partners in charge of the sale of paintings," he wrote to a lawyer friend in New York, "see and observe the market in both Old Masters and French Impressionists every day in their own auctions. . . . Had I known at the beginning what I know today, I would not have shown my paintings to any dealers or to any private individuals and would have dealt straight off with Sotheby's."

The lawyer to whom Goldschmidt wrote was Richard Netter, executor to Wilhelm Weinberg, an Amsterdam Jew who had been in Paris on business in the summer of 1940 when the Germans invaded Holland. Weinberg had been in the process of exporting his pictures and possessions to America, planning to move there with his wife and three children, when events overtook him. He never saw his family again, for they were rounded up in Holland and perished in Nazi concentration camps.

Desperately grieving and guilty, Wilhelm Weinberg devoted the rest of his life to his pictures, concentrating especially on the works of Vincent van Gogh, whose Dutch connections and crippling sense of tragedy struck a special chord with him. Recruiting J. B. de la Faille, an academic who had spent his life compiling van Gogh's *catalogue raisonné,* the definitive inventory of the painter's life and work, Weinberg built a collection of rare pedigree and fame. His van Goghs were featured in *Lust for Life,* the Hollywood version of the painter's biography, based on the novel by Irving Stone.

Peter Wilson and Carmen Gronau got their first glimpse of Weinberg's legendary van Goghs by the light of small, hand-held battery torches, peeling back the dust sheets from the paintings in the collector's deserted home in Scarsdale, New York. It was early in 1957, just a month or so after the sale of the first batch of Goldschmidt pictures in London. Dying without heirs, Weinberg had willed that his entire collection should be sold for charity, and Sotheby's found themselves in Scarsdale thanks to the letter that Erwin Goldschmidt sent to Weinberg's lawyer, Richard Netter — and in return for which Sotheby's paid Goldschmidt an introductory commission.

Netter followed Goldschmidt's advice. He did not negotiate seriously with any other auction house. But he did impose stringent terms on the contract — among them that Sotheby's must retain the services of a professional publicity and public relations agent.

A London auction house had never done anything so transatlantic before, but the London office of J. Walter Thompson, the American advertising agency, took on the contract for the prestige plus £100, mailing invitations to everyone they considered important, starting with the Queen at Buckingham Palace. Neither Sotheby's nor Christie's would have dreamt of anything so impertinent — when the partners saw "The Queen" on the invitation list, they had assumed it referred to the magazine of that name — but Her Majesty was intrigued.

"We've never been to one of these before," she said to her private secretary, Edward Ford. "Why shouldn't we?'

So one summer afternoon in 1957, Elizabeth II came to New Bond Street for her own private view of the Weinberg van Goghs and other paintings, in the company of Prince Philip, Princess Margaret, and a cotillion of attendants. In the course of her four-year reign, the Queen had shown a more lively interest in racehorses than in art, but she seemed to enjoy herself greatly, and she was seen to spend a long time studying one of Weinberg's several non–van Gogh Impressionists — a painting by Degas, *At the Races: The Wounded Jockey.* Her office later confirmed that she went back to the Palace pondering a bid.

On the day of the sale it was clear that she was far from the only one. There had been so many requests for tickets that Sotheby's had had to set up three rooms linked by closed-circuit television, another of Richard Netter's proposals. By the time Peter Wilson knocked down the last lot, he had coaxed out a sales total of £326,520, Sotheby's highest ever. One picture alone, van Gogh's *Les Usines à Clichy,* had fetched £31,000, an auction record, while Degas's *Wounded Jockey* had gone to the Hollywood producer Sam Spiegel for £5,800. No one knew whether the Queen had bid on it or not.

Erwin Goldschmidt had been watching the results of the Weinberg sale very carefully, for his recommendation of Sotheby's to Richard Netter had not been entirely disinterested. Goldschmidt had his father's own van Gogh to sell, the *Jardin Public à Arles,* along with a Renoir, three Manets, and two classic

Cézannes — one of them *Le Garçon au Gilet Rouge,* the boy in the red waistcoat, that had hung in pride of place in the Gold-schmidt mansion in Berlin.

Every picture had a parallel in the Weinberg sale, which had served as the perfect dry run. In the spring of 1958 Erwin Gold-schmidt invited Peter Wilson and Carmen Gronau to New York to let them see his father's seven Impressionist canvases, each of them a masterpiece, and then he started negotiating.

It was a long-drawn process, and the result was a contract un-like any that Sotheby's had drawn up before. It was finally agreed that the reserves on the seven paintings should total £599,000, an unprecedented sum, and that Sotheby's commission should be minimal on this. The auction house would have to raise an-other £100,000 at the same low rate of commission, and they would only see real profit if they managed to push the total above £700,000 — the sum specified being $1.7 million, since the contract was drawn in America. Once that level was reached, however, Goldschmidt and Wolff did concede that Sotheby's could take 100 percent of whatever they could make.

This distant prospect of "overage" was Peter Wilson's remote hope of profit on the deal, for Goldschmidt and Wolff had laid down other onerous and expensive conditions — a defined marketing budget, a sale devoted exclusively to the seven pic-tures, and a late-evening, black-tie sale such as had never been seen before in London.

Wilson was confident that he could make the £700,000. But he would have found it difficult to get the Goldschmidt deal past his partners if there had not been a significant shift of power in New Bond Street. Dissatisfaction with Vere Pilkington had re-sulted in a boardroom putsch. Following a minor quarrel over salaries, Pilkington had offered his resignation, and his offer had been accepted with alacrity — with Wilson being the unani-mous choice as his successor. The handover was scheduled for October 1958, so the sale of Goldschmidt's seven Impressionists would be the testing of the new chairman's mettle.

Erwin Goldschmidt did not make it easy. He flirted with Stavros Niarchos, the Greek ship owner, who had made a side raid, trying to steal the whole collection with a preemptive bid, and he refused to put his own signature on the contract. The signature of his lawyer, Jesse Wolff, was legally binding on its own, but Goldschmidt enjoyed being awkward. When news of the auction leaked out prematurely, he said he would withdraw his pictures, and only minutes before the sale, on the evening of October 15, 1958, he insisted that the entire occasion be cancelled because of an anti-Semitic remark which he had overheard from someone in the audience. He correctly assumed that the comment had been aimed at him, and proceedings were halted until the perpetrator had been ejected.

When Peter Wilson stepped into the auction box just five minutes late, at 9:35 P.M., it was astonishing that he should have conveyed an impression of such calm. But calmness was his keynote for the evening, as he peered out through the barrage of TV lights across an audience that included Somerset Maugham, Dame Margot Fonteyn, Kirk Douglas, Lady Churchill, and art dealers representing the wealthiest buyers in the world. With overflow rooms and closed-circuit television, the arrangements were as elaborate as they had been for Weinberg fifteen months earlier, and when two porters carried in the first canvas, a self-portrait by Manet, the bidding started briskly.

Wilson had the figures in a marked catalogue in front of him, dispensing with his code to make sure there was no mistake and writing the real figures openly in red ink. He had to get £45,000 for the Manet self-portrait, and it went for £65,000. He needed £82,000 for a second Manet, and £90,000 for a third, and with bids of £89,000 and £113,000, it looked as if the gamble was paying off — though according to one newspaper, Somerset Maugham shook his head in amazement when £100,000 was passed.

Lots four and five also made their targets — van Gogh's *Jardin Public à Arles* went for £132,000, £14,000 over its reserve — and then came the red-smeared Cézanne, *Le Garçon au Gilet Rouge,* which, at £125,000, had the highest reserve of the evening. Wilson started the bidding at £20,000, and two New York dealers sprang straight into action, George Keller represented New York's Carstair's Gallery, while Roland Balay represented Knoedler's. Wilson switched his gaze deliberately from one to the other as the bidding went past £100,000, and then moved on past the enormous reserve. On and on the two dealers went — £190,000, £200,000, £210,000. When Keller bid £220,000 there was an awed silence, and Peter Wilson looked out across the audience, almost perplexed. It was a dizzying price.

"Two hundred and twenty thousand. Two hundred and twenty?" he asked. "Will no one offer any more?"

His tone of surprise released the tension with a roar of laughter from the crowd. Two hundred twenty thousand pounds was by far the highest price ever paid for a modern picture at auction. It was the sort of amount that Sotheby's had only recently been delighted to raise on an entire sale. When the final lot, Renoir's *La Pensée,* went for £72,000, a mere £1,000 above its reserve, it was almost an anti-climax.

The sale had taken just twenty-one minutes and had raised £781,000, comfortably more than the $1.7 million ceiling fixed by the contract. Sotheby's had gone so far past the combined reserves they had collected their overage, and the final calculation showed their commission totalled £75,512, an effective rate of 9.2845 percent.

Georges Keller, the dealer who had bought *The Boy in the Red Waistcoat,* refused to say on whose behalf he had been bidding, and the identity of the buyer remained officially a secret for many years. But Jake Carter, who was Sotheby's roving representative in America, suspected that the buyer was the philanthropist Paul Mellon, and he happened to be lunching with Mellon a week later at his club in Washington.

Would he be right, he dared to ask, in congratulating Mr. Mellon on the buying of a certain wonderful picture?

Mellon did not attempt to lie.

"Did I," he asked, "pay too much?"

And before Carter could say anything, Mellon gave his own reply — the timeless secret of the auction business.

"You stand in front of a picture like that," he said, "and what is money?"

Paul Mellon was a collector of the highest calibre. Modest and generous, he did not collect for display, or for reasons of investment, bequeathing *The Boy in the Red Waistcoat* and many other of his treasures to public museums. He collected for the innate pleasure of contact with beauty that he could not personally create, but which, thanks to his money, he could possess. In a bidder like Paul Mellon, Sotheby's had captured the ultimate in class.

10

IN THE AUTUMN OF 1959, Britain went to the polls and re-elected Sir Harold Macmillan's Conservative government on the slogan "You've never had it so good." After nearly thirty years of depression, war, and austerity, the country was feeling rich again, and rising art prices were a reflection of that. It was just a few months after the second of the Goldschmidt sales, and the carnival of spending at Sotheby's seemed emblematic of the general boom. The *Observer* suggested that the radio stock market report should round off the City prices with the latest from the art market: "Renoir, steady; Vlaminck and Manet, mixed."

Trendiness was round the corner. Britain's stuffy traditions were being repackaged as commodities that could be merchandised, and there were striking similarities between "Supermac," the wily Prime Minister who presided over this glossification, and Peter Wilson, the salesman who was bringing wealth and change to Sotheby's. Both men were Eton and Oxford educated, and both appeared to be pillars of the establishment. But Wilson and Macmillan also nursed "flash" streaks which belied their patrician origins, and both based their careers on the ability to identify and, in their different fields, to suck up to the new rich.

The art boom was by no means confined to Sotheby's. On both sides of the Atlantic the demands of the newly affluent stimulated the birth of a new generation of art dealers, since class can take many forms. Once the car, the yacht, and the mistress have been paid for, a man frequently experiences a yearning for something less mortal.

Down in King Street, Christie's turnover grew handsomely, particularly after a group of young partners ousted the antediluvian Sir Alec Martin in 1958. But Christie's had nothing to match the impact of the Goldschmidt and Weinberg sales. New Bond Street's turnover for 1958–59 totalled £5.57 million, an 81 percent improvement on their results for the previous year, and when Sotheby's disclosed these extraordinary figures, they did quietly mention that they had done twice as well as their rivals in St. James.

But this was not their main message. Five and a half million pounds, announced Sotheby's new coffee table–style annual review, was the highest total ever achieved in the history of the art market, and it was "virtually double" the sales achieved by any other auctioneer "in the world." Beating Christie's was no longer the challenge. Peter Wilson had raised his sights higher. He had moved on to his aim of global preeminence, and that meant the art auction conquest of America.

Fine art auctioneering does not reach back far in America's history. A society has to accumulate junk in the cupboards before the auctioneers can move in. But in 1883 the American Art Association (proprietor, Thomas E. Kirby) started offering New Yorkers the transatlantic equivalent of London's great auction houses, and the business soon developed its own flamboyant

style, which drew on the quick-talking patter of the tobacco
sale, with something of the medicine show thrown in.

The American Art Association initially tried to separate itself from these hucksterish traditions. Its high-minded title deliberately avoided the disreputable connotations of "auction" or
"auctioneer" — the A.A.A. sounded almost like an educational
fellowship — and one of its early projects was its 1886 exhibition of "Works in Oil and Pastel by the Impressionists of Paris,"
which lost money and incurred as much knowing derision in
New York as when Manet, Monet, Renoir, and their colleagues
first exhibited their bright and startling canvases at the Salon des
Refusés in Paris in the 1870s.

But the A.A.A. received a crash course in showmanship when
Thomas Kirby's assistant, Rose Lorenz, got her hands on a bolt
of plum-colored damask and thought to enliven an otherwise
mundane set of furniture with a backdrop of plush drapes and
hangings — plus some artfully placed vases of flowers. Working
the same transformation that the Sotheby's Flying Squad were to
effect in England fifty years later, Rose Lorenz rearranged and
amplified the bare elements of used property to create sumptuous, theatrical room sets, and these soon attracted New York's
fashionable and wealthy. Strolling through the displays of the
A.A.A. became a smart Saturday morning diversion, and the
auction house successfully tried another gambit that Sotheby's
only copied decades later — the formal, black tie, evening sale.

The Rose Lorenz room set harmonized neatly with the tastes
of American collectors at the turn of the century, since the robber barons did not just collect Old Masters or porcelain or
French furniture. They collected everything, and in prodigious
quantities, filling their Fifth Avenue mansions with tapestries,
candelabra, suits of armour, rare books, manuscripts, old globes,
and stuffed animals for good measure. They modeled themselves
on the merchant princes of earlier eras, and when the estates of
these latter-day Medicis fell into Rose Lorenz's hands, she did

them proud with displays that were a mixture of a memorial service and the arraying of a pharaoh's treasures.

Ryans, Morgans, Huntingtons — the grandest dynasties of the East Coast bought and sold at the A.A.A., and the house developed an auctioneering style of its own. Its porters were black, and at major sales they would dress up in uniform and station themselves down either side of the room, shouting out and pointing vigorously at bids that the auctioneer might have missed. Lots were not held in the air, as in England, but were displayed on a specially lit stage, and were dramatically revealed by the drawing back of curtains.

With the fairground-like barking of the spotters, it made for a hectic and colorful atmosphere, particularly in the 1920s, when New York's art and antique prices rose even higher than those in London. American prices became so strong that the trustees of Lord Leverhulme, the Lancashire soap magnate, decided to ship his collection across the Atlantic from Britain in 1926, as did the Marquess of Lothian six years later.

As the 1920s progressed, the A.A.A. found its Christie's-like dominance of New York threatened by a Sotheby's-like rival, the Anderson Galleries, a book dealer which had diversified into art — it was Anderson that snared the Leverhulme sale — and in 1929 the two houses amalgamated to create a virtual monopoly, cumbersomely known as the A.A.A.-A.G. This deal was hatched by the financial backers of the two houses, not by the auctioneers and experts themselves, for while some of the hands-on staff held stock or profit-sharing arrangements, most were essentially employees.

This contrasted with the British system, where partners did the business and owned the business, and it would become an important factor when London and New York went head to head in the 1950s. In the 1930s, the consequence for the A.A.A.-A.G. was a breakaway by a pair of veteran auctioneers, Hiram Haney Parke and G. T. Otto Bernet, who wanted more power and equity for themselves. The new house of Parke-Bernet prospered so well that it soon took over the remnants of the A.A.A.-A.G., and became heir to all the traditions of American fine art auctioneering — though its two principals were financed by outside investors, and they were never quite partners with the affection that the linking of their names suggested.

"You're a stone round my neck," growled Hiram Parke to Otto Bernet as he organized the breakaway of 1937, "but you're coming."

Major Hiram Haney Parke came from humble origins, his rank deriving from nothing grander than a spell in the Pennsylvania State Militia. But he carried himself like an aristocrat. Dark of hair and dark of voice, he had the lean good looks of a matinee idol, in striking contrast to the Pickwickian rotundity of his partner Bernet. Fortunately, Bernet was also blessed with Mr. Pickwick's unshakable good humour, and he tolerated his partner's snubs with the stolid philosophy of the Swiss-German peasant stock from which he sprang. As a Swiss-German, Bernet pronounced his name as if it ended with a firm double "t" — which made it incorrect to Frenchify the gallery's name, as many did, to "Parke-Bernay."

Parke-Bernet prospered through World War II with a monopoly on business in the world's only rich city that was isolated from hostilities, and in 1950 the firm moved to new, purpose-built premises at 980 Madison Avenue and Seventy-sixth Street, just opposite the Carlyle Hotel. A sleek edifice of angular white stone, the Parke-Bernet building created a new uptown focus for New York's art dealers and galleries. It had the air of a modern art museum, and above the main door floated the bronze effigy of an amply endowed and scantily-clad Venus, representing the charms of art and culture, with which the goddess was attempting to seduce a muscular male figure who represented Manhattan.

Otto Bernet died before the move, and Parke retired shortly

afterwards, passing the running of the business to three younger partners — Leslie Hyam, Louis Marion, and Mary Vandegrift, who had been Parke's lieutenants in his original breakaway from the A.A.A. The trio had been the guiding spirits behind Parke-Bernet's move to its new premises on Madison Avenue, and it would fall to them to meet the challenge of Sotheby's.

Their leader and chairman was Leslie A. Hyam, who was not unlike Peter Wilson in that he was a tall, unmistakably English Englishman who had not had an idea about what to do with his life until he fell into the auction business — in Hyam's case on a trip to New York in the mid-1930s. His marriage fell victim to his work, as Wilson's did — but Hyam was definitely heterosexual. He had a weakness for *femmes fatales,* entangling himself regularly in unhappy love affairs.

A proud and rather pompous graduate of Cambridge, where he had studied science, Hyam brought an academic approach to American cataloguing, which had not previously been known for its accuracy. As Hyam later put it, "the direction of cataloguing then was to present the object with a description corresponding to the most optimistic expectations of the owner."

After Parke's retirement, Leslie Hyam became the leading light of Parke-Bernet, and in the tradition of the ill-matched character of the original partners, his chief lieutenant was as unlike Hyam as it was possible to be. Un-shy, ungentlemanly, squat, and bow-legged, Louis J. Marion came of Italian stock. His father had changed the family name from Mariano when he encountered difficulties trying to sell insurance in an Irish neighborhood. The red-headed Marion went one better, organising an annual St. Patrick's Day party which became famous as the best in New York. To those who wondered why an Italian should celebrate that feast, Marion would point out that St. Patrick had been Italian before he was Irish.

It seemed to some of his colleagues that Lou Marion celebrated every saint's day in the calendar, but no one could deny his connections. If someone needed to get off a parking ticket or jury duty, Lou knew the man to call at city hall, and he knew how to bring in the business. While Hyam researched the details of Florentine tapestries, the back-slapping Marion got the contracts signed — leaving the day-to-day management of Parke-Bernet in the hands of their third partner, Mary Vandegrift, an efficient and diplomatic woman who smoothed the almost daily disagreements between her two male colleagues. Mary Vandegrift was the sheet anchor of Parke-Bernet.

This idiosyncratic trio successfully attracted major properties to 980 Madison Avenue throughout the 1950s, but as the decade progressed, they found themselves losing deals to Sotheby's — and even to French auction houses on occasions. This was partly a function of the growing strength of the European art market, but it also represented two fundamental handicaps: Parke-Bernet charged high commissions — as much as 25 percent on some sales — and they also refused to countenance the English practice of reserves.

The high commissions originated in the years of being the only game in town. When rich New Yorkers passed away, it was standard practice for their goods to be sold at Parke-Bernet, or one of its earlier incarnations. There was no one offering executors a better rate. This had made the saleroom's overhead fat and happy, and the problem was complicated by the lease that the company held on their Madison Avenue base.

The site had been developed by Robert Dowling, the owner of the Carlyle hotel and apartments across the street, who had courted Parke-Bernet to improve the tone of the neighborhood, and had constructed the new building deliberately low so as not to restrict the light and views of his customers in the Carlyle. To woo Parke-Bernet, Dowling had kept down the rent to some $7,000 per month, requesting only a 2 percent levy on the gross income of the auction house if it were ever to exceed $6 million — a long-term escalator clause.

It had seemed a good deal in the late 1940s. Two percent did not sound very much, and $6 million was a distant dream in the context of postwar art prices. But after Parke-Bernet's heavy expenses, it was not unusual for the company's operating surplus to come out at only 4 percent — which meant that if the day ever came when Parke-Bernet's turnover did reach the $6 million ceiling, Robert Dowling's 2 percent share of gross income would be claiming half of Parke-Bernet's profits.

The $6 million threshold was crossed early in the 1950s, and Parke-Bernet's gross income rose every year after that, reflecting the general rise in art market prices. Hyam, Marion, and Vandergrift had caught themselves coming and going. Their payments to their landlord were both a tax on their own efforts and a permanent levy on the art boom of the 1950s, and by the end of the decade, the trio had little margin to negotiate when Sotheby's came wooing sellers with commission rates of 10 percent, or even less. Parke-Bernet regularly charged double that, and they could not come close to competing with the stringent and risky terms that Peter Wilson agreed to snare the Goldschmidt and Weinberg sales.

Nor could Parke-Bernet offer sellers the security of reserves. New York's high proportion of private bidders meant that dealer rings had never been the problem that they could be in London, so reserves had never been needed. The American spirit found something sneaky in the concept of secret price minimums. To this way of thinking, the appeal of the auction was the certainty that everything must go, giving Parke-Bernet a bargain basement ethos which attracted buyers but could deter the sellers of highly priced goods.

The result was an humiliating paradox for American auctioneering. Thanks to London's reserves and low commission rates, it had become an economic proposition by the late 1950s for Sotheby's — and, to a lesser extent, Christie's — to ship paintings across the Atlantic and sell them in England to a predominantly American group of buyers, many of whom had travelled over for the sale and would ship their purchases straight back.

Peter Wilson had first tried to buy Parke-Bernet for Sotheby's when Major Parke was alive. In 1947 Wilson had been in New York on other business when he heard that the seventy-four-year-old major was thinking of retiring. Wilson met Parke, who seemed amenable to the idea of his auction house becoming part of Sotheby's, and rough terms were agreed.

Rushing home, Wilson was able to secure the cautious agreement of his fellow directors, but when he got back to Parke to conclude the deal, he found that the major's three younger partners were up in arms. Leslie Hyam, Lou Marion, and Mary Vandegrift wanted Parke-Bernet for themselves. The trio put together a consortium of wealthy Manhattan collectors to buy the major out, and they moved into their new premises at 980 Madison, with the Venus over the door.

"I give you to each other," said Major Parke, "and it's all yours."

Peter Wilson was not discouraged. His war years had furnished him with transatlantic contacts that he exploited with frequent trips of his own, and when the British government made a start to the lifting of currency regulations in 1954, he proposed to his partners that this was the time for Sotheby's to have its own man in America.

Their choice fell on John Carter, known as Jake, a rare book expert who had worked as personal assistant — effectively the social secretary — to the British ambassador in Washington. Sporting a monocle and cape, Jake Carter specialized in making himself the American notion of how an Englishman should be, and he had an American wife, Ernestine Carter, a onetime curator at the Museum of Modern Art, who had moved back with her husband to London, where she became fashion editor of the

Sunday Times. Carter had made his name in the book world in the 1930s when his researches helped unmask the forger Thomas Wise.*

Carter filled a briefcase with Sotheby's most impressive catalogues, and set about organizing two annual six-week trips around America that he called his "swings." Taking advantage of speaking invitations from the English Speaking Union, he travelled to such cities as Detroit, Chicago, Charleston, and the richest graveyard of all, Palm Beach. Carter offered a range of lecture titles — "Bull Market at Bond Street," "Sold to the Highest Bidder," "A Renoir Is a Girl's Best Friend"— but whatever topic the branch chose, they got the same talk, a diverting plug for Sotheby's, which would end before time so that Carter could mingle with the audience and cultivate clients.

In New York Carter rented a corner in the office of a friendly lawyer on Wall Street, and by 1957 American consignments were responsible for more than a fifth of Sotheby's turnover. But with the success of the Goldschmidt and Weinberg sales, it became clear to Peter Wilson that Carter's two annual "swings" were not enough. The growing volume of American business called for a full-time Sotheby's representative on the ground.

Peregrine Pollen had a name out of Evelyn Waugh, and he spent his life living up to that. While at Oxford he had won the record for a feat that involved running a mile, riding a mile, and row-

---

* Thomas J. Wise (1859–1937) was a revered figure in the world of rare books until Jake Carter, working with Graham Pollard, demonstrated how the great man had forged a variety of nineteenth-century books and pamphlets, some of which he had successfully sold at Sotheby's. Carter and Pollard showed how the paper and typefaces of these works were more modern than the supposed date of publication, and it later emerged that Wise had also stolen title pages and other leaves from valuable books in the British Museum.

ing a mile in immediate succession. Pollen managed the three miles together in fourteen minutes flat, and his work experience had included spells as a nightclub entertainer and an attendant in a lunatic asylum — both excellent preparations, as Peter Wilson liked to say, for working at Sotheby's.

Taking a leaf from Jake Carter, who continued his "swings," Pollen made himself as flamboyantly English as he could. Bright-eyed, hollow-cheeked, and definitely peregrine-like in the sharp way that he turned his head from side to side, Pollen was an old Etonian like Carter, and the two men delighted in sweeping into Parke-Bernet previews with Sotheby's catalogues stuck ostentatiously under their arms.

Pollen was grandly connected in England. He had grown up at Norton Hall, Mickleton, in the Cotswolds, a handsome estate that he was due to inherit. But he had few contacts in America, so when he arrived in 1960 and the British consulate suggested that Sotheby's might take a stand at that summer's New York trade fair, he jumped at the chance. With his wife, Patricia, he designed a home-made stall which he decorated with large, black-and-white reproductions of Sotheby's recent sales triumphs, mounted in old frames.

"I always thought Rubens painted in colour," remarked puzzled visitors as they admired the superbly framed, but definitely photographic *Adoration of the Magi,* which Sotheby's had recently sold in London for the Duke of Westminster.

One visitor, however, knew a lot about art — and where to get the best prices. Harvey Arneson, curator of the Guggenheim Museum on Fifth Avenue, had more canvases in his museum's storage cupboards than he could hope to exhibit, and he wished to sell the surplus to generate funds for other acquisitions. Feeling it his duty to raise the maximum sum, the curator had decided to get the paintings sold in London — though he was almost furtive as he approached Pollen at his stand, suggesting that the two of them should talk business somewhere more discreet.

The reasons for the curator's fears became clear the moment Parke-Bernet got wind that Sotheby's might be selling surplus Guggenheim material on New Bond Street. The American auction house considered the Guggenheim's willingness to sell abroad a betrayal, and its mouthpiece was Ralph E. Colin, the firm's legal counsel, who was a shareholder and director of the auction house and who also sat on the board of the Guggenheim. Colin managed to delay the sale, but he later resigned from the Guggenheim and orchestrated a press campaign against Sotheby's and its perfidious British practices.

By the early 1960s, Parke-Bernet was feeling the strain. Pollen had set up a permanent Sotheby's office in the Corning Building on Fifth Avenue, and he was getting wind of every significant sale. To fight off the competition, Parke-Bernet were compelled to cut commission rates, promise reserves, and guarantee promotion expenses in a sort of pre-auction auction which the trust lawyers took pleasure in organizing — and in which Christie's also started to participate.

All three houses competed fiercely in 1961 for the extraordinary collection of Old Master paintings assembled by Alfred W. Erickson, a founding partner of McCann Erickson, the advertising agency, and after keen negotiations, Parke-Bernet got the sale. The plum of the collection was one of Rembrandt's masterpieces, *Aristotle Contemplating the Bust of Homer,* a brooding and dramatic canvas showing the philosopher thoughtfully resting his hand on the effigy of the legendary poet.

It was an archetypal image, and Alfred Erickson had had a life-long love affair with the painting. Having purchased it from Duveen for no less than $750,000 in the 1920s, the magnate had had to sell it back at a loss during the Depression, only to reacquire it as soon as he was back in the money. As newspapers picked up this story, the Rembrandt took on an almost mythical status. It was written about as a national heirloom — "a capstone of human culture," as one critic put it — and over twenty thousand people stood in line around the block to file past the

icon when it went on display at 980 Madison. On the evening
of the sale, it took four TV-linked galleries to hold the bidders.

Lou Marion later said that he achieved the ambition of a lifetime when he opened the bidding at $1 million. Chief among
the bidders was James J. Rorimer, director of the Metropolitan
Museum, and the Met got the Rembrandt for $2.3 million,
which, at £831,000, was by far the highest price ever known to
be paid for a painting — more than three times the sum
Sotheby's had secured for *Le Garçon au Gilet Rouge* three years
earlier. Experts criticized Rorimer for paying so much to add
another Rembrandt to a museum which already owned more
than thirty, but public response vindicated his decision. When
Aristotle went on display at the Met after the sale, there were
queues on Fifth Avenue every day for six months.

The sale was a public triumph for Parke-Bernet. But the auction house's commission on the $4.68 million raised by the en-
tire Erickson property added substantially to its turnover, which
meant extra money to the landlord, taking rent to nearly 20 percent of gross income. The sale that the world hailed as a triumph
was actually a financial drain, and according to Robert Woolley,
who was then doing deals with the auction house on behalf of
a Manhattan antique shop, Parke-Bernet started keeping two
sets of books, hiding the sales that it concluded by private treaty
so that it could at least enjoy some meagre revenue free of tribute to the Carlyle.

"There is something faintly deadly about it," said Leslie
Hyam, discussing the 1950s art price explosion, "like the numb-
ing effect of continually listening to an air hammer pulverizing
asphalt."

The rising prices had to be depressing for an auction house
which effectively lost money whenever it broke records. A few
months after the Erickson sale, Alex Hillman, a New York publisher, investor, and collector, made a confidential approach to
try to acquire Parke-Bernet in conjunction with Sotheby's, and

the bid was not rejected. After years of trying to stem the tide, Hyam, Marion, and Vandegrift acknowledged they could not hold off the English forever. All they insisted was that the basis of any merger would have to be an equal, fifty-fifty split.

Peter Wilson talked a little, then broke off negotiations. The framing of an equal partnership, he said, would be the creation of "a dragon with two heads." Wilson knew that Parke-Bernet were on the run. In the spring of the following year, Sotheby's won the collection of René Fribourg, another connoisseur refugee in the tradition of Goldschmidt and Weinberg, with a deal whose keen finances the Americans could not match — zero commission to $1.5 million and 15 percent thereafter. The sale that June grossed more than $3 million, and in anticipation of more Fribourgs, Peter Wilson instructed Pollen to start looking for grander premises in New York.

Then in September 1963, Leslie Hyam committed suicide.

No one could ever quite fathom Leslie Hyam. He kept most people at arm's length. With his elevated stature and his austere style, he reminded some of his colleagues of General de Gaulle.

Many of Hyam's complications stemmed from his work, which consumed him. But there was also his attraction to difficult women, and the strange comfort that he found in unhappy love affairs. Between them, women and work could throw Leslie Hyam into spells of agonising melancholy, and it was some imponderable combination of the two that caused him to get in his car on September 10, 1963, switch on the engine, and poison himself with carbon monoxide fumes from the exhaust.

"Deadly" was the word Hyam had used shortly before his death to describe the stress of steering Parke-Bernet through an art boom that should have been a happy time. The paradox of struggling for profits while gaining business was too much — "a kind of pestilence," he said.

And then there was the exotically named Mrs. Puc-Paris, a divorcée with whom Hyam was involved just as Sotheby's was stealing the René Fribourg sale early in 1963. Jerry Patterson, a young cataloguer in Parke-Bernet's book department, was a guest at Hyam's weekend home in Connecticut that summer, and he could not help noticing how distracted his boss seemed to be.

"It's Mrs. Puc-Paris," explained one of the guests. "She's driving him crazy."

Parke-Bernet was lost without Leslie Hyam. There was no one to match his presence and expertise, while the firm's financial problems made it unlikely that any ordinary investor would be interested in his shares. Peter Wilson was in Japan when he heard of the suicide, and he flew to New York at once to confer with Peregrine Pollen and Jesse Wolff, the canny attorney for Erwin Goldschmidt whom Sotheby's had since retained for themselves. Pollen, Wilson, and Wolff framed an offer for Parke-Bernet, and they went to see Ralph Colin, who, as legal counsel, represented the Parke-Bernet board.

Colin was not encouraging. He made little attempt to hide the dislike of Sotheby's he had nursed since the affair of the surplus Guggenheim canvases, and he accurately reflected the feelings of his fellow stockholders, and particularly of Lou Marion, who had taken over from Hyam as president. Parke-Bernet did not want to be swallowed up by the British, whose piracy of the American market was seen as the root of so many troubles.

Leslie Hyam's executors had estate duty to pay, however. They were professionally obliged to get the best price they could for his stock, so even as Colin and the Parke-Bernet board laboured to keep Sotheby's at arm's length, the lawyers who controlled the votes of the dead partner were seeking exactly the opposite. It was a recipe for deadlock, and as Ralph Colin searched desperately for American investors, Parke-Bernet's auction business slumped. This was no longer good news for

Sotheby's, and in the spring of 1964, after several months of maneuvering and confusion, Peter Wilson summoned a board meeting in London.

Peregrine Pollen flew back for the meeting. He had recently become a director of the company, and he found his partners in disarray. Peter Wilson was as keen to expand in America as ever, and Carmen Gronau was his loyal supporter. But Anthony Hobson, the son of Geoffrey Hobson, was opposed, arguing that buying Parke-Bernet would entirely change the nature of Sotheby's, and he was backed by two experts who had joined the board in the 1950s — Richard Timewell and Fred Rose. With Hobson, both men favoured securing American business and bringing it to London in the traditional fashion, but they feared that a New York auction room involved risk, and, most important, a fundamental change in the character of the firm.

Pollen could sense his cause slipping away. There had scarcely been a day since Hyam's suicide when he had not spoken to Jesse Wolff, working out ways to try to break the deadlock with Parke-Bernet, and he was not going to be frustrated by a similar impasse in London. Pushing back his chair, Peregrine rose to his feet to deliver a speech which, as he later admitted, was heavier on emotion than on reasoned argument — and as he sat down, he heard himself saying, "and if we can't find anyone else to run Parke-Bernet, then I'll run it myself."

Peter Wilson later said that it was "Peregrine's finest hour," and the response of Jim Kiddell, the elder statesman of the board, set the seal.

"I believe the young people in the firm want it," said Kiddell, "and it's their future we should be thinking of."

Pollen flew back to New York with a mandate to push forward with the takeover, and Wilson went out to help negotiate. Peregrine and Patricia Pollen had rented an apartment at Ninety-second and Park, with a guest bedroom for partners and visiting experts, so they saw a lot of Peter Wilson in the summer of 1964. The light would go on early under the chairman's door, while he sat up in bed doing his paperwork, and the rule in the evening was to have dinner ready, but not to expect him until he arrived home. Wilson spent his day out cultivating his contacts, and he would switch dinner plans at five minutes' notice if he sensed a lead to a sale.

By the end of June 1964, a draft merger with Parke-Bernet seemed agreed. A crucial obstacle was crossed in the course of a stormy meeting with Robert Dowling, when Wilson threw a tantrum and dramatically flung his papers in the air. It was a tactic that was familiar to those who knew Wilson well — "You should take acting lessons, Peter," the Weinberg executor, Richard Netter, once remarked — but it scared Robert Dowling. The Carlyle developer finally agreed that if Sotheby's took over Parke-Bernet, he would suspend the escalator clause on 980 Madison in return for a guaranteed rent.

The directors of Parke-Bernet, however, were not so amenable. Colonel Richard Gimbel, a scion of the department store family, was particularly recalcitrant, and on Monday, June 29, 1964, the day the Parke-Bernet board had been expected to approve the merger, Gimbel summoned enough votes to postpone the decision again. The colonel reckoned that some investor could still be found with the money and fighting spirit to keep Parke-Bernet American.

Sotheby's did not respond directly. But the following weekend, the London *Sunday Telegraph* ran a two-column story under the headline "SOTHEBY'S LOOK WEST":

Sotheby's struck the most humiliating blow last week at their American rivals in art auctioneering, the Parke-Bernet Galleries of New York. . . . They blandly announced that their season's turnover for works of art sent from the United States alone already exceeded the Parke-Bernet's entire takings for the year — approximately £3,800,000. Sotheby's is likely to be about £13,000,000. It has been no secret for months that the Parke-Bernet was on the way out, and that substantial holdings in the company were up for sale. The only question was, who would step in? Would it be Sotheby's themselves?

The story had been planted by Stanley Clark, an old-time Fleet Street press agent whom Peter Wilson had hired as Sotheby's publicity consultant in the aftermath of the Goldschmidt sale. Clark had given the *Sunday Telegraph* an exclusive on the battle between the two auction houses, and in return the paper conveyed the real message. It revealed that Sotheby's had successfully renegotiated the lease on 980 Madison, which meant that they were uniquely placed to improve Parke-Bernet's performance, and that if they were still unable to reach a deal, they intended to counter-attack directly by setting up an auction room of their own in New York.

"We will proceed with plans," declared one unnamed director, "which will enable us to hold auctions in New York during the next season."

The following day a storm of New York headlines announced the invasion of the British with their superior financial firepower, and that was the end of any hope that Parke-Bernet could coax outside investors to come to their aid. Less than ten days later, Jesse Wolff was able to phone London with the news that the holders of 78 percent of Parke-Bernet's shares had agreed to sell out to Sotheby's for a total of $1.525 million. The active partners, Lou Marion and Mary Vandegrift, had come on board, as had Ralph Colin. The only holdout was the defiant Colonel Gimbel, who declared that he would never yield up his own 22 percent to the British.

"The American flag has been sold down the river," he complained.

The obstinate Gimbel held out for three months, attending the first board meeting of Parke-Bernet under its new ownership, and managing to raise or oppose no less than eighteen procedural motions in the course of the meeting. But Jesse Wolff discovered the colonel's Achilles' heel. Gimbel was a hopeless book lover. He was an avid collector of Dickens, Conrad, and Edgar Allan Poe, and he could not resist Wolff's offer not just to buy his shares but to supply him with free catalogues from Sotheby's and Parke-Bernet for the rest of his life in galley proof, prior to publication. The colonel could put Sotheby's money in his pocket, and still feel that he had the inside track on the game.

In the spring of 1965, less than six months after resolving the final shareholding complications, Sotheby's opened on Madison Avenue with a spectacular sale. Parke-Bernet was still called Parke-Bernet. For reasons of diplomacy, it had been decided to retain the old name, and Peregrine Pollen had worked hard to keep as many of the existing staff as he could. He shuttled cataloguers and clerks across Madison Avenue to the Bemelmans Bar in the Carlyle, where he listened to their complaints and offered them an expanding Sotheby's future. Pollen was aiming to triple Parke-Bernet's turnover and profitability by the end of the decade.

Lou Marion remained president of Parke-Bernet as a symbol of continuity, but Pollen was the chief executive, and Marion found this difficult to stomach, taking pleasure in mispronouncing the name of his young, English boss, as "Perry Green." What kept Marion moderately civil was the fact that he had brought his son, John, into the firm a few years earlier, dreaming that the boy would one day inherit the kingdom of Parke-Bernet.

The younger Marion was given the honor of taking the rostrum for the ceremonial opening of 980 Madison under English control, a black tie evening on April 14, 1965, starting early and held in two parts, with a formal dinner in between. The highlights of both sales were Impressionist and modern paintings,

many of them sent from Europe, and the dining area was decorated to re-create the Café de la Nouvelle Athènes in Paris
where Manet drank, and where Degas drank and painted.

Around the walls hung large sepia photographs of the great
Impressionist artists, ridiculed, for the most part, in their lifetime, but now the object of feeding frenzy among the super-
rich. The plan was that Lou Marion should take over from his
son once the first set of lots had been sold, but the boy did so
well that his father tapped him on the shoulder and told him to
keep going until dinner time. In the first part of the sale, the
young John Marion managed to sell eighty-seven lots for $2.345
million, a figure Parke-Bernet had not seen for several years.

When Peter Wilson mounted the rostrum to preside over the
auction that followed dinner, it had to be said that the master did
not match young Marion's sturdy and vigorous style. Wilson's
elegant, fade-away voice rang with a certain irrelevance in Manhattan, and though the sale went perfectly well, Wilson was
never to try auctioneering in New York again.

Sotheby's conquest of Parke-Bernet had been in striking
contrast to the post-war pattern of American predators devour-
ing British businesses, but Parke-Bernet had actually been undermined by the monopoly that seemed its strength for so many
years. The New York auction house would not have made its
sloppy deal over rent, nor been allowed to become dependent
on high commission rates, if there had been a Christie's in Manhattan to challenge it. Sotheby's victory showed how wise the
New Bond Street partners had been to keep rejecting the apparently logical merger of the two British auction houses, since
it was competition that had made their sword so sharp.

11

Peter Wilson never had any doubt that art was about money. "Art for art's sake is really awful rot," he liked to say, and he would go on to preach a little sermon on the utility of greed. If human covetousness were ever to be abolished, he would declare, "art would come to an end. It's very rare to be able to appreciate art without wanting to own it. . . . No one who has ever bought a work of art has been exempt from the feeling that it is going to retain its value."

The gospel according to Peter Wilson was that art should yield cash as well as class, and the logical consequence of this philosophy was born in 1967 — the *Times-Sotheby Index,* which charted the progress of art prices with tables and graphs, as if paintings were commodities on the stock market.

The idea was the brainchild of Stanley Clark, the rumpled and portly Fleet Street press agent whom Peter Wilson had recruited soon after becoming chairman. The hiring of Clark as a full-time PR man set the tone for Wilson's stewardship of the auction house, for Clark was not a typical Sotheby's person.

Shuffling around the corridors of New Bond Street with all the elegance of a sack of potatoes, he respectfully addressed his betters as "Sir"— and he brought this awed and definitely non-arty touch to the stories he promoted.

"If the King gave her that tapestry," he would muse, "then he must have been trying to get her into bed."

So a rare Gobelins wall hanging became a key to the seduction of Madame du Barry, and the story won a place on the feature pages. In the years before Clark, auction news was traditionally relegated to the Sales Report, located between the crossword and the bridge column. But Clark saw his stories in headlines and that was what they became.

The notion underlying the *Times-Sotheby Index* had been around for some time. In 1961 Willa Petscheck had pointed out in *The Guardian* how the turning point in Sotheby's fortunes had been the lifting of currency restrictions in the mid-1950s and the free movement of money and art that followed.

"About a quarter of Sotheby's sales total," wrote Petscheck, "is accounted for by America and the nouveau patrons of Europe, the Greek shipping magnates and the tycoons of the industrial boom in Germany and Northern Italy. Swiss and Asians add their quota, but everywhere there are monied people who see, in pictures especially, an attractive alternative to stocks and shares."

Growing wealth meant growing prices, and five years later Clark took this connection a stage further, proposing his index concept to the *Times'* city editor, George Pulay. Pulay hired a young statistician, Geraldine Keen, and she set about dividing the art market into more than a dozen different sectors, from Old Master paintings and Impressionists to Dutch marine pictures and peasant scenes.

It was decided that 1951 should be taken as the base year for comparison, and since this was an historic low point for art prices of almost every sort, the *Times-Sotheby Index* showed some startling leaps in price. By 1968 English glass had multiplied six times in value, old books eight times, and Impressionist paintings nearly ten. Old Master prints had gone up no less than eighteen times — all of which compared very well to the stock markets, which had risen less than four times in the United States, and in the United Kingdom only three. As Keen put it at the end of her report for 1968, the investor in art and artefacts had to conclude that "it is hard to go seriously wrong."

The fallacy of the index was that its dates happened to document a world-wide economic boom, since, with a few rare exceptions, art prices float on the waters of the overall economy, rising and falling with the tides. Longer term studies have shown that art can be a most deceptive investment, particularly when the costs of storage and insurance are written in. But Geraldine Keen's research did shed some interesting light on the buyers who were fuelling the rise of Sotheby's.

At the top of the market, she discovered, were museums, American universities, and millionaire private collectors in the Henry Ford II and Greek shipowner class. They were buying art from £25,000 up to £1 million and beyond, and price rises in this category had been particularly dramatic.

Items priced between £5,000 and £25,000, however, had not shown the same increase. This price band covered categories like French furniture and sub-museum Old Masters, the items that had traditionally been collected by the aristocracy and landed gentry. This elite was evidently less affluent than it once had been.

Below £5,000, however — the sector that belonged, as Keen put it, "to the cultured middle class, with small fortunes or good incomes"— there had been some healthy price increases, reflecting the post-war expansion of this broad middle category on both sides of the Atlantic. Here were the new buyers who read Stanley Clark's stories, along with those whose tastes were more developed than their means, exerting their ingenuity to

buy "artistic junk" in antique shops and markets priced in the
£5 to £200 price bracket.

The *Times-Sotheby Index* gave solid shape to trends that were
previously hunches. Contemplating Keen's category of "artistic
junk," an area that Sotheby's and Christie's had traditionally dis-
dained, it occurred to some of the younger spirits in New Bond
Street that this might represent a new market. A tradition had
developed through the 1960s that the dealers of the Portobello
street market would come to Sotheby's every Friday with the
treasures they had collected in the previous week. Sotheby's
would take what they thought they could auction, and the remainder would go out on the stalls on Saturday.

Many of these discards were items of Victoriana, or even
more modern goods that a few enthusiasts were starting to label
"art nouveau" and "art deco." Howard Ricketts, a young arms
and armour expert, felt strongly that Victorian paintings and furniture were worthy of serious study and would one day generate serious prices. So working with Marcus Linell, a porcelain
specialist, Ricketts sketched plans for a low-budget saleroom in
Motcomb Street, Belgravia, where sales would be organized to
promote and profit from Victoriana and other new categories.
In New York a similar low-budget branch office, PB 84, was already doing well for Parke-Bernet on Eighty-fourth Street. Developing the auction house's business involved the developing of
new customers — and devising new categories to sell to them.

Ricketts and Linell were two of an influx of young staff pre-
cipitated by the dramatic expansion of the company in the
1960s. The most famous was the writer Bruce Chatwin, who
was to leave New Bond Street after only a few years to gild his
own legend rather than Sotheby's. Though scornful of what he
called "Smootherboys," Chatwin carried through his life the
showiness of the auction house expert. Dying of AIDs in 1988,
he returned to the auction world as the setting for his final stories, describing the greed and style of a Peter Wilson–like figure

who used dinner with a Spanish grandee to try to do a deal over the family Goyas.

The new arrivals were selected by Wilson with the same nonchalance that had characterized his own recruitment. There were no selection boards or training courses. Sotheby's in the sixties had something of the atmosphere of a university, and Wilson prowled through it happily, peering over the shoulders of his young protégés like the indulgent dean of the faculty.

"If you didn't know when Piero della Francesca left Perugia," remembers Kenelm Digby Jones, "you might be in trouble. But if you fell down sloshed after lunch, that didn't seem to matter so much."

Peregrine Pollen was struck by the difference between going on visits with the chairman and working with Carmen Gronau: "With Carmen, one was definitely the assistant. With PCW, you felt like the other expert in the room. 'I wonder what my colleague thinks,' he would say, and the client would turn and look at me with awe."

Trips with Wilson were enlivened by his constant habit of darting into antique shops. If possible he would buy something, encouraging his young companions to buy things themselves, so they could learn how to bargain and deal. Auctioneering for Wilson began and ended with the art of the deal, and the skill he taught above all was how to get people to part with their treasures.

"They don't want to sell," reported one trainee in dejection after a visit to a possible client.

"Wrong!" responded the man who had once sold advertising space for Hearst. "They don't *know* that they want to sell. That's what you've got to show them."

Elevenses in New Bond Street would see a good proportion of the staff in the coffee bar opposite the back entrance. Wilson would be poring through a new art book or catalogue, and he would beckon the nearest apprentice to give an opinion. Up in the porcelain department at the end of a Friday, Jim Kiddell would summon his staff and anyone else who was interested for one of his end-of-the-week seminars. It was rather like a parlour game as Kiddell peered over his half-moon glasses and produced some statuette or medallion that had come in during the week.

"Now troops," he would say with relish as he placed the object on the table, "what do we all think of *that*?"

The New Bond Street offices were as cluttered and maze-like as ever, and the outside of the building looked as if it had not been painted since the war. In the middle of the confusing two entrances to numbers 34 and 35 was a kiosk operated by W. H. Smith & Son, and from street level the newsagent's name was more prominent than Sotheby's faded gilt lettering higher up.

The understatement was positively ostentatious, in the shabby chic tradition of the English gentleman who left his paintings dull and uncleaned. When Peter Wilson asked John Fowler of Colefax and Fowler to redesign some of the galleries, the decorator scrapped the prevailing red decor in favor of a subdued, muddy green in the faded style that was Fowler's hallmark. Peter Wilson divided the world into those who wished to appear richer than they were, and those who knew it was smart to seem poorer, and he practiced the auction business as the exploitation of the former by the latter. The boy whose parents had had to rent out the family home took malicious pleasure in parting the swanky from their money.

He was not averse to a bit of swank himself, however. When Peregrine Pollen suggested that Harold Robbins might be tempted to set one of his sagas of power, sex, and money at Sotheby's, Peter Wilson was enthralled.

"Tell him we'll give him complete facilities," he said, "and all his expenses paid."

Wilson's flash side was fascinated by the opulent vulgarity of *The Carpetbaggers*. It held the same appeal for him as James Bond, and he was delighted when Michel Strauss, a young Impressionist expert, commissioned Ian Fleming to devise an 007 adventure in the form of a short story set at Sotheby's. The story was published in Sotheby's annual review, *Art at Auction,* to underline how Sotheby's was the "in" place to be. Wilson was unconcerned that James Bond's parading of short-cuts to status exploited the fantasies of the nouveau riche and the gullible. The same could be said about Sotheby's.

James Bond both glorified and cheapened the cult of the English gentleman, and that was Peter Wilson's game. Aristocrat though he might be, he never seemed at ease with men of his own class. If he had confidants at Sotheby's, they were Stanley Clark, and the equally working-class silver expert, Fred Rose, who had become a full partner but never lost the manner of a tough trade unionist. The plebeian style of these henchmen was that of Harry, the grocer, Wilson's weekend companion — or of John Hewett, an outsize character who lived not far from Mersham and who looked like a poacher in his beard and scruffy cap.

Wilson had first met Hewett through Jack and Putzl Hunt, an erudite couple of dealers whom he had known since the thirties and whose personal collecting had amassed a treasure trove of ancient and curious works of art. Wilson and the Hunts would go antiquing together and they had "discovered" Hewett selling antiques from a barrow in a Chelsea street. So this became the nucleus of Peter Wilson's off-duty family, the bearded Hewett and the scholarly Hunts, friends in thrall to the romantic power of beautiful objects, swapping tips on the telephone, weekending in Mersham — and wheeling, dealing, all the time.

There was a tangible loneliness about Wilson when he was not doing business. "Oh, is it for me?" he would ask almost pleadingly, whenever a telephone rang. One of his colleagues suggests that his obsessiveness stemmed from some deep void he could never fill, and would quote a bizarre and dismissive saying of his mother's. "The boy will never amount to anything. He sits down when he pees."

Nicholas Ward-Jackson, one of the newcomers recruited in these years, remembers an ugly occasion when Wilson was on the phone talking to the heiress Barbara Hutton, who was clearly drunk or drugged. Wilson had the catalogue for a forthcoming sale in front of him, and he was cajoling advance commission bids out of her, for outlandish sums of money.

"'Barbara,' he was saying, 'you should have this marvelous golden box. I really do think you should have it.' She was on the speakerphone. Her speech was slurred and she was completely out of it, and there was Peter, taking down her bids, stifling the laughter. He must have got $750,000 out of her."

It was a complex amorality which drove Peter Wilson to generate, almost single-handed, a new sort of international business that was dominated by the English.

"We knew him well," remembers Patricia Pollen, who had him to stay in New York two months a year for a dozen years, "but we never thought we really knew him."

The closest one could get was to see Peter Wilson as personifying Sotheby's. Whether in bed surrounded by telephones, or whipping a silk handkerchief into his pocket as he embarked on yet another transatlantic flight, he was ceaselessly in motion, the consummate salesman. He knew how to beguile and amuse, to see into the hearts of clients and to play them just as he wanted. Adrian Eeles, a print expert who joined the firm in 1962, remembers being in the chairman's office a few minutes before Wilson was due to sell a collection of eighteenth-century French furniture consigned by the Rothschilds.

"Marie-Hélène de Rothschild, who was a great friend, rang, obviously worried that there were only ten minutes to go and no reserves had been settled. 'Don't worry,' he said soothingly. 'Leave it all to me. I'm sure it will go wonderfully well.'"

It was another example of Wilson exploiting the personal trust of a client, but on this occasion it worked to the client's advantage.

"He put the phone down," remembers Eeles, "and he went out to the rostrum, and he did the whole sale without a single reserve. He was able to sell the first five lots just like that, and when everybody saw they were really going to be able to buy things and that the reserves would not be prohibitive, it changed the whole atmosphere. He got some huge prices."

Wilson's headquarters were his small and disordered office beside the saleroom in New Bond Street. An easel in the corner displayed a prize painting from a coming sale, but there were none of the squawk boxes or maps that might be expected at the nerve center of an expanding international corporation. One German journalist stormed out in fury at having been received in what she took to be a storeroom. Strategically placed near the back of the auction box, PCW's cubby-hole was less a chairman's office than the sacristy behind the altar, and when Wilson was in London, he made a point of coming and going while auctions were in progress, apparently intent on his own business, but never too busy for an encouraging wave to clients that he recognized in the saleroom.

It was the deliberately cultivated ambiance of an enterprise that was constantly in motion, and it reflected the way that Wilson worked himself. Never very patient during formal office meetings, he preferred not to summon staff to his presence, but to go and search them out in their own departments, taking advantage of the visit to enjoy the latest treasures they had snared. He would roll a carved ivory netsuke worth a few pounds between his fingers with the same delight with which he greeted an Old Master worth tens of thousands, for the secret of PCW's eye was his ability to be genuinely interested in almost anything.

Peter Wilson identified so closely with Sotheby's that he could scarcely bear to let the name of Christie's cross his lips. It was "those people" or "the other place," staffed, in his heartfelt opinion, by lazy and inexpert bumblers who were morally inferior — though it was Sotheby's policy to never circulate stories to Christie's discredit. The outside world saw little difference be-tween the two houses, and the story of a failed sale or error on the part of one house could easily get changed in the retelling into a story about the other.

Like Montague Barlow, Peter Wilson realized that success in his curious business depended on adapting to the changing real-ities of a changing world, and, like Barlow, he applied unrelent-ing thought to the process. Having demonstrated the appeal of Impressionist paintings, he subdivided the picture department so there were separate teams dealing with Impressionists and Old Masters.

"People who collect one," he noted, "don't usually collect the other."

He then thought through the consequence of that, noting how many sales were made to museums — and how many new museums were opening around the world, each requiring its own fine example of the major artists and schools of painting.

This was good business for the auction houses in the short-term, but as Wilson once put it, each painting sold to a museum went "into captivity." In the longer perspective, it was a loss to the art market, and as early as 1963, Wilson was predicting a dry-ing up of Old Masters within ten years, and a shortage of good Impressionists in thirty.

"I think we shall find," he said at the end of yet another record year, "when we look back in, say, ten years from now that some of the paintings sold in 1963 went *cheaply.*"

The logic of this was that Sotheby's must look for fresh cat-egories of things for people to treasure and purchase. With the Rembrandts and Rubens virtually all behind bars, the museums and millionaire collectors at the top of the market must be of-fered new "must-haves" like Stubbs and Canaletto, while the lower price categories must be stimulated with initiatives like PB 84 and Sotheby's branch office in Belgravia. There was also a need for totally new categories of collectibles. In 1965 Anthony

Hobson suggested Sotheby's link up with Lord Montagu of Beaulieu to try selling veteran and vintage cars. Across the Atlantic in 1967, Peregrine Pollen staged the world's first ever auction of photographs.

"If collectors cannot get one thing," said Peter Wilson, "they will look for another."

Tax avoidance was something that collectors were always looking for. As the proliferation of welfare legislation in the 1960s drove up tax rates all over the world, the international transfer of art became an increasingly popular means of evasion. Cash in briefcases, numbered bank accounts, off-shore companies — the whole art world played the game. But it particularly appealed to the feline side of Peter Wilson, and there was a relish in his voice as he would explain, "Now, we can't handle this transaction through quite the normal channels."

Sotheby's asked no questions when a lot was successfully bid on by a British or American collector and then acquired in the name of an exotic-sounding company from the Caribbean, and Sotheby's had their own off-shore arrangements. In the 1960s the auction house operated its own numbered account in Switzerland. Certain payments were made through this account to Peter Wilson to help him avoid British tax, and the same facility was offered to important sellers and buyers. It was not proper to ask questions. As Wilson saw it, the good auction house was like a good Swiss bank. It was a facilitator. Its first duty was to the client, and if it could help the client sidestep inconvenient laws and taxes, that was all part of the facilitation.

So the new boys at Sotheby's learned to turn a blind eye to cash transactions — and also to smuggling. As the centre of the world's art market, London offered the best prices on art goods whose export was regulated for reasons of tax, currency, or, sometimes, heritage. Experts dealing with residents of South Africa and Argentina soon learnt there was no market for paintings which could not fit inside a suitcase. Ducking and diving was all part of the game, and PCW's protégés played it in the carefree tradition of Jim Kiddell's pre-war exploits in Germany. Peregrine Pollen boldly carried four French Impressionist canvases out of Buenos Aires on behalf of the owner to pre-empt government confiscation, rolling them inside a Spanish Beatles poster which he tucked under his arm and brought onto the plane. Felix Pryor, who joined the firm a few years later, recalls the complication of manoeuvering antique violins back into Italy after they had been smuggled into London and had failed to make their price. And when it came to Roman urns and vases, both Sotheby's and Christie's regularly accepted consignments from dealers who had cleansed the pedigrees of illegally excavated antiquities by smuggling the goods into Switzerland, then legally re-exporting them.

London was the end of the laundering process. The old-established name of Sotheby's provided the ideal cover for purchasers — particularly museums — who required respectable provenance, and Peter Wilson's willingness to facilitate "complicated" art export deals was part of the dramatic expansion his auction house enjoyed in the 1960s.

Sotheby's had no monopoly of amorality, but, as in so many other areas, they practiced it better than anyone else. Being a privately held company with offices round the world made it possible to offer clients every possible routing of goods and money. French sellers could circumvent their antiquated auction laws by selling in Monaco. If a client had homes in several countries, Sotheby's experts could advise the best place to sell to minimize tax liability. Starting in Toronto in 1967, the firm was to spread a network of branch offices around the world, and was soon holding regular sales in Canada, Monaco, Switzerland, Amsterdam, Hong Kong, Florence, and Madrid, as well as in New York. In parallel domestic expansion, Sotheby's opened branches in Torquay, the Midlands, Edinburgh, and Dublin, and in 1967 had the satisfaction of taking over Hodgson's of Chancery Lane, the booksellers who had spurned Tom Hodge back in 1908 when he had offered them Sotheby's for £30,000.

There was a magic moment in the last few years of the 1960s when just about anything seemed possible for the adventurous auction house on New Bond Street. Beautiful objects fetched beautiful prices. Sellers were happy. Buyers could not wait for the next sale, and breathless newspaper articles extolled the whole process. For Peter Wilson and his bright young men, the auction business seemed the perfect combination of taste, excitement, and money. "Those were the days," remembers Katherine MacLean, Wilson's personal assistant for more than twenty years, "when working for Sotheby's seemed like one long party."

Like Duveen, PCW got his country house in Kent, and it was in these years that he also acquired his estate in the south of France, the Château de Clavary outside Grasse. The entrance hall had a surreal and primitive mosaic of interlaced heads in the form of a clock face, and after the builders went in to start renovations, it was discovered that the mosaic had been the personal work of Picasso. Everyone agreed that Peter Wilson had the luck of the Devil.

12

STEPHEN HIGGINS was an English art dealer based in Paris, where he found that the locals had difficulty pronouncing his name. It came out as "Higgons," and since it was easier for his clients, he let it stay that way. In the 1950s Higgons sold pictures to American collectors, but in the 1960s he found himself more and more occupied on Sotheby's behalf, working with his French-born wife to track down paintings for the auction house's Impressionist sales.

By the end of the decade, Sotheby's was already experiencing the difficulties that Peter Wilson had foreseen in 1963. Good quality paintings were getting harder to find, and one solution was to promote lesser artists to the pantheon. Eugène Boudin proved an ideal candidate — a pre-Impressionist who had churned out sandy-coloured vistas of the dunes and beaches of his native Normandy. When talked up by an enthusiastic expert, Boudin's canvases made ideal auction fodder. They had an inscrutability which hinted at wisdom, or may have concealed nothing at all, and they appealed to the increasing numbers of Japanese buyers coming to London.

Mr. and Mrs. Higgons were able to supply Sotheby's with a number of Boudins and with a steady stream of Impressionist and early-twentieth-century paintings from France. But they purchased many of them through runners and other dealers, who expected to be paid for their merchandise, up front, in cash. The dealers wanted their profit immediately, since the drawback of the auction process is that sellers do not normally get their money (less commission and expenses) until after the auction house has secured payment from the buyer. This is not always as rapid as might be supposed, and first-time consignors have been surprised to learn that, having waited up to six months for a sale, they must hold on a further month or so for their money, because the auction house itself has not yet been paid.

To keep the Higgons paintings coming, Peter Wilson authorized Michel Strauss, the director of the Impressionist department in London, to make direct payments to Mr. and Mrs. Higgons. These payments were technically in the form of advances, but since the Higgons were supplying five or six significant pictures to every Impressionist sale — as many as a dozen canvases a year — these "advances" rolled over in time to become amalgamated into a single, running account. They were, effectively, an investment fund by which Sotheby's bankrolled the couple's purchases. Peter Wilson was gambling, risking the auction house's capital as if he were a dealer, and he concealed the full scope of the Higgons payments from his other partners and from Sotheby's financial director, H. M. Robinow.

The process worked well so long as the Higgons paintings kept selling. But late in 1969, after nearly twenty years of uninterrupted growth, the art boom started to falter. Almost a quarter of the lots in Parke-Bernet's Impressionist sale in New York that autumn failed to sell, and the same happened in London, where a worrying number of the "bought-ins" were canvases provided by Higgons. In normal circumstances, Sotheby's would simply have returned the unsuccessful paintings to the seller with a bill for insurance and photographic expenses.

But this was not possible with the unsold Higgons stock. The advance was too large and diverse, running back through several dozen transactions which had blended into an immensely complicated mess. Willy-nilly, the Higgons had become Sotheby's partners in these deals, and the auction house was now saddled with an inventory of undistinguished paintings which took two years to dispose of.

The loss was shown in that year's accounts as £400,000, wiping out profits and dividends, and when the full story came into the open, experts outside the painting department were furious. Tim Clarke, the veteran porcelain expert, and Howard Ricketts, the inspiration for Sotheby's branch office in Belgravia, were particularly incensed at Wilson's toying with the auction house's funds and reputation.

Feelings had run high in 1964 when the partners debated the acquisition of Parke-Bernet, but everything had been out in the open. The clandestine nature of the Higgons affair left a nasty taste, and after a fierce boardroom row the only agreement was on the need to keep the details of the episode secret. Today it has become routine for the auction houses to "stake" dealers and pay advances to procure interesting stock for their sales, but in the late 1960s it provoked a bitter split. The magic moment was over, and Sotheby's had got its first taste of the price to be paid for breaking the rules.

It was a bad time for internal dissension, since the souring of the market had brought another problem to a head. In traditional fashion, both Parke-Bernet in New York and Sotheby's in London had tried to conceal the comparative failure of their 1969 sales by pretending that their unsold lots, which the Americans called "buy-ins," had actually found successful bidders. Christie's practised the same deception. The sale clerks on each side of the Atlantic had lists of fake names carefully designed not to sound like the names of any of their known clients, and they would enter these in the sale report as if they were genuine purchasers, alongside the final and failed chandelier bid.

In the Parke-Bernet sale of May 1970, however, an invented name and a false price of $60,000 were attached to a painting by Andy Warhol, *Soupcan with Peeling Label*. There was general market interest in the transaction, since it was the first Warhol ever offered at auction, and no dealer had previously secured more than $50,000 for the artist. It became known that there had been a genuine bid in the room at $55,000, so trade scrutiny focused closely on who actually paid $60,000, and the deception was eventually unraveled.

There was widespread surprise and protest, since the mechanism of reserves and "buy-ins" was comparatively new to America. The system had come to New York with Sotheby's takeover of Parke-Bernet, and the row revived the antagonisms of that episode, particularly on the part of Sotheby's old protagonist, Ralph Colin, the one-time counsel to Parke-Bernet, who was now devoting his peppery energies to the interests of the American Art Dealers' Association, which he had founded. Colin took his complaints to New York's state capitol at Albany, where his association protested against the deceptive reporting of "buy-ins" and the whole British-inspired mechanism of reserves.

Lobbying for Parke-Bernet, the lawyer Jesse Wolff was able to argue successfully in defense of the reserve system, justifying it as a business precaution that any seller was entitled to take. But he could not save the disingenuous reporting of "buy-ins" as if they were real purchases. The state regulators insisted that Parke-Bernet should cease pretending if an item failed to sell, and from 1971 onwards, Sotheby's New York subsidiary curtly failed to list any items that it had had to buy in. If you had not been at the auction, you might assume that the lots had never been offered.

Back in London, however, the sale clerks continued to deploy the names on their fictitious list.

"We would go behind a curtain after every sale," remembers Fiona Ford, who was Stanley Clark's assistant as press officer, "and find out from Peter Wilson what we were expected to lie about."

Wilson saw no need to change a centuries-old convention with which London's art trade was quite familiar, but Geraldine Keen, who had branched out from her work on the *Times-Sotheby Index* to produce some probing articles on the auction business, felt otherwise. She had already focused on the deceptive listing of "bought-ins," and she was preparing an exposé on the subject, with the approval of her editor at the *Times,* William Rees-Mogg.

When she told Peter Wilson of her intentions, he felt alarmed enough to join forces with Christie's, overcoming one of his deepest taboos to confer with his opposite number, Peter Chance. The two chairmen made a joint attack on Keen, deploying a mixture of flattery and menaces, which included the threat, on Wilson's part, to ban the *Times* from Sotheby's.

Geraldine Keen and Rees-Mogg called his bluff. The article on "bought-ins" was published in the *Times* — and that was the end of the lying after auctions, and of the *Times-Sotheby Index.*

Peter Wilson did not like to lose. From the schoolboy and student for whom success had held no particular meaning, he had been transformed with the years into a single-minded workaholic for whom failure was unacceptable. He rationalized his megalomania by always talking in terms of the company, but the drive came from his ego, since everyone knew that Sotheby's was Peter Wilson, and vice versa.

When Wilson was travelling, he would send out the hotel bellboy to buy him shirts which would get charged to his room account — and thus be reimbursed by Sotheby's. It was a minor fiddle of the type practiced by many a busy and arrogant executive, but more serious issues were raised by Peter Wilson's personal dealing, and by the selling that he executed through Sotheby's on his own private account.

He had done it from quite early in his career, picking up an interesting curio in an antique shop and putting it into the next Sotheby's sale. It was a game for Wilson, an almost academic exercise to put his judgment to the test. He never made much money from the habit, but it amused him to check on his own taste and to get his instincts confirmed by the marketplace.

But even when Wilson had become chairman of Sotheby's, friends noted small objects from Mersham, his country house, cropping up in New Bond Street sales — a medallion, perhaps, or one of the bronzes that Wilson liked to collect — and they wondered if PCW had tired of them, or if Harry had got himself into trouble again at the betting shop. A day or so before the sale, the chairman would stroll casually into the bids department and ask to look at the commissions book — the ledger in which advance, absentee bids were recorded before the sale — and he would run his eye over the bids that had been sent in for his particular object. If the interest had been healthy, the auctioneer could expect a telephone call some time before the sale.

"I think," Wilson would murmur with his hesitant and charming stutter, "that we might just move the reserve on that lot up a little, don't you agree?" And the reserve would get shifted up to just below the highest of the commission bids.

The point of this adjustment was that an auction house contracts with every absentee bidder to handle his commission as if he were actually in the room, able to see the other bidders and suspend his bidding at the lowest possible price. So though you may place a commission bid for, say, £100 on a particular lot, you do not expect to pay that much if the bidding in the room stops at £60. An unscrupulous auctioneer might take advantage of your absence to "chandelier bid" the price up to the highest you were prepared to pay, but it is a matter of professional obligation for the auction house to get the best possible deal on your behalf.

Wilson was being unscrupulous, taking advantage of the inside knowledge he could command to push up his own reserve and thus ensure that if someone had bid £100, they would have to pay that, or close to it, and not get away with £60. The sums of money involved were never huge, but the chairman was dabbling in deception, and there were other, more serious ways in which the company suffered from Wilson's inability to see where his own interests stopped and those of Sotheby's began.

By the end of 1970, Sotheby's was suddenly short of cash. The score of new offices strung out around the world had not yet produced the revenues to repay their investment, and the creation of the saleroom at Sotheby's Belgravia was proving particularly expensive. The auction house had taken over the Pantechnicon, a bepillared Regency building near Sloane Street, and the conversion was a drain on resources at a moment when the downturn in the market had made money unexpectedly scarce.

Christie's was able to increase its growth in the 1970–71 auction season through tight management and initiatives like the jewelry auctions which it had recently started in Geneva. It expanded its turnover to more than £25 million. But Sotheby's experienced its first real setback in two decades. Turnover fell by 20 percent. At £35.8 million, this was still comfortably ahead of the opposition, but by early 1971, the company overdraft stood at over £1 million.

"We all sat around wondering who to phone up for money," recalled one former director. "We squeezed every single client we could."

It was in the midst of this depression that Peter Wilson produced his solution to the crisis — the Sotheby's Cigarette. Eager to launch a new, upmarket brand, the tobacco giant W. D. & H. O. Wills wished to shortcut the process of building up a brand name, and had commissioned market research to analyse existing names with snob appeal. Their survey had thrown up Fortnum & Mason and Sotheby's, and having been rejected by Fortnum & Mason, who feared that a tobacco connection would compromise the reputation of their food, Wills turned to Sotheby's.

The maker of Woodbines, Capstan, and other largely downmarket brands, Wills made the auction house a straight money offer — £100,000 to use the Sotheby's name on its new, aspirational cigarette, plus several hundred thousand pounds worth of advertising which would not only promote the cigarette, but would spread the name of Sotheby's.

Wilson announced this proposal, which he said he approved, early in 1971 at a meeting of the Sotheby's directors in the boardroom in New Bond Street. It was a small room, without sufficient seats for the twenty or more directors who were now partners in Sotheby's, and out of deference to their seniors, the younger experts left the seats around the boardroom table to the older partners. The newcomers perched on sideboards or leaned uncomfortably on the walls — and the tradition had been that Peter Wilson's proposals were treated with similar deference.

But the Higgons affair had dented the chairman's magic, and the recent financial difficulties had soured things still further. The cigarette proposal provoked uproar, from younger members of the firm concerned at the medical connections that were just being made between cigarettes and lung cancer, to the old guard who were appalled at the vulgarisation of the company name. No one felt enthusiastic about the proposal, but no one realised how strongly Wilson felt committed to the idea, and how determined he was to push the idea through.

"It was bewildering," remembers John Winter, a recently appointed paintings expert who had grown up as a friend of the Wilson family. "We suddenly found ourselves encountering this tremendous pressure over something that seemed relatively unimportant to a lot of people."

Wilson's position was simple. The company was in urgent need of money. There was real anxiety every month as to whether the wage bill could be met. Sotheby's had developed its profitable reputation largely thanks to Wilson's own efforts, and while he was prepared to listen to experts in areas they knew about, this was the area that he considered his own. He had built up the name, and he would exploit it. Fred Rose, the silver expert, PCW's friend and confidant, had died recently of lung cancer, but Wilson was unswayed by the medical arguments, or by the arguments of those who objected to commercialisation. He wanted the Sotheby's cigarette, and he was going to get it.

As the confrontation continued over the course of several directors' meetings, interspersed with furious arguments in offices and corridors, it became clear that the main issue was about Peter Wilson getting his way.

"It just became a question of loyalty," remembers Winter. "He wanted something and he had to have it."

"Suddenly," recalls Adrian Eeles, the print expert, "we saw a side of Peter that we had never seen before. Everything had been going too well, and there were people like Stanley Clark, who was a marvellous person, but who thought Peter could do no wrong, and who had been giving him the wrong kind of flattery. Stanley had constant entrée to Peter's office. He used to sit there for ages, telling him how wonderful he was. No one had ever ventured a word of criticism — there had been no need — and Peter had come to feel a sort of omnipotence."

Marcus Linell, one of the senior and best regarded members of the younger generation, dared to challenge the omnipotence, and rapidly discovered that crossing Peter Wilson was "anything but nice." From being the chairman's blue-eyed boy, Linell found he was treated as the viper in the nest. When Wilson got angry, white spots appeared on his cheeks, and his lips went hard and thin.

"I got a PCW frost from then onwards," remembers David

Ellis-Jones, another paintings expert who dared to speak his mind.

"It was his way of finding out who his friends were," says John Winter. "He could be vicious and dismissive with those who had sided against him."

An immediate show of hands would probably have thrown out the cigarette proposal at the outset, but Wilson was not admitting defeat, and opinions started to change as the chairman went to work. Loyalists like Graham Llewellyn, the jewelry expert, were not enthralled by the idea, but they were willing to rally round the boss, and Wilson openly threatened those who continued to hold out. He went through the mechanics of getting proxy votes from Peregrine Pollen, David Nash, and the partners in America who were involved in running Parke-Bernet, and he pointed out that the one-man, one-vote arrangement at board meetings was not a true reflection of the company's equity structure.

The battle stretched over several months, and Peter Wilson eventually emerged victorious. But it was victory at a severe price. Howard Ricketts, the young inventor of Sotheby's Belgravia, resigned over the issue, and Tim Clarke, the veteran porcelain expert who had once counted himself a friend of Wilson's but who had shared Ricketts's anger over Higgons, also resigned.

These were serious departures, but the damage went deeper than that. "It completely changed the character of the firm," remembers Adrian Eeles. "Peter never forgot who had opposed him — and no one who experienced it could ever forget his bullying."

It marked a loss of innocence. Sotheby's was no longer a university common room or an art seminar. It was a business. Amongst the longest-serving experts, Anthony Hobson and Richard Timewell had already departed in disillusionment, regretful, as old hands, that the character of the auction house was being eroded by the drive for profit. Now their feelings were shared by the new generation.

"When I became a director of Sotheby's," said Michael Webb, one of the several young experts who left soon after the cigarette episode, "I thought it meant something. Now I know better."

13

———

THE SOTHEBY'S CIGARETTE WAS launched in the autumn of 1971 — to Christie's delight. "Sotheby's might affect your health," read a cheeky announcement briefly posted on one King Street noticeboard. The packaging of the new product displayed a stylized silhouette of the facade of the New Bond Street salerooms, prestigiously outlined in gold, plus a title which used auction terminology, but confusingly sounded as if it applied to vintage port: "Sotheby's Special Reserve."

"It tasted disgusting," remembers Fiona Ford — and that proved to be the general verdict of the British smoking public. Sotheby's Special Reserve was withdrawn from the market after only a few years of disappointing sales, and W. D. & H. O. Wills found itself saddled with such a large stock of unsold cigarettes that it surrendered the tobacco to H.M. Customs to secure a refund on the excise tax that it had paid.

Peter Wilson had no comment. From his point of view, the cigarette had accomplished its purpose. The £100,000 royalty fee from Wills — whose founders were the wealthy family who had rented the home of the ten-year-old Peter Wilson forty years earlier — had helped tide Sotheby's over the difficulties of the 1969–70 market downturn. When the market came back in the early seventies, Sotheby's came back with it. The new overseas offices started to generate revenue, and in London, Sotheby's Belgravia was doing all and more than it had promised.

Trying to attract ordinary customers who were not familiar with the auction process, the Belgravia saleroom went for informality, designing catalogues that were more user-friendly than the traditional auction house product. They were sprightly, red-jacketed brochures which deployed as many pictures as possible, and in its second season, the branch office went a stage further. It disclosed its price estimates.

Auction house estimates had never been exactly secret, but there had always been a certain stealth about them. The onus was on the buyer to ask, and it took a certain nerve for a non-professional to tackle a snooty-looking expert to get his views on a price. The auction house wanted to track and engage serious buyers in personal conversation, and Sotheby's operated a working limit — usually five or six — on how many estimates could be given out at a time.

"It was as if," remembers one expert, "we didn't really want to sell everything."

Now the estimates were set out in print — at first on a list of their own, then on a page, and eventually beside each lot as a price guide in the catalogue — and once the disclosure had been made, everyone wondered why it had not been done before. Putting a price on things proved an irresistible hook to the private buyer.

Dealers did not like it, for the disclosure of estimates removed one of their principal advantages over the general public and the novice in the saleroom, and it fractured the cosy insider collusion which had always been part of their ambivalent relationship with the auction process. Now anyone could play the auction game — and they did. The publication of estimates, which soon became standard in the main catalogues of New Bond Street and also at Christie's, was a major step in the shifting of auction house emphasis from wholesale to retail. Estimates were like the racing odds, and knowing the auctioneer's price attracted all the more punters. It lent extra spice to the game.

Other innovations started to pay off. In 1969 a small group of young recruits had been paid to participate in a ten-month, in-house training scheme that involved practical instruction by Sotheby's experts. By year two competition for places was so severe that Sotheby's started charging those accepted, and by year three the "Works of Art Course," later known as "Sotheby's Education" was a thriving money-making division of the company. In 1975, Mrs. Jacqueline Kennedy Onassis paid £850 plus VAT for her eighteen-year-old daughter, Caroline, to attend what came to be seen as the world's most prestigious finishing school.

Wine auctions started in these years, as did the holding of jewelry auctions in Switzerland. Middle-class wine snobbery was another recent hijacking of upper-class tastes, while selling jewelry in Switzerland was a way of sidestepping the import duties and luxury taxes which Labour Chancellors of the Exchequer were devising in these years on an almost annual basis. In all sorts of ways the auction houses were becoming less purely art-centred and more generally user-friendly — the ultimate department stores for luxury and status.

Sotheby's copied both the wine auctions and the Swiss jewelry sales from Christie's, which was continuing to expand, and was holding on to its ability to outshine Sotheby's in the field in which it had always been the leader, the sale of Old Master paintings. In 1970, Christie's auctioned Velázquez's famous portrait of his black servant, *Juan de Pareja,* the property of the Earl of Radnor, for £2.31 million — £1.5 million more than Parke-

Bernet had obtained in 1961 for *Aristotle Contemplating the Bust of Homer.*

Christie's still was not challenging Sotheby's in America, however, and there Parke-Bernet had enjoyed under its English captors an era of expansion and profits such as it had not known in the most glorious years of its founders. In 1966 an office had been opened in Los Angeles, and five years later it pioneered another profitable new auction category. Parke-Bernet's first ever West Coast auction, held in February 1971, was a sale of surplus props from the studios of Twentieth Century Fox — Shirley Temple's teddy bear, a dozen reproduction Japanese World War II fighters, as seen in *Tora, Tora, Tora,* and the bicycle from *Butch Cassidy and the Sundance Kid,* which fetched $3,100.

The news coming out of Sotheby's American subsidiary had been almost universally good, and the credit for that was generally accorded to the brilliant and eccentric Peregrine Pollen. With his long, straight hair, which made him look somehow Red Indian, and his cowboy boots, which he delighted in leaning ostentatiously on his desk, Pollen cut an unconventional figure. When he came back to England in 1972 to resume his career at New Bond Street, he was hailed as a conquering hero. He was generally seen as the next Peter Wilson, and his appointment as deputy chairman seemed to be Wilson's acknowledgement of that.

Lou Marion's son, John, was appointed Pollen's successor as president of Parke-Bernet, so less than a decade after the British takeover, the Madison Avenue auction house had resumed much of its traditional face. Taking its cue from the ferment of creativity in Manhattan, 980 Madison had created the world's first auction market in contemporary art. Pollen had imported New Bond Street experts from time to time, but he had tried to recruit Americans whenever possible, and two of his brightest finds were Robert Woolley and Edward Lee Cave, who each took the company in profitable new directions.

Woolley was cheerfully gay, with the openness that English homosexuals were not to permit themselves for another decade, and he would entertain Wilson at flamboyant cross-dressing costume parties at his Fifth Avenue apartment, where the best sitting room had been turned into an aviary for his collection of brightly plumaged tropical birds.

Woolley had worked at *A la Vieille Russie,* the exclusive antique shop on Fifty-seventh Street, where he had delighted in picking up bargains which slipped past the imperfect expertise of the old Parke-Bernet. Thanks to poor cataloguing, he had regularly been able to walk away with Russian icons and other treasures whose value had not been appreciated.

There were no more bargains once Woolley had moved to Madison Avenue, and there he pursued his enthusiasms to organise an exclusively Russian sale, pulling together furniture, jewelry, paintings, and works of art that would normally have been sold within those separate categories — the first time anyone had thought to reorganize lots on national or ethnic lines. The auction business is about adding value, and this attaching of fresh labels to what were otherwise routine furniture, prints, and paintings generated higher prices and extra sales. Sotheby's department store had gained a profitable new sales department.

Edward Lee Cave, the very first of Pollen's American recruits, took Sotheby Parke Bernet, as Parke-Bernet became known in 1972, into the real estate business. As New York's expert in charge of decorative objects, Lee Cave had laboured long hours on the varied contents of a house sale, only to witness the arrival of a real estate agent who would earn a similar commission, with considerably less effort, by disposing of the house itself.

Sotheby's clientele, it seemed to Lee Cave, were precisely the sort of people who bought and sold grand houses and apartments, and Sotheby's was a name that they had come to trust. So was born the Sotheby Parke Bernet International Realty Corporation, a wholly owned subsidiary which marketed dream homes internationally and was soon brokering deals for a client list that ran from Dupont and Heinz to Liza Minnelli.

In 1960 Sotheby's had been a single auction room in New Bond Street. By the early 1970s it had branches around the world and was turning itself into a supermarket of subsidiary businesses. It took over James Bourlet, the company that handled its packing and storage, and J. J. Patrickson, the picture framers and restorers. Peter Wilson put his son Philip in charge of Sotheby Publications, which turned out art books and *Art at Auction,* the company's annual review of sales.

Most lucrative of all, Wilson secured Sotheby's the contract to advise the British Rail Pension Fund on its programme of art purchases for investment. The auction house earned a basic consultancy fee, the chance to channel many of the pension fund's purchases via New Bond Street, and the undertaking that all eventual sales and profit-taking would be made through Sotheby's — a package of guaranteed income that was tied up for years to come.

By the early 1970s Sotheby's was outgrowing itself. As the auction house prospered, young partners were finding it almost impossible to scrape up the cost of a stake in what was becoming a multinational business empire, and this meant that senior directors could not cash out their own investments when they retired. A succession of ingenious loan schemes attempted to get round the problem, but it was the competition which demonstrated the easiest solution. On November 15, 1973, Christie's issued their shares to the public, floating the auction house on the London stock exchange and making each of their directors a millionaire overnight.

Peter Wilson liked the sound of that. In 1966 he had turned to Jacob Rothschild to help provide cash for the transfer of shares. The son of Lord Victor, the Rothschild who sold 148 Piccadilly in 1937, Jacob put in £250,000 through his investment trust to become Sotheby's first ever outside partner. Like all the working directors, Rothschild stood to profit handsomely if Sotheby's went public, but he explained to Wilson that it could not happen at the flick of a switch. In 1974, Sotheby's was a £90 million business that was still run like a medieval fiefdom. It had to become a controlled and structured company before it could consider approaching the stock exchange, and this was a task which would require an experienced corporate manager.

Peter Spira, a forty-four-year-old vice chairman of Warburg's, the merchant bankers, was the man who got the job. An owl-like and straight-talking character, Spira had the qualifications — a scholarship to Eton, a Cambridge degree, and a spell of military training with the prestigious Green Jackets, the only British regiment with the intelligence not to wear red during the American War of Independence.

In theory Spira had the pedigree to blend into the New Bond Street family without strain. But he was Jewish, one of the first Jews to hold a senior position in a British auction house. Everyone said it made no difference, but somehow it did. And he was also a banker, a figures man by training and instinct, charged with the delicate task of disciplining a complex and creative world that lived by its own rules. It brought Spira head-to-head with some long-cherished corner-cutting, and for many of the old hands at Sotheby's, his arrival marked the day the music died.

"Those were the years," remembers John Winter, "when the meetings started."

Spira arrived in New Bond Street in the autumn of 1974, and he became instantly notorious when, within weeks of joining the firm, he announced the cancellation of the annual Christmas party. The Arab oil embargo of 1973 had had a disastrous impact on the art market, and with revenues slumping, Sotheby's had no choice but to lay off staff. The plan was to make twenty-six people redundant at the end of December, and Spira worked out that saving the expense of the Christmas party could cut that toll by two. He could not say this at the time, however, since the board considered it humane to save news of the dismissals until the last moment. So Spira became the company Scrooge, and that was a reputation that he never lost.

Puzzled as to why the accounts department, which incurred regular bills for weekend overtime, was taking so long to produce figures, he asked John Cann, the director of administration, to investigate.

"They are having orgies," Cann reported. "They are coming in on Sundays and having sex."

The accounts department was housed in a nearby building, and this had become the site of wild socialising at weekends. So there were more redundancies, and the locks were changed, though the reorganised and sex-free staff found it difficult to produce figures with much more speed than their predecessors.

"It was a total, utter shambles," remembers Spira. "There were no real figures, because no proper records had been kept."

Spira uncovered the existence of the company's secret Swiss bank account, which he ordered to be immediately closed, then turned his attention to the directors' expense account claims, which he suspected to be exercises in fantasy. But his attempts to get experts to file proper records of their business-getting expenses provoked outrage.

"It was a clash of philosophies," remembers Peregrine Pollen. "Traditionally we had always taken risks, and we lived on our wits. The record-keeping did not matter, and we didn't worry much about the expenses either. We had learned it all from Peter Wilson. Our view was, 'We're going to get that sale, and if we don't make any money out of it, that doesn't matter. If we've got it, that means somebody else hasn't — and whatever it costs, we'll get the PR out of it.' We didn't worry about the bottom line."

Gross auction turnover was the figure that Peter Wilson was constantly seeking to increase — the total sum of successful bids at all sales in the course of the year. But this was a misleadingly grandiose sum to pursue, since most of it was not Sotheby's money. The auction house only pocketed its commission of 10 to 15 percent of this, and then had to meet all its overheads and expenses. When Spira had been considering joining the auction house in 1974, he was told that the profits on that year's record £90 million turnover were around £5 million before tax. But when the finance director finally tracked down the expenses based on figures that he considered reliable, he discovered that in reality the profits were less than half that.

He also discovered that Sotheby's appeared to be financing most of the major art and book dealers in London. Continuing the tradition that went back to the days of Samuel Baker, the auction house was allowing extended credit to favoured dealers who bought at auction, and this deeply offended the new director of finance.

"We were paying vendors after a month," he remembers, "but the dealers were only paying us after three or four. That meant we were out of our money for two months or more. It was costing us a fortune."

Spira ordained that all dealers would have to settle their accounts within a month, and he sent letters requesting bank references, starting with one of the major creditors, Agnew's.

Next morning, Peter Wilson stalked into Spira's office, the spots on his cheeks glowing white.

"I've been in this company for forty years," he said, icy and furious. "You've been here four weeks, and you're ruining the business. I have Geoffrey Agnew on the phone."

Wilson had recruited Spira personally. The banker had struck him on first meeting as an amenable, flexible fellow, while Spira, for his part, had been won over by the diffident manner with which Wilson approached those that he wished to impress. So both men found themselves saddled with the opposite of what they had expected, and the battles between "Big Peter" and "Little Peter" became regular features of board meetings. Stories filtered back to Spira of Wilson striding round the corridors, King Henry II–style, muttering, "Who will rid me of this turbulent priest?"

Spira got his way over the dealers. Extended credit was reduced. But he incurred his chairman's particular fury when he dared to question Wilson's favouritism towards his sons. Wilson doted on his two boys. His affection for them was a rare incursion of personal feeling into his compulsive professional life. As he had given his younger son Philip charge of Sotheby's publishing business, so, when Sotheby's opened in Monaco, he gave the design work contract to his architect son, Tom.

Everyone in the company knew better than to even touch on the matter. But Spira was appalled by the nepotism. He pointed out to the chairman that his son's publishing operation had swallowed up £70,000, and that, money aside, a crucial principle was involved. The boys survived, but under more stringent financial criteria, since even Wilson could see that a company that handed jobs to the chairman's sons without going through the motions of a comparative tender could not hope to go public.

David Westmorland, Wilson's cousin who had joined the firm in 1967, was the only other director who had ever dared confront Peter Wilson on financial matters. An earl and an eminent figure at court — he was a friend of the Queen, who was shortly to appoint him her Master of the Horse — Westmorland had a background that was financial rather than artistic. He had managed to achieve spending checks during the brief crisis of 1969–70, and now he supported Spira's campaign to impose financial controls over each expert department — though in the eyes of the experts, it was not expense account forms that had made Sotheby's great.

"Of course we were inefficient," says Peregrine Pollen. "But you had to take account of the flair factor." In the on-going war between expert and accountant, the paintings department commissioned a rubber stamp to deal with the relentless stream of memos from the finance director. In large red letters it read "FUCK OFF."

But the memos intensified in the crisis-ridden months that followed the 1973 oil boycott. Sales fell dramatically, while expenses rocketed under the impact of double-digit inflation. Fresh income had to be found from somewhere, and one obvious source was from the commission charged to sellers. Peter Spira calculated that an increase of one and a half percent in the seller's commission would yield a million pounds in the first year, without any increase in expense. But this would give Christie's a competitive edge, and it would also lessen Sotheby's advantage over rival auction houses in Europe.

Europe suggested an answer. It had long been customary there for *buyers* to be charged commission as well as sellers — a straight surcharge of 10 percent on top of their final bid, or "hammer price." Sotheby's and Christie's had both adopted this so-called "buyer's premium" at the jewelry sales they had started holding in Switzerland, and the figures showed that these were among their most profitable sales. When Sotheby's conducted its first auction in Monaco early in May 1975, it was the buyer's premium which made the difference.

"We took over thirty porters and every possible expert hanger-on," remembers Spira, "and we still made a profit."

The downside to a buyer's premium was that it would, theoretically, inhibit bidding. The bidder who kept an eye on his budget might be expected to trim his bids by 10 percent. But in practice, even hard-headed dealers seemed to forget about the premium once the bidding got serious. The extra 10 percent was tolerated, albeit ill-humouredly, as a sort of additional tax.

Sotheby's had been debating the buyer's premium for months, and the first boardroom meeting after Peter Wilson got back from Monaco late in May was scheduled to focus on the possibility of introducing it in England — when on Friday, May 30, Christie's intervened. Late that evening Jo Floyd, Christie's chairman, telephoned New Bond Street to let his rivals know that Christie's would be announcing the introduction of the buyer's premium the following day.

Christie's initiative was a consequence of becoming a public company. They were about to report a 23 percent downturn in their figures, and the only way to break that news to the City was in conjunction with a plausible strategy for stemming the losses. The buyer's premium provided that strategy, and the following Monday, June 2, 1975, Sotheby's announced that it would institute the premium as well.

London's dealers were outraged. Much of their living came from buying at auction to resell at a profit, and they also made bids on behalf of clients, to whom they would now have to charge an extra 10 percent on top of their commission. When the new season opened in the autumn, the silver dealers and the book dealers ostentatiously walked out of the auctions — though Sotheby's noticed no downturn in those sale results, since many of those who walked out had made secret arrangements to bid through nominees or on the telephone.

Some years later, the British Antique Dealer's Association brought a lawsuit charging Sotheby's and Christie's with collusion over the introduction of the buyer's premium. An incriminating letter was rumoured to exist, signed by Peter Wilson. But the dealers could never produce the letter, nor any other "smoking gun." They had to abandon their case for lack of evidence, and the real point at issue was not the possibility of secret correspondence and plotting — which was a lazy, conspiracy theory reaction to how the art world was changing — but the more fundamental collusion of economic self-interest that now linked the auction houses. Sotheby's and Christie's had once been the servants, but they were increasingly becoming the masters — and, in dealers' eyes, the bullies — of the art trade.

"It was so arrogant," said Julian Agnew, summing up the dealers' pain at the realities transforming their increasingly sharp-edged and competitive business.

The introduction of the buyer's premium marked the moment when Christie's and Sotheby's jointly abandoned the notion of the art world as a cosy fraternity in which auction houses and dealers ultimately hung together against everyone else. In taking the public penny, Christie's had made itself answerable to other masters — the outsiders from whom dealers and auctioneers had once profited in tandem — and now Sotheby's was preparing to do the same. In the offer document that the Sotheby Parke Bernet Group Ltd. took to the market in June 1977, the buyer's premium was cited as a major factor in the recent profitability of the auction house.

The document described the extraordinary and still growing company as built by Peter Wilson and his team of experts around the world. As rationalized by Peter Spira and the merchant bankers who handled the flotation, Sotheby's was a success story built around expertise on a scale which Samuel Leigh Sotheby could never have imagined. When Peter Wilson joined the firm in 1936 there had been thirty-six employees. Now there were over a thousand, with sales totalling £98.4 million for the latest twelve months. In the summer of 1977 the auction house offered the public twelve million shares at twenty-five pence, and people rushed to buy. The issue was twenty-eight times over-subscribed. The shares went on sale at 150p, and were trading at close to £2 by the end of the day.

Peter Wilson had held over 1.4 million of those shares, which meant that on June 30, 1977, he became an instant millionaire two times over. But the brilliant, unique and multi-faceted auction house which he had created was no longer his and his partners'. Sotheby's had put themselves on the block, and now they were just another stock market lot. Anyone could come along and buy the business, at the right price, and the future of the quirky and engagingly whimsical old firm was destined to be increasingly corporate.

14

ONE DAY IN THE LATE 1970S, shortly after Sotheby's had become a public company, Peter Wilson was playing croquet with an English couple who were living in Switzerland. Their twin joys in life were a glass collection they were thinking of selling, and their croquet lawn, which was cropped to green and smooth perfection. Wilson was playing in partnership with Simon de Pury, the young Swiss-French head of Sotheby's Geneva office, and the two men had fought a skilful game to get Wilson's ball in front of the very last hoop.

"It was an unmissable shot," remembers de Pury, "totally unmissable. It was the only thing we had to do to win, and I could see Peter bending over with incredible concentration."

Somehow the shot missed and the auctioneers lost the game.

"Maddening!" whispered the chairman to his partner, the very picture of annoyance and regret.

Wilson secured the glass collection for Sotheby's, and sold it for a very good price. He had been flying out to play croquet with the couple on quite a regular basis, as if nothing mattered more to him than afternoons on their beautiful lawn. But once they had signed their contract with the auction house, they could not help noticing how the visits tailed away.

"It's such a shame," they said to de Pury. "He became such a very close friend."

"I know, I know," responded Wilson wearily, when de Pury passed on the couple's mild complaint. "But you know, one just isn't so interested afterwards."

Sixty-five years old in 1978, Peter Wilson could no longer be bothered to pretend.

"One knows perfectly well," he said to John Winter, driving through Italy one day in his later years, "that it has been rubbish all the time. When I go and advise someone to sell their picture because now is the moment to sell it, and they're going to make more money than they'd ever dream of, and there's never going to be another moment like this, I know that I'm giving them the wrong advice. I should be telling them to keep their picture, because isn't that what we are telling our buyers — that now is the ideal moment to invest, and that they should all be buying?"

Winter had known Wilson since his childhood.

"He was always very conscious of what he was doing," remembers Winter, "and to a slightly appalling degree."

Winter's own father, Carl Winter, director of the Fitzwilliam Museum at Cambridge and a friend of Wilson's, had been homosexual, and his marriage had collapsed for that reason about the same time as Wilson's. Like the Wilson boys, John Winter had had the disconcerting experience of a father who had boyfriends, and it made for a particular understanding of the man. When Wilson came pacing off the plane at Pisa, Winter would take him straight to the airport cafeteria and make sure that the chairman had a pastry inside him before they set off in the car.

"Otherwise," remembers Winter, "there'd be trouble. He'd get funny-tempered when his blood sugar dropped."

Peter Wilson had been diagnosed a diabetic in his late forties. "You never thought of him as an invalid," remembers one young paintings expert. "But he'd hang up his jacket, and out of the pocket would fall a syringe."

Wilson took his illness in his stride, handling the mechanics of diabetes in a no-nonsense fashion, and it was at the age of sixty-five that he pulled off his biggest sale of all. The Robert von Hirsch collection was an extraordinary and priceless hoard of medieval art, Impressionist paintings, Old Master paintings and drawings, carpets, caskets, and unique artefacts like the enameled shoulder ornament worn by the Emperor Frederick Barbarossa at his coronation in 1152. Wilson's connection with Hirsch went back to his student days in Germany, and since 1966 he had been courting him through Jurg Wille, the canny founder and director of Sotheby's prosperous operation in Switzerland. A noted connoisseur himself, Wille was a friend of Hirsch, and he effectively became the curator of the old man's collection, selling some of Hirsch's fine Giacomettis under his own name, and handling all the details of the disposal that followed Hirsch's death. When the goods went on the block in New Bond Street they fetched £25 million in a series of spectacular sessions.

It was by far the largest auction haul in history, and it represented a sort of summit in Peter Wilson's long career. The milestones of his life had been the great sales, and it was difficult to see how he could ever top the scale of Hirsch. Slowing down slightly to enjoy the financial benefits of going public, he sold his country house at Mersham and started spending more time in the south of France. He had Harry down to stay with him at Clavary, but he saw less and less of his longtime companion, whom he installed in a retirement villa at Hythe on the south coast.

Peter Wilson got quite angry when people talked of the notion that he himself might retire. "I have no intention of resigning," he declared in 1978 to Geraldine Norman (as Geraldine Keen had been known since her 1971 marriage to the playwright Frank Norman) — adding for good measure "and no need to for many years to come."

But announce his resignation he did, on November 9, 1979, when he surprised even his closest colleagues with the news that he would be relinquishing the chairmanship in just four months' time. He wished to make provision for his sons, he said, by moving permanently to France and becoming non-resident in Britain for tax purposes. He would retire in February 1980, and leave the country before the beginning of the next British tax year.

Wilson's unexpected announcement came five days after the public unmasking as a spy of Sir Anthony Blunt, Surveyor of the Queen's Pictures, who was revealed to have worked for the KGB in concert with Burgess, Maclean, and the so-called "third man," Kim Philby. This made Blunt the fourth man, and the timing of Wilson's resignation renewed suspicions that he might be the fifth, until it was revealed by Barry Penrose in the *Sunday Times* that the fifth man was John Cairncross, a Treasury official who leaked documents to Burgess.

The enduring fancy that Wilson might have been a spy did homage to the deeply tricky nature of the man, but it ignored the fact that, unlike the other traitors, who were all recruited by the same Russian agent while they were at Cambridge and were positively involved in radical socialist activities, Wilson was at Oxford and had no moment of left-wing allegiance in his past. He was apolitical throughout his life. His most obvious use to the Soviets would have been as a channel for the export and laundering of Russian art treasures to the West. But Sotheby's had an unremarkable record in that regard — and the threadbare endings of Philby and his colleagues in their chilly Moscow apartments suggested the conclusive reason why Peter Wilson could never have been a spy. There was not enough money in it.

The best explanation for Wilson's hasty departure was the one that he gave at the time — a desire to build up a tax-free nest-egg for the two sons on whom he doted. It had always been a grievance that his own father had left him nothing. Wilson's entire life could be seen as his struggle to make up for that, and he had a history of unashamedly arranging his affairs in order to avoid tax. Over the years he had set up an offshore company and two trusts whose principal object was the avoidance of tax, and he needed to go offshore himself to guarantee their effectiveness. The haste and lack of dignity of his departure raised suspicions, but haste and lack of dignity are exactly the requirements of most tax avoidance schemes.

It was not as if he was resigning from Sotheby's. His announcement of November 1979 dwelt less on his relinquishing of the chairmanship than on his new position in charge of European business-getting, which had always been his delight. Working out of Clavary with a chauffeur, a secretary, and a salary of £100,000, he would remain very much involved, for as he told Geraldine Norman, he saw himself staying with the company "for many years to come."

The measure of his intended involvement was revealed in the announcement of his successor — not the devil-may-care Peregrine Pollen, whom most people had assumed to be his dauphin, but his other deputy chairman, the courtly and quietly modest David Westmorland, his own cousin, the Queen's Master of the Horse.

Pollen had sabotaged himself since he came back to London, daring to pick fights with Wilson and speaking his mind with a flamboyance that undermined his future, even as he took it for granted. Neither an expert nor an auctioneer, he lacked his own power base, and the long hair and cowboy boots which had charmed America did not go down so well in New Bond Street.

"He used to wear an old overcoat that belonged to his grandfather," remembered Graham Llewellyn. "It was so ancient it was green. It wasn't the mark of someone who was going to lead this firm.'"

Peregrine Pollen was ultimately a free spirit. He had achieved great and original things for Sotheby's, but there was too much of the maverick about him. Having inherited his family estate in the Cotswolds, he never felt the hunger that drove Peter Wilson — which may have been the underlying reason why, some time before his resignation, Wilson wrote a letter to his protégé to warn him that when he did go, it would be Westmorland who succeeded him.

"We were all in New York together," remembers Pollen, "trying to get hold of some collection. He had the letter delivered to me after he had left the building for the weekend. I was a little bit incensed that he didn't tell me to my face, but Peter always hated confrontations. . . ."

It could hardly be said that the 15th Earl Westmorland was hungry for business. Charming and courtly, the gentle Lord-in-Waiting was scrupulous about not exploiting his elevated connections, and Sotheby's was to discover that when it came to securing property from the English establishment, it could actually be a disadvantage to be headed by the man who rode behind the Queen at the Trooping the Colour.

In choosing the unaggressive Westmorland to succeed him, Wilson seemed to abandon several of his most cherished principles, not least his conviction that the auction house should be expert-led. But Westmorland's lack of aggression was the very reason why Wilson chose him, for as the five telephone lines he had installed at Clavary made clear, Peter Wilson did not see himself as retired in any real sense. He intended to go on running Sotheby's through his cousin.

Peter Wilson took up permanent residence at Clavary in the spring of 1980. It was the perfect time of year for gardening, the only relaxation he allowed himself, and on occasions it was possible to imagine that the ex-chairman of Sotheby's really had retired.

"I've just clipped the hedges," he would say proudly, striding into his office with a pair of bright orange, electric clippers in his hand, and work would stop while the hedges were admired.

Wilson devoted long hours to the planning of his Mediterranean garden, which he designed as a symphony in different shades of green, and his office at Clavary was in a farmhouse in the grounds. The eighty-acre estate operated as a compound, with cottages for the sons, Tom and Philip, and a guest house for the endless succession of visitors coming through. The main house itself was quite small, with a finish of inlaid flints and pebbles which made it look, in some lights, like a pavilion cut out of sandpaper.

This quiet oasis amid the creeping suburban villas of Grasse was cared for by Conway Vincent, a gruff, English ex-policeman, whose controlling presence on the estate struck some visitors as mildly sinister. Conway served as butler, chauffeur, general factotum, and security chief, patrolling the grounds at odd hours. "Everything all right, sir?" Philip Astley-Jones, the furniture expert, remembers Conway asking one night, when the caretaker strolled in on a formal dinner party — in full combat kit with a submachine gun over his shoulder. Conway had some hold over Wilson, people felt, in the tradition of the indispensable servant who becomes too indispensable for his master's good, but Wilson would not hear a word against him. He would invite Conway and his French wife in for coffee and drinks after dinner with the most distinguished guests, for Conway was the gatekeeper who protected the little territory that Wilson could finally call his own.

People who saw Wilson relaxing at Clavary understood why he had left Sotheby's in order to move there — but how, in his own mind, he had not moved at all. He still saw himself at the centre of the action. Europe was the true source of culture and cultural merchandise, he liked to argue. Nearly half London's sales came from business gathered by Sotheby's offices on the continent, which was why his new responsibility, the developing of business in Europe, was where the future lay.

Friends who listened to the lecture put it down to Peter rationalising things again. He had to be connected, and the five telephone lines into Clavary were his way of saying that he had not been marginalised. Someone would ring — a friend in New York, perhaps, who was thinking about selling his Picasso — and the gardening gloves would come off in a flash. Conway would get Wilson down to Nice next morning, and the lord of the manor was once again Sotheby's will-o'-the-wisp, jumping onto the plane to Paris in time to connect with the next Concorde to New York.

"He might relax for a day or so," remembers Christine Chauvin, the athletic young French assistant hired to organise Wilson's operations in France, "but he could never let go of Sotheby's. That was his life, his love, his mistress, his friend."

Chauvin found her new boss mesmerising.

"We were in Milan once," she remembers, "on a business-getting trip, when he suddenly asked 'Do you know the Biblioteca Ambrosiana? There's a Caravaggio there. The best he ever did.' And when we got there, he just stood in front of this painting, looking hard at it, not saying a word. It was a still life, a basket of fruits, and he stood there looking at it for what seemed like ten minutes. 'OK,' he said, 'let's go.' And he seemed totally refreshed. He was so happy. He went straight back to the car, and didn't look at anything else. 'When you see a picture like that,' he said, 'you've got to put it inside you and let it live there for a bit.'"

Wilson's salary and expenses were paid in equal parts by Sotheby's London, New York, and Switzerland, and, as a business-getter, he gave value for money. In the course of his

first full year in Clavary, he brought in nearly a tenth of
Sotheby's turnover singlehanded. But business-getting was not
enough. As he saw it, he had not stopped running Sotheby's, and
recapturing that old life was as easy as picking up the phone to
David Westmorland.

"He spoke to David several times a day," remembers Christine Chauvin. "And he had David down to stay as often as he
could."

Graham Llewellyn saw the other end of the process in New
Bond Street.

"You saw David flinch after a time, as the calls came
through," he remembered. "David was such a nice man, thoroughly decent. He could not bear to say no, and especially not
to his cousin."

Llewellyn was one of a group of elder statesmen whom
Westmorland gathered round him on Wilson's departure.
Smooth, grey, and very much a company man, Llewellyn had
joined Sotheby's as an expert in jewelry, which he had once sold
in Harrods. He was set off by Peregrine Pollen, unpredictable as
ever and apparently unabashed at having been passed over for
Westmorland, and by Marcus Linell, who had made a remarkable comeback after daring to oppose Peter Wilson over the
Sotheby's cigarette.

Peter Spira completed this top management group, which
carried an array of confusingly similar titles — two deputy
chairmen, one vice chairman, and a managing director, all reporting to Westmorland. This uneasy equality made for rivalries
and constant jockeyings for power, and Spira was particularly
disliked by Pollen and some of the old, freewheeling style of experts. Recent events in the wider world had provided the finance supremo with a nickname — the Spiratollah.

"Spira was the one chap who was trying to create an agenda
and make the whole thing more businesslike," remembers Gordon Brunton, one of the non-executive directors who had

joined the board after Sotheby's went public. "But he was frowned on by the experts, which was just about everyone — and Peter Wilson disliked him viciously."

Brunton was very much a businessman, chief executive since the 1960s of the Thomson organization, which had flourished under his management, most notably by diversifying from publishing into the package holiday business and North Sea oil. Brunton's willingness to confront the restrictive practices of the print unions at the *Times* and *Sunday Times* had given him a reputation as a tough nut, and when he joined the Sotheby's board he was astonished by the meandering and unfocused style of his fellow directors.

"They'd hire people. They'd fire people. They'd do this. They'd buy that," he remembers. "They could not rise above the details. Someone would say, 'I hear so-and-so is not too well. Someone ought to go and see the estate.' It was gossip and gossip and gossip! And if you said, 'What's the plan here? How much does it cost?' they'd look at you, forgive the expression, as if you were farting in church."

Brunton had to admire the achievement of Peter Wilson. But when he viewed Wilson's legacy from the perspective of a professional manager, he saw it as fatally incomplete.

"He had made himself indispensable," he says, "but he had created no mechanism to succeed him and keep his creation going. It had all been done with hunches and gut instinct, and since there was no chance of finding a successor in the style of Peter Wilson, the only thing you could do was to frame a new and self-sustaining form of management — which was what Spira was trying to do."

This had been the finance director's mission since he joined Sotheby's in 1974, and the company's successful flotation and rising share price could be seen as the vindication of his efforts. But his critics saw these successes as having been achieved despite the bureaucracy and committee meetings which were part of going corporate. It was the instinctive genius of Sotheby's that made the difference, in their opinion — the creative dynamic of 190 hard-working experts who might not chime with an accountant's sensibilities, but who brought in the business — and the conflict between these two philosophies grew worse under the well-meaning but ineffectual chairmanship of David Westmorland.

The quarrels were almost academic to start with, for Sotheby's continued to expand after Wilson's departure to Europe, increasing its turnover for the 1980–81 season to nearly £350 million. This unprecedented figure represented a 33 percent increase in volume. But perceptive analysts were worried to see that profits did not rise in proportion, which meant that the auction house was not controlling its costs.

More worrying still was the league table of market share which analysts had started keeping since the two auction houses went public. In 1977 it showed Sotheby's ahead of Christie's 67 to 33 percent. By 1981 that had fallen to 60/40, and the following year it was 54/46. After two decades of bobbling along as also-rans, Christie's was suddenly catching up.

The reason for the dramatic acceleration in Christie's performance was almost entirely transatlantic, for after years of sending driblets of property back to London through various offices and associates in Manhattan, Christie's had finally bitten the bullet and had opened a full-scale auction room in New York. As Sotheby's was going public with great fanfare in the summer of 1977, its rival — already a public company — was opening its doors on Park Avenue, where it had taken a lease on a corner of the old Delmonico Hotel, and had invested nearly £1 million in creating a stylish American headquarters.

The first sale, on May 16, 1977, had been a catastrophe. Half the goods failed to reach their reserves and had to be withdrawn, to general derision on the part of the American art market, and of Sotheby Parke Bernet in particular. But Christie's went to work doggedly, and they had an unappreciated advantage in their campaign to steal business from their rival — the buyer's premium, which they had decided to import from London.

Charging commission to auction buyers as well as to sellers had never been seen in America, and Christie's initiative was greeted with outrage — with John Marion, chairman of Sotheby Parke Bernet, New York, leading the protests. Marion had declined to adopt the buyer's premium in New York when Sotheby's introduced it in London. He had insisted it was unnecessary. Now he compared the premium to the iniquitous British tax which had provoked the Boston Tea Party, and he promised that it would never be levied in any American auction room in his care.

Marion's bluster was an eerie replay of the process by which Sotheby's had outflanked Parke-Bernet a generation earlier. Then it had been reserves and guarantees. Now it was the buyer's premium which gave the newcomer a foothold, for the income from the premium enabled Christie's to lure sellers with low commission rates, and every season saw Christie's capturing more business in America. When Henry Ford II decided to sell some of his finest Impressionists to pay for his latest divorce, it was not to Sotheby's but to Christie's that he turned.

Back in London, Marion's tactics were viewed with increasing dismay.

"John was a brilliant auctioneer, but he lacked vision," remembers Duncan McLaren, who had spearheaded the opening of Sotheby's European branches. "He thought that Paris and Naples were towns in Florida."

First in Europe, and then in Britain, Sotheby's had discovered how the income from the buyer's premium was an unbeatable business-getting tool, and no one knew how to cope with the almost religious fervor with which Marion insisted that their American operation should foreswear its use.

"John kept digging himself deeper and deeper into the

trench," remembers Peter Spira. "It was just like the Americans in Vietnam. But everyone in London had this 'hands-off' attitude towards him because of the history of him and his father, and all the grand traditions of Parke-Bernet. It was an article of faith."

The bluff and portly Marion traveled across the Atlantic every quarter to attend board meetings in New Bond Street.

"He behaved like one of the blue-born," says Spira. "He'd say, 'Don't worry. Our service is better. Our expertise is better. We understand New York' — and no one dared question him."

In defense of his position, Marion could point out that his American turnover was not actually falling as a result of Christie's arrival. Sotheby Parke Bernet was holding its own when it came to major paintings, and was even increasing its volume in other categories of sales. But this had to be seen in the context of a suddenly booming art market. Christie's was capturing an increasing slice of business that would otherwise have gone to its competitor, and Sotheby Parke Bernet was having to cut sales commissions just to keep pace. This ate into profits, and in the end Marion had to face up to reality. In October 1978, he announced that Sotheby's U.S. operation would be introducing the buyer's premium after all.

The change of heart came too late, for even as it lost market share Sotheby Parke Bernet had been inflating its spending. Long irked by the lack of space inside 980 Madison, the Americans had hatched an ambitious scheme to carve a new auction house out of a derelict warehouse which had once been a cigar factory, and more recently a Kodak camera depository, at 1334 York Avenue in the northeast corner of Manhattan. Robert Woolley was a particular advocate of the venture, which envisioned the conversion of the warehouse into a supplementary saleroom that would handle the furniture, carpets, and other categories which needed large spaces for storage and display.

The York Avenue project was grandiose. A budget of $8.4 million was set aside for the purchase of the lease, the refacing of the building, and the removal of some of the massive, concrete pillars which ran through every floor, and it was assumed that rising sales would absorb the cost of this. But the cost of matching Christie's commission cuts set the scheme awry, and then, early in the 1980s, a second round of oil-price increases provoked general recession — and, in the art world, virtual collapse.

Sotheby Parke Bernet's chief financial officer was Fred Scholtz, a Spira-style figures man who had been hired at Peter Spira's suggestion.

"Fred thought very highly of General Foods," remembers Jerry Patterson, "and that was his model for how to run Sotheby's. He'd say, 'We had these divisions at General Foods in competition with each other, and every month we'd say, "Well, marshmallows sold well this month, but potato chips were down." So that's how it ought to be here. We ought to say, "Silver's a bit slow, but porcelain is really going well. Let's hear it for porcelain!"'"

Scholtz disliked taking orders from London.

"You could always tell when the English were due," remembers one of his staff. "Fred would order these vast detailed reports, double spaced in completely unmanageable binders, so he could wheel out a trolley of them to overwhelm the enemy."

This transatlantic disunity applied throughout a firm which, since Wilson's departure, was headless and increasingly rudderless as well. Accountant versus expert, London versus New York, one leadership contender against another — the disagreements grew more bitter as the early-eighties recession put pressure on the company's figures, and Peter Wilson added to the confusion with his phone calls from the south of France.

"The lines out of Clavary were white hot," remembers his son Philip. "He got infuriated when they would not take his advice."

The former chairman had been watching the confusion at his beloved auction house with mounting annoyance. Christine

Chauvin saw her boss getting so angry on occasions it frightened her.

"He was foaming at the mouth, literally," she remembers. "He was on the phone to Graham Llewellyn, and slammed the receiver down so hard I thought he was having a heart attack."

Llewellyn had incurred Wilson's ire for daring to query the lavish expenses claims that Wilson was sending back to London.

"He could not bear to have lost all his power and authority," remembers Gordon Brunton. "There was something very tough and hard under all that charm, and he used it to bully Westmorland, and an awful lot of other people. There was a degree of evil about him."

The phone calls took their toll on Westmorland, whose sheer niceness deprived him of mechanisms for dealing with his cousin's aggression. Wilson would fly back to London for the board meetings, and he did not hesitate to harangue his successor in front of everyone.

"I remember one meeting in particular," says Peter Spira, "in December 1981. We had adjourned for one of our courtly dinners at Peregrine's club, where we used to have a private room, and Peter was unbelievably offensive to David Westmorland. He was just abusive, telling David that he didn't know what he was talking about, and that he was just ruining the business."

"It was ugly," remembered Graham Llewellyn, who was sitting beside Westmorland at the table, "the way Peter contorted his features. It was so malevolent, it was unreal."

The scene was provoked by the figures that the company had just published. Profits were down from the previous year, from £9 million to £7 million, but, more seriously, internal forecasts were predicting a loss for the year ahead. The cost of the York Avenue warehouse conversion had ballooned to $15 million, and revenues were falling.

In the early months of 1982, Peter Spira initiated some cost cutting, to which his colleagues reluctantly agreed. It was announced that Sotheby's Belgravia would be closed, and some of the regional British offices slimmed down. The Belgravia operation would be moved into New Bond Street, and there would be staff cuts in England, and in America as well.

"Is Sotheby's in trouble?" asked *Barron's,* the influential New York financial magazine, and the Sotheby's share price fell forty-three pence on the news. It became known that Jacob Rothschild, whose investment trust had held 10 percent of the shares since the company went public, had been quietly selling his stake and now owned only half of one percent.

"Going, going . . ." commented the *Sunday Telegraph.*

The falling share price was worrying in its own right, but it also had business implications, since there was a risk that consignors would stop sending material to the auction house altogether if they thought it was in financial trouble. The share price sank further.

"My influence at Sotheby's really started," remembers Gordon Brunton, "when they became scared. . . ."

15

GORDON BRUNTON HAD FELT honoured when first invited to join the board of Sotheby's as a non-executive director in 1978.

"It was like being asked to join the Guards," he recalls. "Sotheby's was a famous name and, frankly, it flattered my vanity."

Having built up Lord Thomson's empire of newspaper, magazine, and book publishing companies, Brunton reckoned he had some expertise in the tricky area of harnessing creative people to the commercial requirements of a business. But he knew nothing about auctioneering, and in the early days he kept his counsel about the confusion and, as he saw it, the irrelevance of so many things that were discussed by the Sotheby's board.

"It wasn't for me to lock horns with Peter Wilson," he says. "But then Wilson left, and things started to slide. That was when I started to speak my mind."

Though affable in manner, Brunton was capable of charging like a rhinoceros where business was involved. He was a tall and square-shouldered character who had studied under Harold Laski, the Marxist thinker, at the London School of Economics, and he could be detached and almost academic in his analysis of a problem. But once Gordon Brunton had decided on a strategy, he was famous for pursuing his goals with intimidating focus, and the Sotheby's board turned to him when things looked their blackest in the early months of 1982.

"I offered to carry out an exercise in consultancy," he remembers, "without charge. Peter Wilson said, 'What about fees?' and I said, 'Let's see first of all if I can make a contribution.'"

Starting with Wilson, Brunton interviewed every member of the Sotheby's hierarchy in England and America, all the principal experts, and the managers of the European offices as well. He spoke privately to everyone for an hour or more, encouraging them to spill out every grievance and suggestion, and in less than a month he had seventy files packed with ideas, opinions, and complaints.

"I promised that everything would be absolutely confidential," he remembers. "I wanted everyone to be totally frank."

The result was a report which took its cue from his interviews, painting a picture of extraordinary disunity and divisiveness — which all stemmed, in Brunton's opinion, from poor leadership. "There are no bad troops, only bad officers," he wrote in his opening paragraphs, quoting an adage from his army days.

"Sotheby's has had strong leaders throughout its history," he continued. "The highly individualistic, rather talented, often difficult and temperamental people who are the real strength of the company react to strong leadership, and expect it."

Everyone he spoke to liked David Westmorland as a person. They found him "polite and charming and kind." But they did not feel he was a strong leader, and the clear inference of the report was that Westmorland should step down.

John Marion in New York had "unique skills as an auctioneer and a business-getter." But he was much criticised as a manager, and Brunton recommended that Marion should move to a more representative function and leave the money and the running of the U.S. company to a new chief executive in New York.

Brunton identified four directors whom he considered surplus to requirements — Peregrine Pollen, Marcus Linell, Robert Woolley, and David Nash, the English expert who ran the Impressionist department in New York — and he was scathing about the clubby and unbusinesslike fashion in which the board as a whole operated. The array of vice chairmen, deputy chairmen, and assistant chairmen titles, he said, was "sheer Gilbert & Sullivan farce."

Brunton went on to make specific suggestions as to how the company should be restructured, and who should hold the new jobs. He made the startling suggestions that Julian Thompson, the oriental expert based in London, and Jim Lally, his equivalent in New York, should be elevated to be chief executive in their respective cities. Of the many experts he interviewed, Thompson and Lally had most impressed him with their business abilities, and the fact that the two men had worked closely together in the development of business in the Far East would address another of the problems he had identified — the appalling degree of antagonism between London and New York.

"Of all the problems that the company faces," he wrote, "I regard that as the most serious. The most urgent need of all is to heal the wounds and repair the bridges."

The report made for tough reading, and after Brunton presented it to the board at the end of April, he withdrew to let them consider it in his absence. When they called him back into the room, their response was unanimous. They accepted every criticism and proposal he had made, and they now wanted him to become chairman, and to put it all into practice.

Gordon Brunton became chairman of Sotheby's in April 1982, working in an unpaid capacity, and retaining his position as chief executive of the Thomson organisation.

"Thomson's was a well-run company," he says. "I was chief executive, but I had set up five major divisions, each with chief executives who each ran things very well."

At Sotheby's, the immediate consequence of Brunton becoming chairman was that David Westmorland stepped down.

"David looked ten years younger overnight," remembers Peter Spira.

Brunton went down to Clavary to offer Peter Wilson the position of Honorary Life President, which would be printed in a prominent position on the notepaper of the reorganized holding company and its four subsidiaries that would now be set up in Britain, Europe, America, and the Far East. Brunton felt it important to harness the magic of the Wilson name. But he made it clear that there was a new team running Sotheby's, and that the interference from Clavary would have to stop.

Wilson had no option. He could hardly imagine that he would get far placing phone calls to Gordon Brunton, nor to Graham Llewellyn, whom Brunton had named as his number two.

Llewellyn had the task of telling Peregrine Pollen that he was sacked from the board of the holding company. There were stringent staff cuts ahead, and Brunton had laid down the principle that the cuts should be at every level.

"I didn't enjoy it," remembered Llewellyn, "and neither did Peregrine. The other directors who went were all experts, so there were jobs for them to do. But when Gordon called the whole company together in the auction room to explain his report and announce the changes, it was Peregrine who led the applause. That was very generous. He knew that he was going, but he stood up and said that this was the way ahead."

Over in New York, Jim Lally, the expert-turned-executive, was rapidly confronted by the headaches that went with his new eminence. Lally was a sardonic business graduate who had joined Sotheby's as a manager in the 1970s, running the Los Angeles office, and the closing of that office now became the first of his tasks. He had studied to become an expert — his specialty was Chinese porcelain — and he had been well respected by his peers. But the biggest decision in New York was what to do about the converted warehouse on York Avenue — the ideal machine for auctions, in the opinion of some, a grandiose folly in the opinion of others.

York Avenue was so far east in Manhattan that the numbering ran out. A block beyond First, it was technically Zero Avenue, and there could be little hope that an auction house there would attract passing trade. It was surrounded by hospitals and nursing homes. Christie's gloated at Sotheby's shifting of its low-budget auctions to such an unpromising location, publicizing stories of rich visitors from out of town whose eye was caught by Christie's Delmonico salerooms while strolling down Park Avenue, and who popped in to bid a few hundred thousand dollars.

Sotheby's continued to auction paintings and jewelry in the old Parke-Bernet building on Madison, and David Nash, the Impressionist expert, argued that the company's business should be restricted to these. Paintings and jewelry were always the most profitable auction categories, and in 1982 they were the only categories not making a loss. Nash argued that York Avenue was a white elephant, and should be shut down. Tough times called for tough decisions.

In the event, a tough decision was taken, but it went the other way. The lease on Madison Avenue was complicated, and there was no possible way of expanding the building. The division of sales between Madison and York Avenue made no sense, and no one else endorsed Nash's elitist argument for jettisoning all but the top ticket sales.

That left no alternative. Not quite knowing how they had painted themselves into this corner, Sotheby's American board decided that their whole operation would be shifted east to the hospital district. The lease on Madison Avenue would be sur- rendered — with the careful provision, negotiated by Jesse

Wolff, that no other auction house could occupy the site — and the new headquarters of Sotheby Parke Bernet would be set among the concrete pillars in the converted camera warehouse at York and Seventy-second.

Like many of the decisions taken under the aegis of Gordon Brunton, the move from Madison Avenue felt like a living limb being chopped off. Some 350 staff were made redundant, nearly a sixth of the labour force. By the autumn of 1982, Sotheby's had cut nearly £8 million, the equivalent of a good year's profits, from the expense side of its balance sheet, and was in fitter shape than it had been since the early 1960s.

But this was only apparent to insiders. The outside world was still focussing on the inefficiencies which had made the cuts necessary. "Sotheby's Lost Art — Management," ran one scathing article in *Fortune* magazine — and the stock market took its cue from this. Sotheby's share price sank to £2.60, lower than it had been for four years.

"A company is at its most vulnerable," remarks Gordon Brunton, "when it is putting its house in order, but has not managed to get those improvements reflected in its price on the stock exchange."

Sotheby's, in other words, was ripe for a takeover.

Christine Chauvin still remembers the excitement with which Peter Wilson came into the office one morning at Clavary.

"You must keep this very secret," he said. "We've discovered this amazing Roman silver."

By "we," Wilson was referring to himself and a frequent visitor to Clavary, Rainer Zietz, a talented young German dealer who shared Wilson's charm and his fascination with early works of art. Zietz's specialty was von Hirsch territory, rare artefacts of the Middle Ages and the Renaissance, and towards the end of 1980 he came across a most unusual object, a beautiful silver ewer, full-bellied and thin-necked, almost Byzantine in appearance, dating from the fourth or early fifth century A.D.

Wilson was so taken with the ewer that he bought it for £48,000 through Art Consultancy of St. Peter's Port, Guernsey, in the Channel Islands, part of his personal network of offshore companies and trusts, and in the months that followed he splashed out on more, notably a grand and elaborate silver platter more than two feet wide, decorated with hunting, fishing, and picnicking scenes. The platter bore a Latin inscription: "Let these dishes last for you, oh Sevso, through many centuries so that they may be worthy of and benefit your descendants."

There is no record of Sevso in the barely documented history of late Roman times, but the date of his silver service suggests that he was a high official administering some corner of the empire of Constantine the Great. Exactly which corner was open to question. When Zietz had located the first ewer, it was in excavated and corroded condition, broken in three pieces and wrapped in a cloth on a table in the Mansour Gallery in Davies Street, one of the Jewish Persian galleries established in London following the fall of the Shah.

Zietz had called in Richard Falkiner, an eminent coin and medal expert, to help establish the identity of the silver. But the chain of dealers and go-betweens that led back from Davies Street to the treasure's original find-spot, wherever that might be, was uncertain and remains a mystery to this day. Halim Korban, the dealer who had placed the ewer on consignment with Mansour, said it had been found in Lebanon, and he was Lebanese himself. But Korban operated out of Vienna, where one of his associates was a Yugoslav who later told a tale of the hoard having been found in Croatia by gypsies.

To judge from its style, the treasure could have come from anywhere in the Roman Empire. For its age, it was extraordinarily well preserved. The dishes appeared to have been stored through the centuries in a huge, purpose-shaped, bronze cauldron which had kept the collection intact and made it the late Roman equivalent of Tutankhamen's treasures. Some of the ewers were of majestic proportions. When unveiled to the world, it would certainly cause a sensation.

"I remember the excitement," says Christine Chauvin, "as they kept buying more — one piece, two pieces, and so on. He'd go off to see them, and come back so excited and enthusiastic. 'It's so beautiful,' he'd say. 'It's fantastic.'"

In his semi-retirement, Wilson seemed to have stumbled on a personal coup to cap his career — breathtakingly beautiful objects, a ground-breaking historical discovery, and the chance to make a fortune on his own account. As he embarked on his Sevso adventure, Peter Wilson, private dealer, took over from PCW, auction house chief, and he started to detach himself from Sotheby's.

"This is something that cannot be sold at auction," Wilson confided to Chauvin. "It has to be sold privately."

But this was the catch in Sevso's silver. Wilson did not have clear and legal provenance to the treasures he was collecting, since there were no papers to back the story of the hoard having been unearthed in Lebanon. The salvers and ewers were so exceptional that whether they came from the Middle East, Yugoslavia, or anywhere else in the Roman Empire, they were almost certainly governed by local laws restricting the export and sale of classical antiquities.

This was no novelty to Wilson, who had always relished the less respectable aspects of the antiquities trade. Plunder was its motto, from the local tomb-robbers who unearthed fresh material to the mega-rich collectors who hid their choicest prizes from the eyes of the world. Smuggling was its modus vivendi, and after four decades in the business, Wilson had become pleasurably skilled at the game. He loved the trickery of it, keeping his own private treasure cabinet at Clavary in which he stored sensitive items that he was willing to transport and sell "off the

books" on behalf of special clients and friends. He was a particular expert in the sleights of hand whereby antiquities were
channeled through secrecy-favouring jurisdictions like Switzerland.

But as each new item made Sevso's silver that much more
noteworthy, secrecy became less of an option. Wilson could easily have sold a couple of dishes to a private collector, but he
came to see that the full value of the hoard could only be realised by going public. Where and how the silver was found
would be intrinsic to its eventual unveiling, so at Wilson's request, Zietz asked Halim Korban to provide proper licenses
for all the items he was selling them. These licences were being
requested after the event, but on June 11, 1981, they were duly
forthcoming, and the authenticity of the paperwork was confirmed by the Lebanese consulate in London.

Wilson already knew the ideal home for Sevso — the recently established J. Paul Getty Museum in Malibu, California,
which was beginning to purchase its collections with endowments that made it by far the richest art museum on earth. It
could easily afford $10 million or more for a unique find like
Sevso — and Wilson invested accordingly. He had already spent
the best part of a million pounds on the project, but he was running short of money, so he turned to a collector he had met
at the von Hirsch sale, the thirty-six-year-old Spencer Douglas
David Compton, 7th Marquess of Northampton.

Known as "Spenny" to his friends and ex-wives, the eccentric and volatile Northampton had done well out of art. Wilson
had helped him turn a healthy profit on a von Hirsch Renoir,
and the Marquess sniffed big money in Sevso. He bought a geo-
metric vase to match the first that Wilson had purchased, along
with three other lavishly decorated items which brought his
own investment to around £1 million. This, plus a finder's fee,
was the price of his partnership with Wilson and Zietz, and the
trio formalized their arrangement through the creation of yet

another offshore entity, the Abraham Trust, registered in Liechtenstein.

It was an expensive and complicated enterprise, but Wilson
felt certain his investment would pay off, since he had given a
glimpse of the silver to Jiri Frel, the Getty's curator in charge of
antiquities. Frel had been as exhilarated by the treasures as everyone else who set eyes on them, and the Getty purchase seemed
a certainty. Wilson only needed to fund his share of the project
— and he did so by selling a million pounds worth of his shares
in Sotheby's.

If a date were to be set on Peter Wilson's decisive distancing
of himself from the company he had built, it would be the moment when he decided to transfer a major proportion of his assets out of Sotheby's shares in order to gamble with the money
on his own account. He was finally cashing in his chips, and
when he unloaded his shareholding in the summer of 1981, it
was, typically, at an instant of maximum advantage to himself,
for at over £4, the share price did not reflect the poor figures
which he and the directors already knew would be coming at
the end of the year.

For this very reason, however, Wilson should not have sold
his shares without first notifying and securing the permission of
the board.

"We had laid down strict rules about this," remembers Peter
Spira. "We announced our results every year in the middle of
December, and it was agreed that directors could only deal on
their own account for a week or two after that. At any other
time they had to go through the company secretary, because
there was such scope for insider advantage. The moment you
knew that a big sale was coming, you knew that the profit from
that would be going straight to the bottom line."

In 1981, however, Peter Wilson did not bother to get permission to sell the shares he needed to finance Sevso. Sotheby's
picked up news of the transaction in a panicky call from the

stock exchange, and Peter Spira got straight on the phone to
David Westmorland. It was a few months before the board
changes made by Gordon Brunton, and Westmorland was still in
charge.

"You're the chairman," said Spira. "He's your first cousin.
You'd better ring him up and tell him he just can't behave like
this."

Westmorland was in Hawaii when Spira reached him. It was
three o'clock in the morning, and the chairman pleaded the inconvenience of time zones. So, not for the first time, it was Spira
who had to confront Peter Wilson.

"I had to do it for personal reasons," explained Wilson apolo-
getically, launching into the story of a Japanese investment he
said he had decided to pursue, and that was what Peter Spira believed until, many years later, the complicated truth emerged
about Peter Wilson and Sevso's silver. Wilson was lying about his
Japanese investment — and about virtually every other aspect of
his Sevso adventure.

The problem with Peter Wilson selling his shares was that so
many other insiders were doing the same. When Sotheby's went
public in 1977, some 53 percent of the stock was in the hands of
directors and friends of the company. Five years later, that proportion had fallen to 14 percent, and coupled with a falling share
price, it made the perfect recipe for takeover. Sotheby's shares
were a bargain, and they were floating freely on the market for
anyone who took the trouble to gather them up.

As Gordon Brunton saw it, the right sort of takeover or
merger might be a shrewd way ahead for the auction house. A
buyout or partnership with a prosperous company would take
care of Sotheby's balance sheet and the share price in the short
term, and it would also protect the auction house against a hostile predator who might decide that the company's weakness
made it a candidate for asset-stripping.

Sotheby's had already been buzzed by one worrying suitor, Steve Ross, the quick-talking chief executive of Warner Communications, who had flown into London one evening at the beginning of 1982 in his private jet, and had dazzled the board with talk of video catalogues, two-way cabling, and bidding by home computer.

"He kept using this word 'synergy,'" remembers Peregrine Pollen, "which I don't think at that time any of us had heard before."

Sotheby's never heard from Ross again. But as the share price continued to fall through the summer and autumn of 1982, there were other investors eyeing the ailing British auction house. With more than 80 percent of the shares floating freely, an investment of £20 million would secure control of Sotheby's.

Twenty million pounds was just about $40 million at 1982 rates of exchange, and this figure had caught the eye of Marshall Cogan and Stephen Swid, two Jewish-American entrepreneurs in their forties who had made their fortunes by snapping up undervalued businesses. Their most profitable coup had been their venture into industrial felt and carpet underlay through General Felt Industries, a private Delaware corporation which they controlled. But the project they liked to talk about was their turnaround of Knoll International, America's leading manufacturer of classic, modern furniture. Originally designed by such masters as Mies Van Der Rohe and Marcel Breuer, the spindly steel and black leather creations which Knoll manufactured had been exhibited at both the Louvre and the Museum of Modern Art in New York.

Cogan and Swid were proud of their taste. Cogan was on the board of the Museum of Modern Art, and was a noted contemporary art collector. But both men were essentially traders, operating from their office perched high over Manhattan on the fifty-seventh floor of the Citicorp Building. Sitting side by side at a large partners' desk, the pair kept an eye on video screens that tracked the movements of stock markets in New York,

London, and around the world, and through the summer and autumn of 1982 they had been keeping a particular eye on Sotheby's, picking up parcels of shares until, unbeknownst to anyone, they controlled nearly 15 percent of the company, the level at which London's stock exchange rules required them to disclose their holding.

Cogan and Swid disclaimed any hostile or asset-stripping ambitions.

"It was our intention," says Cogan today, "to own a position and to be invited to participate in the management. Sotheby's was losing money at the time, and we thought we could bring a love of art and our management capabilities."

But the Americans were not aware that Gordon Brunton already considered himself the sympathetic outsider who had brought management salvation to Sotheby's. Brunton's reforms were in place. He saw no need for further management advice, and the style of Cogan and Swid when they arrived in London in December 1982 with a retinue of limousines bearing merchant bankers, lawyers, and PR advisors, aroused his suspicions. Ostensibly the Americans were on an informal "get-to-know-you" mission to discuss the shareholding they had recently disclosed, but the array of hired guns bore all the hallmarks of a corporate boarding party.

"We could not believe there were so many of them," remembered Graham Llewellyn. "A whole crew of sharpies in a caravan of hired automobiles."

It was just before Christmas, and there are two versions of the encounter between the opposing sides at Brunton's Thomson offices in Stratford Place, the windows lit by the flashing Christmas decorations of Oxford Street. The Americans felt snubbed by the English establishment. They recall a perceptible sneer whenever reference was made to their carpet felt and underlay manufacturing business. Nor were the Sotheby's directors impressed by Cogan and Swid's involvement with Knoll, which, to

English ears, sounded like Parker Knoll, the British manufacturer of banal, high street furniture. Stephen Swid later said he felt patronised in the worst sort of way.

Brunton, for his part, could not understand why a pair of friendly investors should have felt the need to retain a merchant bank, Morgan Grenfell, and, in particular, Roger Seelig, one of Morgan Grenfell's most aggressive and thrusting young partners, who already had a reputation for no-holds-barred business tactics.

"Is this an informal meeting?" Brunton asked Seelig. "Can I confirm that none of us are talking to the press?"

"Yes," replied Seelig after a pause and consultation with his American clients. "This is informal and private. We shall not be issuing statements."

But three hours later, after the meeting had broken up and the two Americans were heading back to New York on the Concorde, Brunton received a phone call from Gordon Newton, editor of the *Financial Times*.

"Can you tell me," he asked, "about your meeting this afternoon with Morgan Grenfell and Mr. Cogan and Mr. Swid, who have bought a share in Sotheby's? I have their statement in front of me."

Newton dispatched a messenger so that Brunton could read the press release — a six-page statement that had clearly been prepared in advance by the Americans, setting out their criticisms of the Sotheby's board. The recent programme of economies, declared Cogan and Swid, "appeared to have been motivated by short term considerations, and little of a constructive nature has been announced to enhance overall growth and development." Even at its existing, low level, said the Americans, the price of the auction house's shares, "could not be justified by Sotheby's current financial performance."

To Brunton, outraged by what he considered a deliberate deception by Seelig, there could only be one interpretation of what Cogan and Swid were saying.

"They were trying to get the world to lose confidence in Sotheby's," he says, "and drive the share price down still lower so they could buy more shares. From that point onwards, it was war."

16

GORDON BRUNTON WAS ON holiday in the south of France when he got the news that General Felt Industries was launching a full-scale bid for Sotheby's. It was the spring of 1983. Nearly four months had elapsed since Marshall Cogan and Stephen Swid had made their Christmas foray into London, and the two Americans had not been idle.

"They hadn't even pretended to listen to us," says Marshall Cogan. "They'd told us to go away, but we saw no reason why we should. So we decided to go for the whole thing."

Cogan and Swid raised a war chest of nearly $100 million from Citicorp and a consortium of other banks, and announced their intention of making a bid for Sotheby's. On April 15, 1983, Morgan Grenfell revealed the details — £5.20 for each share of Sotheby's stock. City analysts pronounced the offer reasonable, and judged that it had a fair chance of success.

Brunton met up with Peter Wilson at Nice Airport, and as the two men flew back to London together, they discussed the forthcoming board meeting, at which Cogan and Swid would be formally presenting their offer.

"You know, Peter," Brunton remembers saying, "these people are totally unacceptable. They might be rich. They might have raised money, but they are not right for Sotheby's, and I've not the slightest doubt that one of the things they will have worked out is that they need to get you on their side. They'll probably say to you, 'Peter, come back into Sotheby's. We need you.'"

Brunton was looking at Wilson as he sketched this scenario.

"I imagined he would look shocked at the idea," remembers Brunton. "I thought he'd say something like, 'God, I'd have nothing to do with that.' But, I'll never forget it, he actually looked eager. 'Do you think so?' he said. 'Do you think so?' He looked really excited at the prospect."

Wilson was not alone in his ambivalence. The tone of the takeover battle for Sotheby's had been set by the quasi-religious fervor with which Brunton, Llewellyn, and a hard-core group of directors had come to mistrust Cogan and Swid. But many at the auction house saw things more dispassionately. Brunton, to them, was another outsider. They tended to agree with the Americans' criticism that the Brunton cuts had been panic measures, and they liked the way in which Cogan and Swid, citing their turnaround of Knoll, promised to take their cue from the experts. Marshall Cogan rented a service flat in Mayfair, a few blocks from Sotheby's, as the working headquarters of his takeover campaign, and he invited experts there for secret meetings.

"I felt I had to find out for myself what these guys were like," says Julian Barran, an Impressionist expert. "You have to make decisions based on information you gather for yourself, rather than on what you're told. So I met with Cogan, and he seemed to make perfectly good sense to me."

Cogan invited Peregrine Pollen to his South Audley Street hideaway. As a major shareholder who, unlike Wilson, had hung on to his stock, Pollen was much in demand.

"I got this phone call from New York when I was in the kitchen in Gloucestershire," he remembers. "It was from Ivan Boesky, saying he wanted to buy my shares."

Pollen liked Cogan, but he could not see Sotheby's maintaining its preeminence if General Felt Industries took over the auction house. Auction houses need prestige and provenance, just like the goods they sell, and there was something ultimately colourless about Cogan. Flying to New York, Pollen hatched a plan with David Nash to set up a breakaway auction room which would specialize in nothing but Impressionist paintings and jewelry. They courted two of the top experts at Christie's, and they offered the running of the money side to a dynamic young banker who had recently joined Sotheby's finance department in New York, Mrs. Diana D. Brooks — known as "Dede" Brooks.

"We wanted to be prepared," remembers Dede Brooks, "in case they wanted to get rid of everyone, lock, stock and barrel. We had no clue what to expect. All we knew was what we read."

Fancies and anxiety gripped the auction house on both sides of the Atlantic as it entered the unsettling limbo of takeover. Employees huddled in corridors and offices, arguing the pros and cons of working under "Toboggan and Skid," as their detractors had taken to calling them.

"It was a lousy time," remembered Graham Llewellyn. Richard Camber, a medieval and decorative arts expert, composed an emotional letter which promised his resignation in the event of the takeover being successful, and he got more than fifty of the London staff to join him in the pledge. Jim Lally organized a similar petition among the experts in New York, but he encountered resistance to what some considered a Joseph McCarthy–like test of orthodoxy.

"It was like a revivalist meeting," remembers Anne Horton, the expert who founded the New York photography department. "The way they talked about Cogan, the 'vulgar felt and underlay merchant,' you could practically picture the man on his knees, pounding in the carpet tacks."

Graham Llewellyn organized resistance in London, and he made no attempt to hide where his sympathies lay. Asked by Geraldine Norman what he would do if Cogan and Swid were successful, he replied, "I would go home and blow my brains out."

"Where would he aim?" was the reaction in New Bond Street when his comment appeared in the *Times* next day. But John Hignett, the head of London's takeover panel, took a less flippant view.

"It is extremely important," declared Hignett, "for people to say precisely what they mean during a takeover. I don't believe Llewellyn meant what he said at all. For that reason, I must censure him immediately."

The confrontation with the raiders, as they had now become, took place in New Bond Street on a Sunday. The alarm system in the galleries had been set for the weekend, so Cogan, Swid, Seelig, and their advisors were asked to come in by an entrance at the rear of the building. This was the route by which the Queen Mother and other important guests were regularly welcomed into New Bond Street for lunches and private viewings, but feelings were now running so high that Cogan and Swid interpreted this as yet another snub.

No one pretended on either side. Brunton reiterated his several objections, chief among them the low price that the Americans were offering for the auction house, but it was left to Julian Thompson, the Chinese art expert who was now managing director of Sotheby's, to deliver the line that Cogan and Swid took away as the keynote of the encounter.

"It will not work," enunciated Thompson with a politeness and precision which made his disdain all the more cutting. "You are simply not our kind of Americans."

It was at this point that Cogan and Swid made the play Brun-

Samuel Baker, the founder of
Sotheby's, and the Exeter
Exchange in the Strand, London,
site of his first book auction in
March 1745.

A world of goods. James Christie, who opened his Pall Mall auction rooms in 1766. *Below:* Books only for Samuel Baker and John Sotheby. Thomas Rowlandson's "Dispersal of an Antique Library at Baker's Old Auction Room," circa 1800.

The first Sotheby, John Sotheby, who inherited Samuel Baker's share of the business in 1778. *Below:* an eighteenth-century French fashion doll, and George Leigh, partner to Samuel Baker and to John Sotheby.

Last of the saleroom Sothebys —
Samuel Leigh Sotheby (died
1861). *Below:* title page from the
sale of the library of Napoleon.

A CATALOGUE

OF THE REMAINING

LIBRARY

The late EMPEROR NAPOLEON,

REMOVED FROM

The Island of St. Helena,

BY ORDER OF HIS MAJESTY'S GOVERNMENT:

ALSO,

HIS WALKING STICK,

Formed of one Piece of Tortoise-shell, with a Marked Head

To which is added,

AN INTERESTING COLLECTION OF BOOKS,

Recently Imported from Paris.

WHICH WILL BE SOLD BY AUCTION

BY MR. SOTHEBY,

At his House,

WELLINGTON STREET, WATERLOO BRIDGE, STRAND,

On WEDNESDAY, the 23d of JULY, 1823,
at Twelve o'Clock.

To be viewed, and Catalogues had at the place of Sale.

Montague Barlow, who transferred Sotheby's to the West End—while also cutting commission on paintings and the other goods that Sotheby's wished to capture from Christie's.

Messrs. SOTHEBY & CO. beg to announce that their charges for offering the following categories of property for sale are in general 7½ %

> *Pictures, Modern Drawings and all other Works of Art, including Armour and Bronzes, Ceramics and Glass, Objects of Vertu, Furniture, Silver, Jewellery, Miniatures, Tapestries, Rugs and other Textiles.*

A commission of 10 % is charged on every lot of the above which does not realize £100.

12½ % is charged for offering the following :—

> *Antiquities, Autograph letters, Books and Manuscripts, Book-plates, Coins and Medals, Engravings, Etchings and Old Drawings, Japanese colour prints, and Japanese Works of Art, Persian and Indian Miniatures.*

All the above charges include cataloguing, advertising and all other expenses of the sale after the property is received, except insurance and illustrations in catalogues should such be desired.

In the case of lots which are not sold, a reduced commission is charged on the amount actually bid at the Sale.

Messrs. SOTHEBY & CO. receive and inspect Property

𝕿𝖍𝖊 𝕭𝖗𝖔𝖜𝖓𝖎𝖓𝖌 𝕮𝖔𝖑𝖑𝖊𝖈𝖙𝖎𝖔𝖓𝖘.

CATALOGUE
OF

OIL PAINTINGS, DRAWINGS & PRINTS;
AUTOGRAPH LETTERS AND
MANUSCRIPTS;
BOOKS;
STATUARY, FURNITURE, TAPESTRIES,
AND WORKS OF ART;

THE PROPERTY OF

R. W. BARRETT BROWNING, ESQ. (DECEASED),
of Asolo, Veneto, and La Torre all' Antella, near Florence, Italy
(SOLD BY ORDER OF THE ADMINISTRATORS OF HIS ESTATE),

INCLUDING MANY RELICS OF HIS PARENTS
ROBERT AND ELIZABETH BARRETT BROWNING.

WHICH WILL BE SOLD BY AUCTION
BY MESSRS.

SOTHEBY, WILKINSON & HODGE
𝕬uctioneers of 𝕷iterary 𝕻roperty & 𝕸orks illustrative of the 𝕱ine 𝕬rts.

AT THEIR HOUSE, No. 13, WELLINGTON STREET, STRAND, W.C.

PICTURES, &c. ...	Thursday, 1st May, 1913.
AUTOGRAPHS, &c....	Friday, 2nd May.
BOOKS	Monday, 5th May, and Two following Days.
WORKS OF ART ...	Thursday, 8th May.

AT ONE O'CLOCK PRECISELY.

May be Viewed : PICTURES, &c. ...	Tuesday and Wednesday, 29th and 30th April.
AUTOGRAPHS, &c.	Tues., Wed. & Thurs., 29th & 30th April, & 1st May.
BOOKS	Friday and Saturday, 2nd and 3rd May.
WORKS OF ART ...	Tuesday and Wednesday, 6th and 7th May.

DRYDEN PRESS: J. DAVY AND SONS, 8-9, FRITH-STREET, SOHO-SQUARE, W.

The title page of Sotheby's first modern celebrity sale. *Opposite:* lot 7, a portrait of Robert Browning, and a page from the sale ledger showing the price paid for the Barrett-Browning love letters, and the buyer, Frank Sabin the book dealer.

writing to Miss Blagden on the 19th of every month, and this
habit continued till her death in 1872. His letters are largely
concerned with his daily doings, his son, his health, his furniture
left in Florence, etc., but there are many interesting references to
things and people of social and literary interest. He mentions,
for example, a call of four hours duration paid him by Swinburne,
a meeting with Thackeray a fortnight before the latter's death,
and going with Dickens to see the illuminations on the Prince
of Wales's marriage.

BROWNING (ROBERT AND ELIZABETH BARRETT) THE LOVE
   LETTERS, a series of Two Hundred and Eighty-four from
   Robert and Two Hundred and Eighty-seven from Elizabeth
   Barrett Browning, *in the original cases where they were always
   kept until sent for publication, her letters being kept by him in a
   marqueterie box, and his by her in a collapsible gold tooled leather case*

* It is impossible to exaggerate the importance of this, probably the
   most famous series of letters in the world. We may, however,
   point out that it is unique in a double sense, for not only are these
   the only love letters which have passed between two great poets,
   but also they are the only letters which passed between Browning
   and his wife, for after their marriage they were never separated
   for a day. We reproduce the first and last letters of the series.

                    [*See Illustrations.*]

BROWNING (R.) and Mrs. BROWNING. Copy by Robert Browning of
   a Letter written by his wife to John Forster [*May* 1860], (printed
   in the Letters of Mrs. Browning, II, 383); Copy, also by Browning, of an allusion to his wife in "The Parisians" as "the greatest
   of English poetesses married to a great English poet"; and Copy
   by him, in pencil, of a Poem to her on her later sonnets; in all
   6 pp., 8vo and 4to

BROWNING (R.) A. L. s. 2¼ pp. 8vo, from *New Cross, Hatcham,* to
   Mr. Kenyon, *n. d.* [1843], *with envelope,* on which Miss Barrett

6 50		Sabin
8 10		Dove
55		Young

Sotheby's lucky mascot, the Egyptian lion goddess Sekhmet, first placed over the door at 3 Wellington Street, then moved to 34–35 New Bond Street in 1917. *Below:* an advertisement for Sotheby's first major sale in the West End.

Peter Cecil Wilson, architect of
Sotheby's modern pre-eminence,
taking an auction at 34–35 New
Bond Street.
Below: Ronald Searle's impression
of Wilson presiding over the saleroom in the 1950s.

Opposite: the picture that Sotheby's took a loss on, to make a spectacular gain: Poussin's *Nativity,* sold in July 1956 for £29,000, and now in the National Gallery, London.
Below: elder statesman and inspirer of the "Flying Squad," Jim Kiddell.
This page: "Will no one offer any more?" The first of Sotheby's modern record breakers — Paul Cézanne's *Boy in a Red Waistcoat,* purchased by Paul Mellon, October 15, 1958, for £220,000, and the title page of the catalogue.

Hiram Parke (left) and Otto Bernet, and (*opposite*) the painting that brought their saleroom down: Rembrandt's *Aristotle Contemplating the Bust of Homer,* sold in November 1961 at the Parke-Bernet Gallery, Madison Avenue, for $2,300,000.

Top: the Sotheby's cigarette. *Middle and bottom:* the Kodak Depository on York Avenue in Manhatttan, and the building as transformed in 1977, now the world-wide headquarters of Sotheby's.

Peter Wilson with his successor, the Earl of Westmorland (to his right), and Peter Spira, foreground. *Below:* Wilson's Riviera retreat, the Château de Clavary, near Grasse, France.

Takeover battlers. Sotheby's champion, Sir Gordon Brunton.
Below: the raiders from New Jersey, Marshall Cogan and Stephen Swid (standing).

"It's like buying the throne." Alfred Taubman outside Sotheby's, London, soon after his acquistion of the auction house in 1983.

No more shabby chic: Judy, the second Mrs. Alfred Taubman. *Below:* Back in the money. John Marion (left) and David Nash celebrate the $9.9 million sale of van Gogh's *Wheat Field with Rising Sun* at the Gould auction, April 1985. Rumor had it that Alfred Taubman bought the picture. In fact, he bought the Toulouse-Lautrec, a portion of which can be seen below.

Sold for $53.9 million — but half
the money was lent by Sotheby's.
Australian tycoon Alan Bond
poses in 1989 with van Gogh's
Irises.
Left: "The right sort of American"
—Michael Ainslie, Chief
Executive Officer, Sotheby's,
1984–93.

SOTHEBY'S
FOUNDED 1744

Contemporary Art

NEW YORK
MONDAY AND TUESDAY, MAY 2 AND 3, 1988

The
Andy Warhol
Collection

Sotheby's blonde bombshells. *Opposite:* Lucy Mitchell-Innes, Director of Contemporary Art, 1981–94, with a sculpture by Allen Jones, and, below, a catalogue from the sale of the Andy Warhol collection in 1988. *Left:* Diana D. "Dede" Brooks, appointed CEO in 1994. *Below:* Dede Brooks celebrates Sotheby's 250th birthday with Henry Wyndham (left), Chairman of Sotheby's UK, and Simon de Pury, Chairman, Sotheby's Europe.

SOTHEBY'S
FOUNDED 1744

ROMAN SILVER
BOWL WITH
WELL-KNOWN MYTH

"Timothy's at art school
but we're terrified he
might drift into
auctioneering"

Top: $29.2 million — Picasso's *Angel Fernandez de Soto,* purchased
at Sotheby's in 1995 by composer Andrew Lloyd Webber.
Left: The *Independent* on Sevso's silver.
Right: The *Times* comments on Sotheby's smuggling scandal.

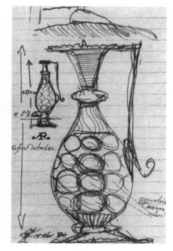

Poisoned chalice. *Top:* the Sevso silver hoard, shown off by senior director Marcus Linell. *Left:* Spencer Douglas David Compton, 7th Marquess of Northampton. *Right:* the first sketch, by expert Richard Falkiner, of the silver ewer spotted by Rainer Zietz in the Mansour Gallery in London in November 1980.

Selling celebrity. Jacqueline Kennedy Onassis, 1996, and the Duke and Duchess of Windsor, 1998—plus a couple of recent grocery products.

ton had anticipated, requesting permission to have a private meeting with Sotheby's two elder statesmen, Peter Wilson and John Marion.

"They had done their homework," remembered Graham Llewellyn, who, by this stage, was bitterly estranged from Wilson, "because Peter was ambivalent."

By British takeover law, suitors for a company could only talk to individual directors with the permission of their board, and Brunton used this convention to insist that Julian Thompson and Jim Lally should join Wilson and Marion as "working directors."

"Those were two people," he says, "whose integrity I totally trusted."

The four men left the boardroom with Cogan and Swid to confer in the little kitchen next door, still scented with the lingering aroma of the last boardroom lunch, and there Cogan and Swid made what they hoped would be their winning pitch — a profit-sharing incentive scheme they had devised to get the experts more motivated and involved in the fortunes of the company.

Lally, Marion, and Thompson listened noncommittally, but Peter Wilson responded with a speech of strange ambivalence. Rising from his kitchen chair, the President for Life responded quite positively to the ideas of the newcomers. He was thinking only of the future of the firm, he said, though they should appreciate that he was now just one voice in a decision that would be made by many.

Nothing Wilson said could be taken as directly contradicting the line that had been laid down by Brunton, Llewellyn, and Thompson, but he was clearly opening a door of his own to the Americans, and as the group walked back into the boardroom, he underlined it by taking Cogan to one side.

"I have not spoken with Brunton," he said quietly, "in more than six months."

The Americans left soon afterwards, and Gordon Brunton moved swiftly to establish Sotheby's formal rejection of General Felt's offer — with no waivers or doubts expressed.

"There weren't allowed to be," remembers Brunton. "Sometimes you don't bother with the niceties. When you feel very strongly about something, you express an opinion, you get one or two other people to express a strong opinion, and that's that."

Within twelve months of being asked to run Sotheby's as the cool and dispassionate outsider, Gordon Brunton was fighting heart and soul for the auction house, his emotions ferociously engaged. He was defending his own reputation as a businessman, but he was also fighting for the less tangible mystique of Sotheby's — the cachet he had once compared to belonging to one of the Guards regiments. It was part snobbery and part old-fashioned patriotism. His long-time boss Lord Thomson had taken great pride as a Canadian in his ownership of the *Times* newspaper. Now Brunton, a different sort of outsider, saw himself as the custodian of another corner of the national heritage.

"In one sense Sotheby's was any other company with a balance sheet," says Peter Spira. "But we were also part of what Britain is about, for better or worse. We saw ourselves, and a lot of people certainly regarded us, as a sort of mixture of the Church Commissioners and Westminster Abbey."

There was profound hypocrisy in this claim to saintliness. Sotheby's had a good name — a name to match Christie's and a sparkling name when compared to the expertise and practices of many non-British auction houses. But a company that manufactured bids and non-existent buyers, turned a blind eye to smuggled goods, and routinely connived in tax evasion had an uncertain claim on virtue. It was the same combination of greed and grandiosity that built the British Empire, and Britain's old boy network understood it perfectly when Gordon Brunton played the final card in his campaign to fight off the Americans.

At the end of April 1983, Sotheby's emergency chairman contacted GJW, a partnership of political lobbyists at Westminster.

GJW stood for Gifford, Jeger, and Weeks, a trio of agile young political operators who had, between them, worked as personal assistants to the leaders of Britain's three principal parties — David Steel (Liberal), James Callaghan (Labour), and Edward Heath (Conservative). Telephoned on a Friday, they presented their proposed strategy to the Sotheby's board on the following Sunday evening, and in the politest possible way, they told Brunton and Llewellyn that they were the wrong people. The defence of Sotheby's required a more low-key, establishment touch — which could only mean Peter Wilson, whom the lobbyists proposed to flank with Julian Thompson, as the voice of youth and expertise, and David Westmorland. What could be more British than the Master of Her Majesty's Horse? Presenting the auction house as an ancient and priceless national asset was part of the lobbyists' strategy, though they realized there were limitations to this.

"How can Sotheby's claim to be part of the national heritage," commented the Conservative MP Anthony Beaumont-Dark, "when they have made so much money selling off bits of it?"

These were the years of Margaret Thatcher, who had little time for companies who got themselves into trouble and came crying to the government for help. The traditional way to frustrate, or at least delay, a takeover bid, was to get the proposed merger referred to the Monopolies Commission. But no one could argue that an American takeover of the ailing Sotheby's would create a monopoly in the London art market. The Americans were only doing what Sotheby's had done when they took over Parke-Bernet.

Brunton's lobbyists, however, could see another route, since, monopolies aside, the Monopolies Commission had a brief to uphold the vague but emotive concept of "the public interest." An American takeover could not help but shift Sotheby's center of gravity to New York. This would, arguably, jeopardize London's preeminence in the art market, and provoke a loss of jobs. Still more significantly, there was a lingering question mark over Marshall Cogan and a brush he had had with the Securities and Exchange Commission in New York.

It was Jesse Wolff who had discovered this. Several years earlier, when Cogan was a broker, he had pleaded "no contest" to a charge that he had mishandled the monies in one of his client's accounts.

"It was a technical violation," says Cogan today. "It was irrelevant."

Pleading no contest meant that Cogan did not admit guilt. But by failing to contest the case, he had also failed to clear his name, and the SEC had not only suspended him from engaging in the brokerage business for nine months, they had also banned him permanently from ever handling discretionary accounts again.

Graham Llewellyn immediately grasped what this might mean for Sotheby's — "A foreign boss with this black mark over his head? What would Christie's make of it? And what were we to tell clients? They'd say, 'This new chap of yours — has he been inside or something?' That's the way it works. And what else does an auction house do but handle the assets of clients in trust?"

Trust and the public interest. It was enough for the lobbyists to work with, and they started with Patrick Cormack, a Conservative MP who was chairman of the all-party Heritage Committee, and who listed his recreation in *Who's Who* as "fighting Philistines." Cormack agreed to buttonhole the small but vocal group of MPs who tended to pronounce on cultural matters, the most vocal being Andrew Faulds, the flamboyant ex-actor who was Labour party spokesman on the arts. Within a few days Faulds and Cormack had tabled a bipartisan Commons motion calling on the Minister of Trade to take "immediate steps to refer the proposed takeover of Sotheby's to the Monopolies and Mergers Commission."

The Minister of Trade was Lord Cockfield, the former Arthur Cockfield, a one-time tax inspector, who had also been managing director of Boots, the chemists. Edward Heath had brought Cockfield into public life to run the Prices Commission in the 1970s, and Margaret Thatcher had been impressed with his precision. "He thought in paragraphs," she once said admiringly, and she had promoted him to be her minister for trade. Cockfield, however, had proved a quixotic minister, tending to take his own line on policy, particularly when it came to referrals to the Monopolies Commission, and he now became the focus of the lobbying efforts.

Sotheby's directors called in every connection. Their contacts on the boards of eminent museums and at the National Trust produced appeals to Cockfield that made impressive reading. But the key figure proved to be the former Prime Minister, Edward Heath, for whom Wilfred Weeks the lobbyist had once worked, and who had been Cockfield's original mentor.

"He was a sort of extension of GJW that week," said Weeks of his old boss, "phoning up several times a day, rallying support in the Lords."

Heath knew Peter Wilson. He had been a guest at Clavary, and was also close to Earl Jellicoe, one of Sotheby's non-executive directors, who had once served in Heath's government. This was the Tory high command that had been ousted by Mrs. Thatcher, and they relished demonstrating their power through the defence of Sotheby's — the more so, perhaps, because it contradicted the principles of the Iron Lady.

The Director of Fair Trading, who answered to Cockfield, had already made his recommendation. There was no reason, he felt, for the Sotheby's takeover to be referred to the Monopolies Commission. But as GJW got the letters and phone calls piling up on the other side of the balance, it was the lobbyists who won the day. On May 4, 1983, Cockfield announced that he had found sufficient grounds for the takeover to be investigated, and a week later Mrs. Thatcher's disclosure that she was planning a general election explained why the Iron Lady had, for once, allowed one of her ministers to give shelter to a lame duck.

"It is inconceivable that Mrs. Thatcher did not take a personal interest in the Sotheby's affair," said one senior Tory. "With election fever building up fast, it would be politically disastrous to allow a national asset like Sotheby's to be sold to foreigners."

Marshall Cogan has a very clear memory of what happened that morning.

"I got a phone call from Morgan Grenfell," he recalls, "telling me the good news that we had received sufficient votes to take control of Sotheby's, and the bad news that the Monopolies Commission had acted, so we were not legally able to take control of the stock."

The referral did not kill Cogan and Swid's takeover stone dead. It deferred it for the three or four months that the Monopolies Commission would take to decide whether their bid was in the "public interest." But the delay would give Sotheby's time to find a bidder that they viewed more favourably, and the auction house was, in fact, already talking to such a "white knight," a midwestern shopping mall magnate by the name of A. Alfred Taubman.

A self-confessed rough diamond from Pontiac, Michigan, Alfred Taubman did not sound like an obvious saviour. But by May 1983, the Sotheby's board was desperate. In their eyes, almost anyone was preferable to Messrs. "Toboggan and Skid."

PART FOUR

A. Alfred Taubman

17

L IKE PETER WILSON, Adolph Alfred Taubman was born into comfort, only to have it stripped away from him early. Life on Ottawa Drive, Pontiac, Michigan, in the late 1920s did not, to be sure, compare with the grandeur of Eshton Hall, Gargrave in Craven, Lancs, but Ottawa Drive was a spaciously verged and respectable street, and the Taubman residence at number 300 was the sort of inviting and slightly fanciful residence which made people move to the suburbs. Standing well back behind a wide green lawn, it was fronted by a curving, whimsical gable reminiscent of the dwarves' cottage in *Snow White* — a dream cabin to come home to at the end of a hard day's work.

Philip Taubman worked hard. A first-generation Jewish immigrant, he ran fruit farms and orchards in the Michigan lake country, north of Pontiac, then branched out as a builder, constructing custom-built houses for the workers and managers of the nearby General Motors plants. But the Depression caught him when he was most extended, and it was back to the orchards and share-cropping for the Taubman family — a Michigan *Grapes of Wrath* whose memory is still painful.

"My father," says Alfred Taubman, "never really recovered."

In the opinion of Al Taubman's friends, the profoundest effect was upon Al himself.

"If you want to understand him," says one of his former business partners, "you have to understand those years when his family lost everything. Even when he had millions, he would worry that he could lose it all, just like his father. That was the insecurity behind the bluster, and that's where his drive came from."

Al Taubman needed all the drive he could get in his years at school, where he stuttered, misspelled words, and had difficulty reading. Nowadays he would be diagnosed as dyslexic. In the 1920s and '30s Al Taubman was just a slow and clumsy student, left-handed, and only good for the art class. He was a large boy, unkindly remembered by one classmate as "porky." Drawing and design were his great consolation. As with many dyslexia sufferers, he found that visual connections could liberate him from the frustrating confusion of numbers and words.

Alfred Taubman concentrated on his strong points. He worked hard at his drawing classes, and he finished quite a popular student at Pontiac High.

"For a fat boy," remembers one of his female classmates, "he was a wonderful dancer. So light on his feet. You would never call Al handsome, but he didn't seem to realize that. He had this enormous confidence in himself. He just sort of swept you along with him."

Friends from these days remember him as "Al," but his birth certificate had saddled him with the encumbrance of "Adolph," a name that history has rendered embarrassing, particularly for Jews. Over the years Taubman experimented with various ways to jettison it, finally settling on "A. Alfred," which somehow raises more questions than it answers.

Taubman was one of the few students in the class of '42 to go on to college — to U of M's art and architecture department, where he paid his own way. He had worked in a shoe shop during high school, and at Ann Arbor he brought the shoes onto campus, displaying them up and down the staircases of the female sorority houses. He had the knack of guessing shoe size on sight — but would always propose one size smaller to his customer.

At cotillion time, he took orders for corsages and boutonnieres, undercutting the prices of the local florists, and driving the forty miles to Detroit in an old Ford to get the orders made up in the flower market there. Back on the campus, he had a network of bicyclists working on commission to deliver the flowers, and when he left Ann Arbor he was able to sell the business.

He left the university without graduating, a fact that his corporate CV failed to mention until 1981, when Taubman was prompted by the digging of a *Detroit News* reporter. Taubman had interrupted his studies to do his military service. He wanted to start earning, and he had also fallen in love with Reva Kolodney, a calm and attractive young woman to whom he had proposed marriage. So he took a job with a construction company, working on site as a muddy boots field engineer while he tried to complete his architectural studies in the evenings at Lawrence Institute of Technology, whose classes were held in the old Henry Ford factory in Highland Park, Detroit.

Alfred never completed his studies. Borrowing $5,000 from the bank, he set up in business in his own right. The quick-talking shoe salesman became the quick-talking retail developer, designing and building the small stores and strip shopping centres that were proliferating in the expanding suburbs of 1950s Detroit.

Taubman's father was his first partner and construction manager, coming out of retirement to help his son by supervising work on site. This made it possible for Al to run the office and go out in search of new business, and he had to search far afield, since major shopping centre development in the Detroit area was tied up by Hudson's, the city's traditional department store. The Taubman Company set up an office in California, the new frontier for developers. New towns were springing up overnight. It was a land made for shops.

Back in Detroit, Reva Taubman did not see much of her husband. She now had three children to look after, and she played a lot of bridge.

But Detroit remained Al Taubman's base. The burly boy from the Pontiac lake country enjoyed cultivating the image of the raw-cut midwesterner — and he maintained his business in Michigan. He built and renovated service stations for Speedway, one of the companies owned by Max Fisher, a legendary local oil and property tycoon whose gentle manner and generous philanthropy had enabled him to pull off the unusual feat of being both extraordinarily wealthy and widely beloved. Seventeen years older than Taubman, Fisher became a friend and mentor to the brash young builder when he recruited him to Franklin Hills, his exclusive Jewish country club.

"You'd better join," Fisher said, "before the other members get to know you," and Taubman was so overawed he dared not ask Fisher what he meant.

Fisher today says it was his commentary on the other members.

"I always knew Al was special," he says. "He had this gift for seeing three-dimensionally. He could pull out a piece of tissue paper and draw on it anything you wanted. So when I told him that I didn't like the looks of these gas stations we had acquired, he came up with the right design."

Taubman designed Fisher a huge, lighted fluorescent facing for his gas stations, making use of a new transformer which had recently made it possible to site standard fluorescent tubing out of doors. It lit the forecourts brightly and cheaply, giving Speedway stations an instant style and uniformity, and could be repaired without calling in an electrician.

"You stood on a ladder," remembers Taubman, "opened up the door, and slapped in new tubes when they burned out."

Attention to the minutest detail marked the shopping malls that Taubman began building in California in the early 1960s. His first contract involved the extending of an existing centre, but soon he was building his own — finding the real estate, arranging the financing, pulling in the anchor stores, and dealing with all the problems of local zoning. When stiletto heels became a craze, he designed small, cushioned floor tiles that were stiletto-friendly, and he also insisted that he personally approve the location of every shop and ice cream vendor. Trees, fountains, and lightwells brought the outdoors indoors, and when people started tossing coins into the fountains, Taubman contacted the local Boy Scouts to collect the money, clean it, and take it away.

Alfred Taubman is sometimes credited with the invention of the modern shopping mall, but he is quick to pass that ambiguous honour to others, among them Hudson's, whose energetic malling of the Detroit suburbs drove him to California in the 1950s. Not that he would be ashamed of such a distinction, for he is inordinately proud of the Taubman Company's clean, bright piazzas, which can claim, in many senses, to serve as the principal social centres of their communities. Everyone comes together in the food court. The Taubman public relations department has a helpful stock of *Arcades,* a treatise by Johann Friedrich Geist, the German architect and teacher who traces the distinguished history of the enclosed shopping arcade back to its origins in the eighteenth century.

It is no coincidence that shopping arcades and the art auction houses got their start in the same century, for both sprang up to accommodate the appetites of the newly affluent middle class. Samuel Baker held his first auction in one of London's earliest

arcades, the Exeter Exchange, which from 1773 onwards boasted
a menagerie of exotic beasts, a billiard room, a shellfish restaurant, and its own under-cover street of shops. Entertainment,
food, and a climate-controlled environment in which to stroll
and meet and spend — all that it lacked was thirty acres of as-
phalted car parking space. Adding the automobile to the traditional, covered retail arcade was what created the modern
shopping mall, and it was in the marrying of the two that Alfred
Taubman did make a unique contribution.

When you enter a Taubman mall you may possibly find yourself on the ground floor or, mysteriously, and just as possibly, you
may find that you have walked in on one of the upper floors, for
wondering how he might coax shoppers upstairs — and thus
charge their retailers prime, ground floor rents — Taubman
worked out that he could use earth-moving equipment to
"birm" or ramp his car parks so that they fed customers into the
building at the desired level. "Flow" was his specialty. The car
parking ramps of a Taubman mall are designed to feed shoppers
into the building in the precisely desired proportions — and to
let them drive away quickly, so they do not arrive home with the
memory of a traffic jam, but still tingling with the joy of shopping.

Technically, a shopping mall does not include the three or
four department stores that are its anchors. The mall is the network of galleries and communal areas that link them, and it was
Taubman's art to mould this potentially chaotic area into a department store of his own, enrolling the correct blend of Gaps
and cookie stores and Victoria's Secrets, not just as tenants but as
partners. Stores in Taubman malls had to pay a percentage of
turnover, in addition to their rent, and if turnover fell, a Taubman "Retail Energy" squad would arrive to analyse the business
and suggest ways to improve. There were larger mall empires in
America, but none squeezed out such a consistently high revenue per square foot.

By the late 1970s, Al Taubman was the prosperous owner of twenty mall developments — one of them, at Woodfield, outside Chicago, the largest in the world. Through Max Fisher he had become a friend of Henry Ford II, and he was numbered among the great and the good of Detroit who, following the riots of 1967, laboured to redeem the inner city. He had a home in Bloomfield Hills, Michigan's most exclusive zip code, and he was building another in Palm Beach, a starkly contemporary creation whose white walls and portholes made guests feel they were entering the boiler room of the Queen Mary. Al Taubman was wealthy by anybody's standards, but it was not until he got involved in pure real estate speculation that he could be numbered in the ranks of the super-rich.

In retrospect, it was a simple case of buying and selling. In 1977 people thought that Al Taubman was crazy to outbid the Mobil Corporation and pay $337.4 million, in partnership with Max Fisher, Henry Ford II, and some East Coast investors, to acquire the Irvine Ranch, 77,000 acres of orange groves and development land in southern California. It took six months of tough negotiation and legal battling to secure the deal, but when he and his partners sold their investment six years later for a profit of $1 billion, Alfred Taubman was suddenly a businessman to be reckoned with.

The Irvine Ranch sale was completed in April 1983, the month in which Sotheby's was searching with increasing desperation for the white knight to save them from Cogan and Swid — and the connection was made by David Metcalfe, a lanky and legendary figure in transatlantic society who was the son of Fruity Metcalfe, the Duke of Windsor's aide and friend. A friend of David Westmorland, with whom he shared the distinction of being a godchild of the ex-king, Metcalfe had long known the Detroit trio of Ford, Fisher, and Taubman, and he had been with them the previous winter as they anticipated the bonanza of the Irvine deal. Taubman had actually asked Metcalfe if he had any venture in which he needed backing, for once the Irvine deal closed, he said, he would have a tidy sum of money to invest.

Back in London, Metcalfe found everyone talking about the American raid on Sotheby's.

"They were desperately looking for someone to rescue them," he remembers, "and so were Warburg's. But nobody managed to do a thing. So I rang Al, and he was interested. So right away I rang David Westmorland, who was staying at Lyford Cay, and said, 'Listen. Al Taubman would like to meet you. So get on a plane immediately and go up and see him in Detroit.' Which was exactly what he did. At the time, the Sotheby's board, including Westmorland, had absolutely no idea who Al Taubman was."

In this, the Sotheby's board were not alone. In 1983, with the Irvine Ranch deal only just making headlines, A. Alfred Taubman was a backwoods character scarcely known outside Detroit. He had recently dabbled with that rich man's plaything, a sports team, buying the Michigan Panthers, one of the franchises in the short-lived USFL, and, having been divorced by Reva in 1973, he had found himself the classic trophy wife, Judy Runick, a stunning blonde who was a former Israeli beauty queen. He served on worthy boards in Detroit, Palm Beach, and New York. But when it was disclosed in May 1983 that A. Alfred Taubman had become a possible suitor for New Bond Street's ailing auction house, the predominant reaction was, "Alfred who?"

Which was one of the reasons Alfred Taubman was attracted to the notion of taking over Sotheby's.

Alfred Taubman had been an art collector since before he could afford to become one. Max Fisher remembers the pride with which the young Al would show him sinuous, abstract creations by cutting-edge artists like Jean Arp, which Taubman was purchasing by instalments, paying off $1,000 a month. By the time he moved to Bloomfield Hills, Taubman's home resembled an overstocked museum, the walls jammed with canvases, and all serious names — Jackson Pollock, Rauschenberg, Jasper Johns, plus some significant Impressionists. Taubman's reputation as a discerning collector of modern and contemporary art won him a place on the board of the Whitney Museum in New York — and he also collected Chinese figures and porcelain.

There was no doubt that Alfred Taubman had the credentials to be the owner of an art auction house like Sotheby's. But precisely the same could be said of Marshall Cogan, with his seat on the board of MoMA and his own fine collection of contemporary art. The Earl of Westmorland got back from Detroit to report enthusiastically to his colleagues on his meeting with Taubman. He felt sure that Sotheby's had found their white knight. But it was difficult to explain why a Jewish-American shopping mall developer would make a better owner of the auction house than a Jewish-American manufacturer of carpet felt.

"Chemistry" was the answer that Graham Llewellyn and Julian Thompson gave early in June 1983, when they held a press conference to announce that A. Alfred Taubman had emerged as a new bidder for Sotheby's shares, and that the board supported his bid.

"In a people business," Llewellyn explained, "chemistry plays an extremely important role. That did not exist in the previous bid. But it does in this one."

The fallacy of this was that the bad chemistry had come almost exclusively from Sotheby's itself and from the intransigent reaction of its directors to Cogan and Swid's initial approach. How would Brunton, Llewellyn, and their colleagues have reacted the previous December if Big Al from Michigan had bought up some Sotheby's shares and flown over in his private jet?

The fundamental difference, of course, was that events had made the Sotheby's directors humble. They were desperate to be saved — and Al Taubman had the money to save them, since the weak spot of Cogan and Swid's bid was that, having criticized the existing management for running up the overdraft, they were proposing to load the company with still more debt. They had to borrow heavily to accomplish their takeover.

Alfred Taubman, by contrast, had ready cash. He was proposing to underpin his own bid with borrowing, but he and his partners could buy Sotheby's several times over with their profit from the Irvine Ranch — and the partners made a difference. Max Fisher carried gravitas, while Henry Ford II had unique cachet. Only recently retired from the running of the motor company, Ford was not, in fact, keen to get involved with the acquisition of Sotheby's, but he knew that Taubman had done him a favour by taking him into the Irvine deal, and that this was the payback.

"I'll be the token Gentile," he said.

Cogan and Swid did not intend to go quietly. Their reaction to the news that Taubman would be bidding against them was to raise their own bid for the auction house, from 520p to 630p a share. If Taubman was going to outgun them, he would have to pay for it. Negotiating face to face with his rivals in New York one Sunday afternoon at the end of June, Taubman offered Cogan and Swid 700p for each of their shares, and the pair walked away from their ten-month Sotheby adventure with a profit of £7 million — though Marshall Cogan today says that their decision to sell to Taubman involved more than just money.

"Stephen and I *chose* Taubman," he says. "There were several other buyers who were interested in our block of stock."

It is doubtful whether any of the speculators who were hoping to make a quick killing on the Sotheby's takeover in the summer of 1983 would have paid Cogan and Swid as much as 700p for each of their shares, but the pair had become convinced that anti-Semitism lay behind their rejection by the Sotheby's board. It was their frequent complaint to the reporters covering their side of the story, and they liked the idea, as Cogan today puts it, that "Al Taubman was Jewish as well."

"They rejected us," he says. "We wanted the British establishment to have Taubman."

All that remained was for the establishment to pronounce on the white knight in the form of a hearing in front of the Monopolies Commission, and with the Sotheby's board supporting Taubman's bid, the result was a formality. In September 1983, Taubman and his partners — Henry Ford II, Max Fisher, and a consortium of smaller investors — offered shareholders £7 a share, the same price Taubman had paid to Cogan and Swid, which meant that the purchase of the auction house would cost their group just over £80 million. Reckoning this was a lot for a company whose assets were worth £20 million at the most, and had lost £4 million in its last year of trading, analysts wondered if Al Taubman knew what he was taking on.

"Is it true," asked one journalist, "that you are buying the business out of petty cash?"

"No cash is petty," replied the new owner of Sotheby's.

18

———

GRAHAM LLEWELLYN KNEW THAT Alfred Taubman had taken control of Sotheby's when he glanced out of his office window one day and saw the considerable bulk of his new American boss teetering precariously on the roof. Taubman was looking down at the jumble of chimneys and roof extensions that reflected the auction house's growth over the years. Flow had been the secret of his success in the mall business, and he made the redesign and reordering of New Bond Street's rabbit warrens one of his first priorities.

It was a metaphor for his objectives for the company as a whole. A few days after he secured the share acceptances which gave him control of Sotheby's, Taubman organized a double pep talk to the staff on both sides of the Atlantic. Starting in London in the morning, then taking the Concorde so that he could address his New York employees the same day, he had the entire staff, from directors to porters, summoned to the main saleroom, where he issued the welcome news that everyone would get a pay rise.

But the principal import of the new chairman's speech was

bracing. Never in his life, he said, had he been treated so snootily as he had been on the occasions he had been a customer at Sotheby's — though he was prepared to admit that Christie's ran a close second when it came to superiority and general unhelpfulness. Those days, he said, were now over. He had made his living in a service business. Sotheby's was a service business, and service would now be the name of the game.

"When he finished," remembered Llewellyn, "everybody applauded heartily, which was not Sotheby's wont. He was very well clapped."

Taubman was equally clapped in New York, where his proposal for enlivening the drab, concrete architecture of the York Avenue warehouse headquarters, unkindly dubbed the People's Palace, was to open up walls to create "skyboxes," American football–style, that would house special clients around the top of the two-storey auction room.

"After all the months of agony," remembered Robert Woolley, "it was such a relief to have someone who was really in charge. Cogan and Swid were not as bad as they were painted. But Alfred had a personal touch — and he had a hell of a lot more money."

Sotheby's felt surprisingly comfortable with its rich new boss. Taubman displayed all the delight of a happy child as he went round the different departments being shown the latest books and paintings and musical instruments. He disconcerted Graham Wells, the London expert, when he paused in the middle of examining a beautiful Ruggieri cello to ask, "So how much do you gross?"— which after translation turned out to be a query about the annual turnover of the music department. It was the sort of thing that tycoons were expected to say.

The tycoon's wife also lived up to expectations. Married once before, Judy Taubman had spent one of her between-marriage years working part-time on Christie's front counter in New York, answering inquiries. As at Sotheby's, the front counter girls were chosen to be as glossy and desirable as the goods they were promoting, and they worked for very little money. The legendary perk was a chance to snap up a rich husband — and Sotheby's staff rather enjoyed the fact that their new chairman's wife had made this cherished legend come true.

"Drop your napkin and see if they're genuine," whispered Peter Spira to Graham Llewellyn, the longtime jewelry expert, when Mrs. Taubman arrived for lunch with the board wearing shoes which appeared to be studded with genuine diamonds and sapphires. Llewellyn did and reported that they were not — though they were very good copies.

Those in the know confided that the former beauty queen used a computer to keep an inventory of the furs and gems and other fabulous gifts that Mr. Taubman showered on her. Every time she made a purchase, the paperwork went off to be entered in the electronic Aladdin's cave — and soon after the takeover, Mrs. Taubman generously revealed the charms that had won her Israeli beauty title by posing in swimsuits in the pages of *Town & Country*. The saucy cover of the usually staid magazine was pinned to bulletin boards in London and New York the morning it came out.

Experts discovered, however, that Judy Taubman had a highly sophisticated taste for Chinese Imperial monochromes, austere porcelain that was made exclusively for the Emperor, in a single colour and of the finest quality — and that she had a refreshing gift for self-mockery.

"It's shabby genteel," explained one expert, discussing the possible changes to the colour scheme of the New Bond Street galleries and explaining the history of Sotheby's green.

"Well, that won't do, will it?" asked the chairman's wife in feigned disapproval. "We're supposed to be nouveau glitzy now."

The general welcome to the Taubmans was shared down in Clavary, where Peter Wilson was prepared to take personal credit for the advent of the new regime. Within days of David Westmorland's initial pilgrimage to Detroit, Wilson had made one of his phone calls to Taubman's office in America, saying that he happened to be due in New York shortly on other business, and wondered if he might, perhaps, just pop in.

"I met him in my apartment," remembers Taubman. "I didn't know him, and he was a pretty amazing character. He was quite tall and had a wonderful voice. He was an incredible salesman."

Wilson invited the Taubmans to stay at Clavary next time they were in the south of France, and they duly arrived, Conway barely managing to get the car back from the airport. The suspension was scraping the road under the weight of leather-bound Vuitton suitcases.

The estate had been turned upside down in preparation for the royal visit, with Conway at his most military, organizing a special room at the top of the house where the Taubmans would sleep. Wilson had raided the château to fill the guest suite with his finest things, and after dinner that evening he led Taubman off to the library for a long business chat.

"Peter always used to say," remembers John Winter, "that it would end up with a rich American, and Al Taubman was exactly his idea of how a rich American should be."

There were those who wondered whether Wilson did not see Taubman's arrival as a way to reestablish his old power in the company. But Taubman had no such role in mind for the charming President Emeritus, and from the viewpoint of Wilson's health, any such prospect was too late. Christine Chauvin noticed how easily her boss was tiring.

"I'll just go and lie down," he would say after lunch, "and have a little rest."

One day early in 1984, Chauvin was in Monte Carlo organizing the sale of the furniture and possessions of the American heiress Florence Gould. Securing the Gould sale for Sotheby's had been the latest of Wilson's coups, and she was expecting him in the Sotheby's office at 6:00 P.M. to go through some details. By 6:05 he had not appeared, and she started getting worried.

"Peter was an unbelievably punctual person," she remembers. "When you were driving him anywhere he kept saying, 'Will we make it on time?' It was very nerve-wracking. So I telephoned where he was staying — it was Somerset Maugham's secretary's house — and the butler said, 'Oh Madame, thank God you've called. Monsieur has collapsed.' So I said, 'Give him some sugar and I'll be straight over.' When they took him to hospital, that was how we found out. They gave him a blood test and you could hear the doctors whispering 'Plaquettes.'"

"Plaquettes" is French for platelets. Peter Wilson had leukemia. He flew back to London to see his doctor, who confirmed the diagnosis and gave him a blood transfusion.

"He looked much better when he came back," remembers Chauvin, "but he didn't talk to me about what his doctor had said. I heard it through Conway. He took me aside one day and told me. 'Frankly,' he said, 'Mr. Wilson doesn't have that long to live.'"

Illness was something that Peter Wilson had never acknowledged. Throughout his time at Sotheby's, he had ploughed straight ahead through headaches and flu. Work was his medicine, and he tried the same remedy with his cancer, losing himself in the arranging of his affairs — and particularly in the accomplishing of his supreme coup, the selling of the great Roman silver hoard of Sevso.

Through a Swiss dealer, and hiding their identity behind their Liechtenstein trust, Wilson and his associates Rainer Zietz and Lord Northampton had sent slides of their silver to the new Getty Museum in Malibu, California, which had responded excitedly. Late in 1983, the main board of the museum voted $11 million to acquire the treasure, subject to satisfactory documentation and verification of the objects, offering the prospect of a handsome profit to Wilson, Zeitz, and Northampton. In dollar terms the investors had paid out nearly $5 million to acquire the hoard, so if they sold at $11 million they would be more than doubling their money.

On March 14, 1984, however, the Getty received a telex from the Lebanese lawyer to whom they had sent Sevso's export licences for verification. The licences, reported the lawyer, had not been registered with the Directorate General of Antiquities in Beirut. The director's signature on the licences had been forged, and, having been shown the bogus documents, the director was furious and had decided "to refer the matter to the public prosecutor's office for investigation."

Wilson had always known that the Sevso paperwork was secured after the event. But he took a casual view of such formalities, which had not existed for most of his auction career. What did it matter whether the hoard was found by an Arab farmer or a Croatian gypsy? Export regulations were like taxes. They existed to be got round. The important thing was that the silver itself existed, and was genuine. It was ancient, unique, and breathtakingly beautiful, and what always mattered most to Peter Wilson was the beauty.

Peter Wilson never found out that the last of his great adventures turning art into money had come to grief, for the Getty kept its doubt about Sevso to itself while it pondered the next step. The museum board wished to buy the silver as badly as the partners in the Abraham Trust wished to sell it, and their hesitation did at least do Peter Wilson the kindness of letting him imagine that he had really pulled off his coup. Early in June 1984, he was taken ill at Clavary.

"He booked a ticket for Paris," remembers Colin Mackay, who had spoken to him that morning on the phone, "and I think he knew that he was not going to return. Conway told me later how he realized it was the end as they were driving down to Nice Airport. Peter was sitting next to him with the tears streaming down his cheeks, and Conway said, 'Would you like me to come to Paris with you, Mr. Wilson? I'll keep you company on the flight.' Peter said, 'No, no, Conway. You go back and look after Clavary for me.' "

That evening, Mackay spoke to Wilson on the phone again in Paris: " 'I've got this bloody awful headache,' he told me. 'I feel ghastly.' "

Wilson was meeting with Jean Chouraqui, a dealer friend, and Marc Blondeau, the head of Sotheby's Paris office, and when he suffered a haemorrhage in the course of the night, they phoned his cancer specialist at the Institut Pasteur.

"It sounds like the end," the doctor told them. "Bring him in. We can take care of him better here."

The two men went into the bedroom to get Wilson ready for the hospital, to find him with the telephone receiver in his hand. He had been listening to every word. But he said nothing, putting down the receiver guiltily, remembered Blondeau — "just like a small kid"— and talking business normally as they waited for the ambulance.

"Be careful with the reserve at that next sale," Wilson said as they escorted him out on the stretcher.

At the hospital the two men took turns to sit beside his bed. Wilson was waning visibly, but then the phone rang, and he seemed magically to regain strength.

"Is that for me?" he asked, turning round and reaching for the receiver. They were the last words he spoke.

Peter Cecil Wilson was buried near Clavary in a brief, private ceremony early in June 1984. A few weeks later his family, friends, and colleagues gathered for his memorial service in London, and sang the old hymns — "He Who Would Valiant Be," "For All the Saints," and the "Nunc Dimittis."

Everyone was there. There was a full-dress representation from Christie's. It was a brilliant midsummer's day, and afterwards the congregation filtered out into the sunlight, to gossip, invite each other to lunch, exchange tips on likely deals, and, as Geraldine Norman put it, generally keep alive the London art market which was so very much Peter Wilson's creation.

19

THE PRINCESS WAS DUE AT ANY moment, and Alfred Taubman still had not arrived. It was an opening at London's Hayward Gallery in the mid-1980s, an exhibition that Sotheby's had sponsored and at which Princess Alexandra, cousin to the Queen, was guest of honour. The princess's husband, the Hon. Sir Angus Ogilvy, was a fairly recent appointment to the Sotheby's board — £6,000 a year, plus expenses, for director and spouse to travel to board meetings in locations like New York and Palm Beach.

Mr. Taubman was evidently unaware of the British protocol whereby *all* guests are expected to be on parade at least a quarter of an hour before royalty arrives, and when he did show up, twenty minutes after the princess, it was also clear that he not been instructed in the distinction between private and public etiquette. Striding across the gallery to join the royal party with a cheery wave, Big Al from Michigan reached out both arms to Her Royal Highness and, without a trace of a nod or a "By your leave," kissed her warmly on both cheeks.

"It's like buying the throne," Alfred Taubman had said when he first announced his bid for Sotheby's, and he made no secret of his red-blooded delight in his acquisition of this slice of English taste and breeding.

"It was a dream come true for Alfred," remembers one of his friends. "Sotheby's rounded off what he started when he married Judy — he was well and truly *launched.*"

Loud and wide with his cigars and his white-whiskered sideburns, Taubman was a tycoon by central casting. He had always enjoyed the rather sexy aura of power that went with his money, and he had the intelligence to see the funny side. Soon after he took over Sotheby's he threw a party in Palm Beach which *everyone* attended. Big Al the mall king had sometimes had difficulty attracting the full social cast list to his gatherings, but for A. Alfred Taubman, the new owner of Sotheby's, attendance was 100 percent.

"Look at this crowd," he said with a grin, a sleek and happy shark suddenly thronged about with pilot fish. "How did *I* get invited?"

Owning the world's largest art auction house opened so many doors. From shooting duck in the Michigan marshes, the new American chairman went to beaten drives on Scotland's finest grouse moors. Having learned his golf in Detroit's Jewish country clubs, he found himself playing on the WASPyest links on Long Island — though usually as a guest. Membership was not open to Jews, even to the owner of Sotheby's.

Tangling with the racist snobberies of America's social register was brave if you could laugh about it, but it was rather pathetic if you actually cared, and the evidence suggested that Mrs. Taubman did.

"I'm really Greek," the former Israeli beauty queen was heard to explain earnestly at dinner parties, apparently upset that she could not crack the charmed circle represented by Palm Beach's snooty and anti-Semitic Everglades Club. The jet-set tittered endlessly — though that did not prevent them accepting trips on the Taubman jet.

Alfred Taubman shared Peter Wilson's familiarity with the rich, and though he came at it from a different angle, he was to prove Wilson's equal in the profitable serving of their needs. Relishing his own money and the new dimensions that it gave to his life, he grasped how the auction business was fueled by people like him. Most newly rich people seek to reinvent themselves, and the auction houses provide the merchandise for the expensive accomplishment of that need.

It is the aura surrounding the merchandise, however, that people are really purchasing — the Sotheby's stamp of approval built from history, tradition, and the authoritative command of style developed by the likes of Peter Wilson — and there was an obvious danger that an American takeover might jeopardise that. So one of Taubman's first moves after he acquired Sotheby Parke Bernet was to drop the American component and make the name of the company simply "Sotheby's." Samuel Sotheby and Son; Sotheby, Wilkinson & Hodge; Sotheby and Co. — never in its history had the company been officially named what people actually called it. Sotheby's was so simple, but in its Englishness, solidity, and slight fustiness, it summed up what the company meant to people, and it took a boy from Pontiac to see it clearly.

Taubman's other innovation was to embellish Sotheby's board with glamorous-sounding outside directors who formalised the combination of social and artistic connections that Peter Wilson had kept in his head. Titles were welcome. Early recruits, joining Sir Angus Ogilvy, included the German millionaire art collector Baron Thyssen, the Infanta of Spain, HRH Pilar de Borbon, the Duchess of Badajoz, and a previously unheard of Earl Smith, who puzzled English aristocracy spotters when his name was first announced. He turned out to be Mr. Earl E. T. Smith, Al Taubman's friend, the mayor of Palm Beach.

They made an impressive array at the front of the catalogue, reducing threshold resistance in the finest Taubman tradition, and lending the company the tone of an exclusive and desirable club. Soon after he took over Sotheby's, Taubman was invited to address the Harvard Business School on his secrets of success, and he compared the merchandising of art to the selling of root beer. It was a question of stimulating appetite, he explained. His business empire included the A&W fast food and root beer franchise, and he pointed out how the seller of both art and root beer faces the same problem. Nobody *needs* a painting on the wall, any more than they need a drink of root beer. They have to be persuaded that they *want* it.

This elemental observation drew derision from the art world at the time, prompting Taubman to become uncharacteristically shame-faced and to issue complicated "clarifications" of what he had said. But his root beer comparison summed up the business of art precisely. It was a Michigan version of what Peter Wilson was always saying. Art may be art, but business is business.

Within three months of taking over Sotheby's, Alfred Taubman was able to announce that the previous year's loss of £4 million had been turned into a healthy profit.

"Alfred's timing was immaculate," remembered Graham Llewellyn. "He came in after six hundred jobs had been shed — and he bought at the very bottom of the cycle. Even before he appeared on the horizon, the consignments were starting to come in."

The new chairman was generous in his praise of the cost-cutting initiated by Gordon Brunton, who had reverted to being a non-executive director, and also of the Sotheby's experts who, at the height of the takeover crisis, had kept on working and had managed to pick up some remarkable sales. From sources that were never revealed, New Bond Street came up with the Gospels of Henry the Lion, a richly illuminated medieval manuscript which was purchased by the West German government for £8.14 million (over $11 million), by far the highest price ever secured for any item sold at auction, while New York secured some of the Impressionist paintings in the famous collection of the Havemeyer family.

One of the Havemeyer trustees later revealed that Christie's and Sotheby's submitted almost identical bids, but that what won them over was the auctioneering ability of John Marion and the care taken by two Impressionist experts, Michel Strauss and David Nash. They had been alarmed to see that a flake of paint was about to fall off one of the canvases, and suggested that the painting should be taken off the wall and laid flat on the dining table, pending the attentions of a restorer — whom Sotheby's were happy to send along, free of charge.

Taubman took an excited part in the promotion of the Havemeyer sale, encouraging his rich friends to bid. But he had never intended to run the company on a day-to-day basis, and in the spring of 1984 he announced the appointment of a new chief executive, Michael L. Ainslie, a businessman who had been working as president of the American National Trust for Historic Preservation. Ainslie was not Taubman's first choice. The magnate had had a headhunter out for months looking for potential CEOs, but the promising candidates had all demanded long-term, guaranteed employment contracts that Taubman was not prepared to give.

A formal and courteous, definitely English-style American, Ainslie was prepared to take the risk. In his business career, he had an impressive record of turning round ailing companies, and he negotiated a contract which gave him no more than one year's job security in return for stock options on a share of Sotheby's that could amount to as much as 4 percent.

This was an extraordinary proportion of equity for someone

who was an employee. Taubman's own stake in his consortium was 60 percent, which meant that for every fifteen dollars Taubman made, Ainslie would make one. But more than a year had elapsed since Taubman had been first approached by the Sotheby's board. He wanted results, and he felt that the way to achieve them was through an experienced CEO who was not an auction house person.

"Al had a clear idea of where he wanted to go," recalls Ainslie, "but he had no desire to do it himself."

June 1984, the month when Michael Ainslie, aged forty-one, first walked into his office in York Avenue to take up his duties as chief executive officer, marked the moment when, after 240 years of trading in London, the headquarters of Sotheby's effectively moved to New York. Ainslie softened the blow by spending at least one week of every month in London, where he kept a permanent office and secretary, and in 1990 he went to live there for a year. But his brief was clear. While maintaining the antique and British prestige of Sotheby's, his job was to turn the auction house into a businesslike American corporation.

As a newcomer to the auction business, Ainslie started from first principles. The practice of "chandelier bidding"— the inventing of bids until the reserve had been reached — was that actually legal? Ainslie commissioned legal opinions in England and America. If Sotheby's contract was with the seller, what were its obligations to the buyer, who was being charged the buyer's premium and who might later discover that his purchase was a forgery which the auction house should have detected? The traditional rule was "buyer beware," but what was the value of a Sotheby's opinion that a particular canvas was, say, a Renoir painted in 1895, if the auction house was not prepared to back that opinion with some sort of guarantee?

The new chief executive was facing the same sort of challenges that had faced Peter Spira. Alfred Taubman had bought up all the publicly held shares of the auction house so he could operate Sotheby's as a privately held firm. But if the enterprise flourished, the company could scarcely avoid going back to the stock exchange, and that made it Ainslie's responsibility to harmonise the age-old tricks of a sometimes dubious trade with the requirements of a modern, publicly accountable corporation.

His ultimate duty, however, was to deliver profits. The American economy was on the mend, gathering momentum for the Reagan boom that was to push art prices to unprecedented levels, and as the cycle swung upwards, the new Taubman team was ready for it. "Retail Energy" came to Sotheby's. The first auction of the Ainslie era was the April 1985 sale of the Impressionist paintings of Florence Gould, the property on which Christine Chauvin and Peter Wilson had been working at the time of Wilson's death. The Gould jewels had gone to Christie's because of the anxiety the lawyers felt at entrusting too much to Sotheby's in its pre-takeover state, and the selling of the Gould paintings gave the new team the chance to test some of its ideas.

As a retailer with design flair, Alfred Taubman knew all about the power of strong visual display. Graphic catalogues were one of his earliest priorities for Sotheby's, and under his aegis they became slick and essentially populist documents that would not have disgraced *The Sharper Image*. Michael Ainslie had used mail shots and list sampling to expand the membership of the National Trust, and the same techniques now brought in tens of thousands of new catalogue subscribers, spreading Sotheby-awareness through America's wealthiest zip codes.

The tasty young ladies of "Client Advisory" were the next step in the process — the conversion of the rich and curious into solid bidders and buyers. "Get in the goods and the bidders will follow," had been the philosophy of the Wilson years. The emphasis had been on snaring the star properties and letting their desirability do the rest. Client Advisory focussed on buyers, analysing art market surveys which showed that 60 percent of serious art collectors were American (followed by the Japanese and the Germans), but that when it came to American millionaires, only one percent had ever bought at auction. For the Gould sale Client Advisory set itself the mission of tracking down the other 99 percent — and of offering all bidders the facilities of Taubman's most controversial innovation, Sotheby's Credit.

"Why should you be able to borrow on a home or stock," asked Taubman in a 1985 interview with the *Wall Street Journal,* "and not on art, which, in most cases, is more liquid than real estate?"

For the Gould sale, Client Advisory helped identify more than three dozen creditworthy buyers who were offered the chance to bid and pay for their purchases by instalments. It had always been an unpublicised facility of auction houses to negotiate staggered payments from buyers whose bidding had got too enthusiastic and had outrun their immediate capacity to pay. It was the logical consequence of the overheated atmosphere that the auction process seeks to create, and Sotheby's Credit formalised the arrangement ahead of time. Glossy brochures explained how Sotheby's new Financial Services Department was prepared to advance up to 40 percent against the auction house's valuation of a painting, piece of jewelry, furniture, or virtually any auctionable property.

Dealers expressed themselves outraged, and Christie's went so far as to deliver a rebuke in their annual report for 1985.

"We will resist the temptation," declared its chairman, Jo Floyd, "to branch out into quasi-related financial services, lest they should provide an undue influence on demand, and create an artificial level for works of art."

But it was not as if Christie's had never negotiated instalments when a buyer had had difficulty meeting his bid, and Christie's clients soon discovered that if they inquired about credit in advance, the auction house was happy to put them directly in touch with an agent who would lend on terms that were competitive with Sotheby's.

Dealers' principles proved even more flexible.

"It's mostly dealers that take our credit," reported Dede Brooks, the young financial executive who helped create Sotheby's Financial Services, at the end of the new department's first year of business. "Our figures show that 75 percent of our loans are to the trade."

The Gould sale was a success. Presiding fluently in the auction box, John Marion sold every painting, and the star lot of the evening, van Gogh's *Landscape with Rising Sun,* was knocked down for the highest price Sotheby's had ever achieved in America. At $9.9 million, it went to the secretive Argentine collector Amalia Lacroze de Fortabat, who refused to let Sotheby's link her name to the sale.

In the absence of a name, art world rumour decided that Alfred Taubman had bought the picture for himself to get his auction house off to a good start, and though Taubman strenuously denied the story, no one believed him. The notion of the new chairman boosting his auction room's prices with his own, private, multi-million-dollar bids was so appealing — and it did no harm at all when it came to Sotheby's chances of picking up future sales.

As the economy turned ever upwards, the mid-1980s at York Avenue turned out to be much like the late 1950s in New Bond Street — hectic years of applause, when overflow crowds cheered gladiatorial contests of spending. Raising your paddle became the symbol of the times. When Tom Wolfe was in search of characters for *Bonfire of the Vanities,* his memorable novel of the age, he went to Sotheby's to study the throngs. Junk bonds, green-mail, leveraged buyouts — New York was generating more paper wealth in the mid-1980s, remarked the art critic Robert Hughes, than any other city at any other time in human history. Credit became a way of life, and as the Reagan boom gathered momentum, the easy money splashed its way uptown to the auction houses, much of it in pursuit of the Impressionist paintings whose brightness appealed to the newest of the nouveau riche. A junk bond trader would hardly feel comfortable with a crucifixion over the mantelpiece.

The skyboxes of the People's Palace witnessed some of the defining moments of the decade. Bidders fought to pay as much as $20,000 for the cookie jars which Andy Warhol had picked up from his local drugstore, while queues lined around the block to inspect the jewels of the Duchess of Windsor which Sotheby's later sold in Geneva for ten or twelve times their estimates. Celebrity was added to the definitions of classiness, and the new glossy, coffee table–style catalogues memorialised each sale. The limousines could find their way to Zero Avenue after all.

20

"NATURE HERE IS SO *extraordinarily* beautiful!" wrote the thirty-six-year-old Vincent van Gogh in 1889. "Everywhere and over all, the vault of the sky is a marvellous blue, and the sun sheds a radiance of pure sulphur."

Vincent van Gogh had been wandering the Provençal countryside, painting nature as it inspired him, and *Irises,* his passionate depiction of an otherwise simple clump of violet flowers, was the masterpiece of this turbulent climax to his brief painting career. Using colours more fiercely than he had ever done before, van Gogh brought the irises to life in a swirling panoply of sharp green stems and purple blooms, handling the paint in bold, slashing brushstrokes which cascaded across the canvas like the waves in a Japanese print.

In the writhing tubers of *Irises* one could sense van Gogh's own personal agony, the legendary mental disturbance which had recently caused him to mutilate his ear. A year later he would commit suicide. The intensity of his painting was almost physical. To set eyes on *Irises* was to gasp, and when the canvas came up for auction at Sotheby's, New York, in November 1987, David Nash had no hesitation in describing it as "the finest painting Sotheby's has sold since I started here twenty-five years ago." The world's greatest auction house was selling one of the world's greatest paintings, and Nash estimated that *Irises* could fetch as much as $39 million.

The reason for this extraordinary estimate — and the reason why the painting came to auction at this particular moment in 1987 — was the explosion that had been occurring in the mid-1980s art boom. *Irises* had hung for many years on the walls of Westbrook College in Maine, on loan from its owner, John Whitney Payson, until the spring of 1987, when one of van Gogh's famous series of sunflower paintings was sold in London by Christie's for the unprecedented sum of £24.75 million ($39.9 million). This was nearly three times the previous record of £8.14 million set at Sotheby's only four years earlier by the Gospels of Henry the Lion.

Sunflowers had been purchased by the Yasuda Fire & Marine Insurance Company of Tokyo, after a fierce bidding battle with Alan Bond, the Australian beer and property tycoon, and the sale pushed art prices into an undreamt-of stratosphere. A few months later quite an ordinary van Gogh, *The Bridge at Trinquetaille,* went at Christie's for £12.6 million ($20.2 million), and John Whitney Payson, a canny art dealer with galleries in New York and Hobe Sound, Florida, decided that the time had come to cash in on the wonderful painting which the people of Maine had been enjoying for so many years. Announcing that a proportion of the proceeds would go to Westbrook, he consigned *Irises* to Sotheby's for sale in November 1987.

The fact that two non-Americans had been the principal bidders for *Sunflowers* a few months earlier marked a significant shift in a market hitherto dominated by the new rich of Wall Street. Foreigners were picking up America's leveraging devices, and they were adding some twists of their own. The Japanese

were particularly inventive. Western art critics saw a charming link between the sudden Japanese appetite for Impressionists
and the historic impact of Japanese prints on painters like van
Gogh, but the truth was more prosaic. Impressionists were good
collateral. Compared with Old Masters, their precise, modern
pedigrees made them acceptable security to banks — and in the
burgeoning "bubble culture" of mid-1980s Japan, they had an
additional dimension. They were the ideal currency for bribery
and fraud. When Michael Ainslie later analysed the top twenty
Japanese buyers at Sotheby's in the years 1984–92, he discovered
they had each spent sums ranging from $22 million to well over
$100 million — and that seventeen of them were either bank-
rupt, in jail, or under serious investigation.

Many Japanese used paintings as straightforward bribes to
politicians and other businessmen, as under-the-table payments
to get round the government ceilings on property prices, and as
old fashioned devices for looting and tax evasion. They were
precisely valued and extremely portable. A tycoon concerned to
sidestep inheritance tax would use company money to build up
a collection of Impressionists, then employ creative bookkeep-
ing — "zaiteku," or "financial engineering," as it was known —
to slip the choicest specimens to his children.

A favourable exchange rate magnified the sums involved, and
easy credit completed the process, for Japanese banks accepted
the prices bid at Sotheby's and Christie's as holy writ. Much
more adventurous than Sotheby's Credit, some Japanese banks
were prepared to lend as much as 80 or 90 percent against the
prices paid in the New York auction houses, and this drew still
more money into the market. When the surplus cash was com-
bined with lack of knowledge on the part of the new purchasers, the result was prices which not only rose sharply, but
madly as well.

"Want Green Lady! Want Green Lady!" exclaimed one
Japanese buyer after a visit to the Museum of Modern Art,
where he had seen de Kooning's famous painting of that name.

David Nash explained to him that there were no further copies of the painting available, but showed him a small de Kooning painting of a pink lady that was coming up in the sale the following week.

"Want Pink Lady!" said the businessman, smiling happily, and next week he bid furiously to drive up the price of the pink lady to $3.7 million, setting a new record for a small de Kooning.

"Sometimes we had to laugh behind our hands," remembers Michael Ainslie, "at the prices paid for really mediocre things."

No possible aspersion, however, could be cast on the quality of *Irises*.

"It was magic," remembers Billy Keating, the rakish male half of the Nevill-Keating dealership based in London. "It was lying on the floor, propped up against the wall, in a small basement room in Sotheby's, York Avenue, when I first saw it. When they flipped on the light, it was as if the painting came to life. Everything was in motion, all those leaves and flowers. It was so much better than the reproductions."

Billy Keating and his partner Angela Nevill represented Alan Bond, the flamboyant Australian who had bid up the price of *Sunflowers* a few months earlier at Christie's. The epitome of a piratical 1980s entrepreneur, Bond had financed the Australian yacht which captured the America's Cup, and as a new adventurer in the field of art, he was building up not one, but two collections with the help of Nevill-Keating — a collection of Australian paintings and a collection of Impressionists.

Having failed to capture *Sunflowers*, Nevill and Keating had also been outbid on *The Bridge at Trinquetaille* a few months later, so they were the obvious candidates for Sotheby's to call the moment that *Irises* reached York Avenue. The painting was about to start on a worldwide promotional tour, and the couple arranged for Bond to view the picture when it came to London.

The canvas — Sotheby's most valuable property ever — was hanging near the boardroom, not far from the portrait of old Samuel Baker, and the dealers had coached Alan Bond on the importance of not showing his feelings when he set eyes on the painting. They knew that the Sotheby's experts would be scanning every facial twitch for clues about the Australian's bidding intentions, and that there was no need at this stage for Bond to tip his hand.

The exuberant winner of the America's Cup did his best to be po-faced, but he confessed afterwards that he nearly died under the strain. He found *Irises* incredible. This was the ultimate painting, Bond told his two dealers, and he must have it at any price.

On the night of November 11, 1987, Keating and Nevill were sitting in one of the darkened skyboxes overlooking the York Avenue auction room, with their patron's authority to bid over $50 million. Keating was bidding by telephone down a line to David Nash on the auction floor, while Nevill was scanning the audience. After $20 million, there were no more bids from the floor, their only competition being another bidder on the telephone.

"Just buy the fucker," muttered Keating down the phone when the bidding passed the record $40 million level — and finally, at $49 million, David Nash did.

It took twenty-four hours to track down Alan Bond next day and tell him he was the owner of the world's most expensive painting, and it was then that the serious negotiations started. Before the sale, Angela Nevill had asked Sotheby's about the possibility of "terms," since Bond had told his dealer that although he had the full sum "organised," he wanted to pay in stages. He would put down a deposit, with the balance to follow.

Dede Brooks responded, on behalf of Sotheby's Credit, with a lending proposal, and this became the basis of Alan Bond's purchase of *Irises*. In the event, Sotheby's lent the Australian 50 percent of the purchase price, against the security of *Irises* and other paintings from his existing collection.

These details became significant when it emerged, two years later, that Bond had paid his record price with the help of Sotheby's money, for the sale of *Irises* had provoked a boom on top of a boom, pushing every price level still higher. So far as dealers were concerned, the success of *Irises* had further increased the auction house share of the art market to their detriment, and they were outraged to discover, as they saw it, that Sotheby's had inflated the price by putting its own money into Alan Bond's pot. Already complaining about the competition from Sotheby's Credit, they reckoned they had caught the auction house red-handed.

Sotheby's defence was that they had only agreed to lend Bond money *after* the event, since the credit deal had not been sealed until Dede Brooks met Alan Bond in London a few days after the sale — in the tradition of an auction house agreeing terms with a buyer whose enthusiasm had exceeded his immediate resources. By this argument, Bond could not be said to have based his bidding on the loan — while Nevill-Keating have always insisted, for their part, that their man was willing to go over $50 million from the start, before he knew that Sotheby's were prepared to offer him terms.

But these were technicalities. Angela Nevill's account makes clear that her client's bidding always depended on his assumption that Sotheby's would accept some sort of payment in stages, while the auction house did formally offer Bond the option, before the auction, of paying on credit. Dede Brooks's original credit offer — sealed after the event — was conveyed to Angela Nevill by David Nash on the eve of the sale. There is no getting round the fact that Sotheby's offered Bond their money prior to the sale, and that when the time came to pay, he accepted their offer. Of every two dollars that he bid, one was provided by Sotheby's. Credit provided by the auction house clearly inflated the market — not to mention the $4.9 million buyer's premium which was Sotheby's cut on the deal.

From being a triumph for Sotheby's, the record-breaking sale of *Irises* turned into a public relations disaster, for, as accomplices in the inflated sale, Sotheby's became tainted, willy-nilly, by the collapse of Alan Bond's empire, which led first to the revelation of the credit arrangement, and then to the ignominious repossession of the painting by Sotheby's. Billy Keating had to go to Perth and bring *Irises* back in its original packing case. Since Bond had defaulted on the loan, people wondered, was the sale really a record?

The paperwork showed that John Whitney Payson, together with Westbrook College, received their $49 million in full, while Sotheby's later retrieved and sold other paintings from Bond in order to settle his full debt, plus interest. One of these paintings was Edouard Manet's *La Promenade,* which went to auction at Sotheby's in November 1989, and raised $14.85 million. After *Irises* had taken yet another trip halfway around the world to Brunei, where the Sultan had expressed interest, it ended up in Malibu, at the Getty Museum, for a price which has never been disclosed, but which completed a process whereby Sotheby's got back every dollar of their outlay, including interest and expenses.

"In any other industry," says David Nash, "this would be the perfectly normal situation of a well-calculated loan which started to go wrong, but where the lender made all the right steps and came out of it whole. We did not lose a penny — in fact, it was a very profitable deal. But in this particular business, because of the novelty of the scheme and all the rest of it, it was wildly contested. So at the end of it all, I recommended to the firm that we abandon lending on bids. Not because it didn't work. It worked beautifully. But because it was getting so much bad publicity."

"When we looked in the records," adds Michael Ainslie, "we saw that Sotheby's Credit had financed only six purchases of more than $1 million, which told me that the financing of purchases was not central to our credit business or to our auction business.

"Alfred and Dede thought we had done nothing to be ashamed of, and I agreed with that. But I also agreed with David. We were taking a beating for nothing. So we announced that Sotheby's Credit would no longer take the object being bid on as collateral, and would not lend on any art within twelve months of purchase — though that would not stop people putting up some other painting that they already owned as security. Sotheby's remained willing to take bids on credit."

Irises today hangs in the new Getty Museum overlooking Los Angeles — green, sharp, and vital as ever. Now "in captivity," most probably, forever, its raw, fierce brushstrokes keep it energizingly wild. The canvas remains a creation of extraordinary passion, its purity unsullied by its misadventures at the height of the late 1980s art boom.

"I went to see it last time I was in California," remembers Angela Nevill. "It was like visiting an old friend. It had been very badly hung, in my opinion, with too much natural light crowding in. But it was still incredibly beautiful. Whatever you do to that painting, you can't kill the magic."

21

IT WAS IN THE SPRING OF 1987 that the Marquess of Northampton approached Alfred Taubman, and asked him if he would care to purchase some old Roman silver. His lordship did not inform Sotheby's new owner that the goblets and salvers in his wonderful hoard had originally been assembled by Peter Wilson and the dealer Rainer Zietz, and he also kept quiet about the complicated Sevso partnership that he had formed five years earlier with Zietz and Wilson, whose interest had been organised in a trust in favor of his son Philip.

The unconventional Marquess had spent the years since Wilson's death trying his hand at being a dealer, unsuccessfully seeking to offload Sevso's treasure on a variety of clients, the last of whom had been Christie's. The King Street auction house had handled some spectacular previous art sales for Northampton — they had sold his family Mantegna, *The Adoration of the Magi,* for a record £8.1 million — but after consideration, they decided, like everyone else, that they would prefer to pass on Sevso. It was Sotheby's who went for the booty — and the risk.

Northampton approached Taubman personally, in the classic tradition of the fading aristocrat seeking to unload an heirloom on a gullible-looking moneybags. But Sotheby's had already had professional contact with the treasure through Peter Mimpriss, Peter Wilson's lawyer at Allen & Overy, the top people's solicitors who represented many of the British aristocracy as well as the royal family. In 1986, Mimpriss had taken Richard Camber, Sotheby's medieval expert, to inspect the silver, without disclosing who the owner was.

"It was breathtaking," remembers Camber, who flew to the Channel Islands to inspect the silver in the vaults of a Guernsey bank. "I told Mimpriss that one of our private clients might be very interested."

Camber was in touch with some of the world's principal antiquities collectors, secretive characters who often preferred private treaty deals to purchases at auction, and who would certainly appreciate the mystery of a hoard like Sevso's. The expert made two more trips to Guernsey with clients who both expressed astonishment at the beauty and extent of the silver, but who both decided, on reflection, that they did not wish to get involved. The provenance was the problem.

Camber knew nothing about Lord Northampton's stake in the silver, but in the spring of 1987 he was summoned to Alfred Taubman's office in New Bond Street, where he discovered that Northampton knew all about him.

"So you're Richard Camber," said his lordship. "You're the one who's been going to see my treasure."

Taubman's attitude was clear-cut. He had no interest in acquiring the hoard personally, but he thought that it might be a project for Sotheby's if the sums made sense.

"Get a proper valuation done," he said to Camber, "and let's see."

Camber was, in fact, in the process of leaving Sotheby's to set up in business on his own, but he accepted a contract as consultant on the Sevso project, and he arranged an expedition to

Guernsey for himself, Julian Thompson, Marcus Linell, and
Simon de Pury.

"We were the valuation team," he recalls. "We spent a day in
Guernsey in the vault, looking at everything, each working out
our own estimate, and then looking at each other's figures. The
sum that we came up with was £40 million."

Sotheby's income from a £40 million sale would be £4 million in buyer's premium, plus the sales commission — a heady
profit in heady times. The Duchess of Windsor's jewels had just
broken records in Geneva. The sale of *Irises* was a few months
away. Four million pounds was a prospect well worth going for,
and Camber was put in charge of the academic analysis of the
silver. On Sotheby's behalf he commissioned research from Dr.
Marlia Mango, an Oxford art historian, who came up with interesting evidence that linked the hoard with the eastern European élite surrounding the succession of self-made strongmen
who dominated the Roman Empire in its battles with the Huns
in the fourth and fifth centuries. One of the most highly decorated plates carried the name "Pelso" above the image of a fish
swimming, Pelso being the Latin name for Lake Balaton in
modern Hungary, where archaeologists have unearthed the
ruins of grandiose Roman palaces and villas.

This interpretation was both illuminating and plausible. But
it did not explain how Sevso's silver might have found its way to
the Bekaa Valley in Lebanon, the ostensible country of origin
which had supplied its export licences, and it soon became apparent that clearing the muddled history of Sevso's title would
be the key to any successful sale.

"That's Peter's silver!" Christine Chauvin exclaimed when
the name of Sevso started cropping up in correspondence.
Chauvin was now working for Michael Ainslie in New York,
having been transferred to America soon after Peter Wilson's
death. Chauvin did not know whether her former boss had been
involved with the silver as an owner or as some sort of advisor,
but she did remember his warning.

"Peter always said there were complications," she told Ainslie, "and that it couldn't be sold at auction."

Ainslie seemed unconcerned. "Marcus Linell is clearing all that," he said.

In one sense, Sotheby's was acting very prudently. Following the £40 million valuation and the beginning of historical research, the auction house had commissioned radiocarbon and metallurgical tests from laboratories in Oxford and at the United Kingdom Atomic Energy Authority at Harwell. These confirmed the age and authenticity of the silver, and had also detected mineral traces which suggested that the hoard had been stored for many years in a limestone cave or cellar.

But that was only part of the story. Richard Camber had got wind of worrying subplots in his own dealings with the silver. Four more pieces had turned up from somewhere and had been acquired by Northampton — and there now appeared to be two sets of Lebanese documentation: the original export licences queried by the Getty Museum, and some new, improved licences secured at a later date.

Something smelled wrong. It was not unusual for the ownership details of a valuable property to be hidden behind a trust, but there were strange imprecisions in the stories being told, and there was also the involvement of Wilson's original advisor partner, Rainer Zietz, who was now presenting himself as Northampton's advisor on the hoard, with no mention of any personal interest.

"Make sure the stuff is all right," hissed Alfred Taubman to Richard Camber after a spectacular night of entertainment at Northampton's Tudor mansion, Compton Wynyates.

Sotheby's solution, after discussions at board level involving Michael Ainslie and Taubman himself, was that Sevso's treasure should be subjected to what Joe Och, the London company secretary and a veteran of property title disputes, described as clearance by "the blaze of publicity." The auction house should invite all possible claimants to the hoard to state their case. A map was drawn up of the Roman Empire at the time of Sevso, and Christine Chauvin typed letters to the twenty-nine modern countries that lay in the area, enclosing photographs. Did they recognize the treasure? Did they have any suspicion that it might have been stolen or smuggled from their jurisdiction?

The letters, which were hand-delivered to the countries' representatives at the United Nations, were carefully modelled on a clearance process drawn up by the Getty Museum in response to criticisms that it had been purchasing antiquities of questionable provenance. It was difficult to see what further precautions Sotheby's could take.

But the auction house still knew nothing of the silver's complicated history — including the fact that the Getty had rejected the hoard five years earlier — and there was a dangerous ambiguity in the "blaze of publicity" strategy, which became clear when Marcus Linell, who was in charge of the title-vetting, proposed a further step in the discovery process.

"It was Marlia Mango," he remembers, "who told us about a major archaeological conference that was scheduled for February 1990, in New York, and it seemed ideal to announce the sale when we had several hundred archaeologists from all over the world in one place. The one thing that was completely clear was that if you were ever going to get any sort of clear title, you had to trumpet it from the rooftops."

This was fine if the title truly was clear. But it would magnify the embarrassment to Sotheby's if complications emerged — and less than a week before the New York announcement, the lawyer Joe Och discovered a ten-page paper that Peter Wilson had written in 1982 for the benefit of Lord Northampton:

In 1980 [Wilson began] farm workers in the Lebanon discovered on their land an underground chamber. This contained silver objects of the highest importance, portrait heads in limestone and possibly in marble, and, according to the labourers' accounts, gold cups, a bust of an emperor inlaid with gold and silver, a bronze bed also inlaid, and some jewellery. Until now only eight objects have come to Europe, and all of these have been purchased by the author of this note and a friend of his, an expert in early works of art. . . .

The paper went on to discuss "Possible purchasers," "The question of export regulations," "What remains to be purchased?" and "Suggested course of action"— which proposed the three-way arrangement between Wilson, Zietz, and Northampton that resulted in the creation of the Abraham Trust. It made clear that Peter Wilson had been involved in Sevso as considerably more than an outside observer.

Confronted with this evidence, Lord Northampton acknowledged that he had originally been invited into the Sevso project as an associate of Wilson and Zietz. But he insisted that he had since bought out both their interests — and at this late stage Sotheby's had little choice but to cross its fingers and go ahead with the sale. Catalogues had been distributed. The silver had been shipped to New York. The opening party was a few days away, and the press releases had gone out. The vast momentum of a £40 million sale was rolling inexorably — and was also making a nonsense of the "blaze of publicity" as a credible way of uncovering the truth.

That strategy had been valid until Sotheby's signed a sale contract with Northampton. To that point, the auction house could take the silver or leave it. But once the contract had been signed and the sale set in motion, Sotheby's was only paying lip service to the idea that it was still welcoming challenges — as it proved by the defensive way it reacted to the challenges that began the moment the sale was announced. Art trade reporters like Geraldine Norman began uncovering embarrassing evidence about the mysterious origins and history of Sevso, and Sotheby's curt "no comments" were anything but welcoming to the truth that was revealed.

Publicity and a round of letter-writing proved to have been no substitute for serious research and thought. The auction house had over-casually tied its name to Northampton's ambiguous package, and as the complex tale became public in the months that followed, the auction house twisted miserably in the wind. Among other details which had eluded Sotheby's in its trumpeted search for the truth, it emerged that, following the rejection of the silver by the Getty Museum, the Abraham Trust syndicate had paid fees totalling £628,000 in order to secure the second set of Lebanese papers, and that Peter Wilson's son Philip had gone out to Beirut to make the payment.

Sotheby's error was compounded by its decision to bring the treasure to New York. The sale was technically being organized by Sotheby's Swiss company, Sotheby's A.G., under Swiss law — in itself an admission that the auction house felt defensive about Sevso and wanted to sell the silver in a country which discouraged challenges to title.

But flying the silver to New York had deposited the treasure in the most lawsuit-happy city on earth, and within hours of the hoard going on show in York Avenue, three countries who had received but who had failed to reply to Michael Ainslie's Roman Empire round-robin decided that they *did* have a claim to the silver after all. Lawyers representing the governments of Lebanon, Yugoslavia, and Hungary all filed claim to Sevso's silver. The treasure was impounded by the New York courts, and instead of several million dollars of sales commission, Sotheby's was embroiled in legal action and scandal. Hungary's lawsuit included the sensational claim that the original finder of the hoard had been murdered by rival dealers.

Great was the indignation in Sotheby's boardroom at the behaviour of Lord Northampton.

"He never gave us the full picture," says one director. "He should have told us right from the start about Wilson's involvement, and the rejection by the Getty."

But this was a feeble excuse from the world's largest auction house. Sotheby's entanglement with the Sevso tar baby stemmed from the gap between the profit motive and experience. Alfred Taubman and Michael Ainslie, the two men who set the pace and who made the key decisions about Sevso, were both total innocents when it came to the wiles and pitfalls of the classical antiquities trade. They made the mistake of assuming that Sotheby's was like any other business, and found themselves floundering when they ventured into the quicksands of cunning and sharp practice that are part of auction house expertise. With their business plans and marketing strategies, they had imagined they could emulate Peter Wilson — but the old twister had the last laugh in the end.

At the time of writing, Sotheby's and Lord Northampton have parted company on less than cordial terms. None of the countries who claimed Sevso's silver were able to prove their case, and the entire hoard, which was returned to Lord Northampton, remains unsold. The silver service today reposes in its bank vault, a vast and unrealized investment, and it is difficult to see who could actually buy the treasures. As of early 1998, Northampton has a court case pending against Peter Mimpriss and the law firm of Allen & Overy, alleging mismanagement of his affairs in relation to the silver, and if his Lordship wins the financial compensation he is demanding, he may decide to off-load his embarrassing treasure for whatever the market may yield.

But Sotheby's are not in line for that fascinating transaction. In disentangling themselves from Lord Northampton, they have recused themselves from the deal. If Sevso's silver ever goes to auction, the tragi-comic involvement of Peter Wilson and his less adroit successors means that Christie's will almost certainly get the sale.

22

RISES AND SEVSO WERE THE follies of an art boom that
was out of control. By the end of the 1980s, remarked Robert
Hughes, it had become routine for auction prices to offend the
ordinary person's sense of decency. In the spring of 1990, Saito
Ryoei, a Tokyo paper magnate, went on a spending spree in
New York in which he surpassed *Irises*'s record on two occa-
sions, paying $82.5 million at Christie's for van Gogh's *Portrait of
Dr. Gachet,* and $78.1 million a few nights later for Renoir's *Au
Moulin de la Galette* at Sotheby's. Saito's career was to end, like
Alan Bond's, in bankruptcy — which meant that all three of the
world's most expensive paintings suffered the ignominy of being
repossessed.

The day of reckoning came in the summer of 1990, when
the world-wide intake of breath provoked by Iraq's invasion of
Kuwait undermined an art market that was already showing
signs of shakiness. The sales that winter were disasters. In London Sotheby's failed to sell more than fifty percent of the Impressionist paintings that it offered. Turnover was halved at both

auction houses, and at Christmas there were firings. Sotheby's dismissed 119 staff, Christie's 140.

This was the sort of collapse that had proved nearly fatal to Sotheby's ten years earlier. From $2.9 billion turnover in 1989 at the height of the boom, the annual turnover dropped to little more than a third of that. But, as reorganized by Michael Ainslie and particularly by Dede Brooks, who had become Ainslie's principal lieutenant, the auction house weathered the storm. Profits fell as low as $4 million in 1992, but Sotheby's never posted a loss.

"Show me a business which can take a seventy percent cut in sales and still make a profit," says Ainslie proudly, "and I'll show you a well-managed business."

The same could not be said, however, for the other investments of Alfred Taubman. In September 1985, two years after he took over Sotheby's, Taubman had pledged half his mall business to the pension funds of General Motors and AT&T, to raise $600 million that he wanted to spend on new ventures. He had media dreams, negotiating an option with members of the Pulitzer family to invest in their newspaper empire. He was eyeing Manhattan real estate in a scheme involving a chic Fifth Avenue office building, and he had ambitions in the department store business. He had recently acquired "Woody's" — Woodward & Lothrop — the Washington, D.C., retailer, and, through another partnership, he held 5 percent of Macy's.

It was too much to handle, even for Alfred Taubman. After bitter family infighting, the Pulitzers rejected his takeover. His New York office building proved a lossmaker for several years, and when it came to the department stores, the mall-meister seemed to lose his touch completely.

"Al tried his normal trick," says one of Taubman's several business colleagues who prefer to go off-the-record at this stage of the story. "He slapped marble and glass everywhere to take the stores upmarket, but the customers never came."

The mid-1980s was a good time to be taking over an auction house, but a bad moment to invest in the traditional department store business, and as Woody's losses swelled in Washington, Taubman compounded the problem by purchasing Wanamaker's, the flagship Philadelphia store. His idea was to create regional economies of scale, but the conglomerate went on losing money, which Taubman had to supply personally. By the late 1980s, he was paying out cash in multi-million-dollar instalments to keep his stores afloat.

It was fortunate that Sotheby's had proved a profitable investment. In 1988 the auction house had gone public, transforming Taubman's original $38.5 million stake into $285 million, including dividends, and as the art market continued to grow, Sotheby's share price grew with it. At the peak of the boom in 1989, Taubman's personal 60 percent holding in the auction house had stood at $536 million.

But when art prices collapsed, the share price fell as well, and this was precisely when Taubman needed money to keep his department stores afloat. Having failed in an attempt to sell his A&W root beer and fast food franchise, he turned to Sotheby's for ready cash. In 1991, a year in which Sotheby's reported a profit of only $13 million, Taubman got the company to pay out $36 million in dividends, of which his share was $21.6 million.

Stock analysts raised their eyebrows at the auction house giving money away at the beginning of what could prove to be a long recession — and next year the annual report disclosed why. Sotheby's proxy statements to shareholders revealed that the chairman had pledged the bulk of his personal stockholding, now worth only $132 million, as security to guarantee loans on other parts of his business empire — and that he was also selling some of his shares.

Max Fisher had not joined his old associate in his department store ventures.

"I looked at the figures Al showed me," he says diplomatically, "and for me they didn't make sense."

Fisher was in no need of money, but in a gesture of solidarity with his friend, he now joined in a public issue of ten million Sotheby's shares. In the spring of 1992, the two men announced they were selling off portions of their individual holdings in Sotheby's, and as chief executive of the auction house, Michael Ainslie repeated the road show he had gone through at the time of the first public offering, flying by Lear jet to twenty-seven cities to talk up the Sotheby's stock to analysts and brokers.

Why were Mr. Taubman and Mr. Fisher selling their shares at such a difficult time? was the question at every stop.

"To diversify their investments" was the answer, and at a price of just over $12 per share, Al Taubman raised himself $105 million. In the summer of 1992 it was estimated that his fifty-three storey Manhattan office tower was worth $75 million less than the mortgage he held on it, and later that year Macy's went into protective bankruptcy.

The heaviest blow came when Woody's and Wanamaker's followed. Taubman's original deal with the GM and AT&T pension funds had been structured to leave him with half his shopping mall empire, but his business misfortunes compelled him to surrender a further share. By 1994, Alfred Taubman's only significant business assets were 26 percent of the shopping mall empire of which he had once been the sole owner, along with his stake in Sotheby's — and all of his Sotheby's shares were still pledged to the banks.

In 1989, at the height of the art boom, *Fortune* magazine had gauged Alfred Taubman's wealth at $2.15 billion, which put him level pegging with William Gates III, the czar of Microsoft. This was almost certainly an over-estimate, but by 1991, the magazine had reduced its Taubman figure to $600 million, and by 1994 it had sunk still lower, to $405 million — a notional loss of over one and a half billion dollars in five years.

Alfred Taubman still had his jet and his homes in Manhattan, Bloomfield Hills, and Palm Beach, but his anxiety that he might one day lose everything as his father had done had not proved totally wide of the mark. From 1988 to 1994 it was the $250 million that Sotheby's paid him which kept him afloat — an income of nearly $40 million a year in dividends and stock offerings. Ten years earlier the mall developer had saved the auction house. Now Sotheby's returned the compliment.

Michael Ainslie had done considerably better for Alfred Taubman than the executives that Taubman chose to run Woody's. As CEO from 1984 onwards, Ainslie had guided Sotheby's to the 1,500 percent return that Taubman made on his money, and, in accordance with the 4 percent stock option deal that Ainslie had negotiated in his employment contract, he had made himself one dollar in every fifteen of that. His gamble paid off handsomely.

Ainslie's $35 million in salary, stock, and dividends compared quite modestly to some of the executive packages on Wall Street in the 1980s and '90s. The payment was spread over ten years. But it was more than anyone had ever earned for working in an auction house, and it provoked some bitter resentments.

"It galled the hell out of everyone," remembered Robert Woolley, who pointedly omitted any mention of Ainslie from his memoir of his years at Sotheby's. "He knew nothing about the auction business. He came in after we had all been through the tough times and made the tough decisions — and he pocketed more than everyone else put together."

Apparently anticipating this reaction, Alfred Taubman called Ainslie for a meeting in the summer of 1987 when the company was preparing to go public — when the details of Ainslie's hitherto secret package would have to be disclosed.

"You've got a problem, Michael," Ainslie recalls him saying. "Your deal is going to blow the lid off this place."

"I think," Ainslie remembers replying, "that you and I have a problem — not just me."

Ainslie was due to collect $10 million on Sotheby's going public, and he proposed that he should use $3 million of this to create a bonus fund for senior managers — and that Taubman should match this $3 million with $3 million of his own. Ainslie remembers Taubman agreeing to the proposal. Taubman denied any such agreement.

"I was furious," remembers Ainslie. "I felt betrayed."

"Al simply didn't share Ainslie's agonising over this," recalls one of Taubman's associates. "That guiltiness gene is not in his body. He knew that going public offered the staff all sorts of chances to get rich, and that no one was mad at *him*."

When Sotheby's went public in 1988, its offer document disclosed a $3 million bonus fund for senior managers by which Ainslie personally distributed payments of $100,000 or more each to Dede Brooks, John Marion, and a score of other senior colleagues. Ainslie had gone ahead with his bonus plan without Taubman, and he made a point of letting his colleagues know how, in his opinion, the fund should have been twice as large. His relationship with Alfred Taubman was never quite the same after that.

"At the start," remembers Ainslie, "Alfred was like a father to me. His good side is a man of incredible sensitivity and generosity — much more than the world realises. But there is a darker side, and that's what I started seeing after we went public. I could only explain it in terms of the money."

Alfred Taubman quite rejects that explanation.

"I think he was very fortunate," he says. "When he came on board there were two pay options he could have taken. He could have gotten more base salary and less future opportunity. He took the risk. He took less base salary and the company made a lot of money, and he was entitled. . . . I don't think anybody makes too much money. I think if they've taken the risk to make the money, God bless them. . . . On the same basis, I make too much money too."

In the summer of 1988 Ainslie and his second wife, Suzanne, rented a house in Southampton not far from where the Taubmans were staying.

"We made Michael rich," Judy Taubman was heard to say at parties, apparently annoyed that an employee should be living in such style — and should also be a member of exclusive fraternities that only admitted WASPs.

Relations between Taubman and Ainslie continued to go downhill.

"Watch out, Michael," one of Al's confidants would warn the Chief Executive. "Al's in his Ainslie-bashing mode this morning."

Ainslie saw no need to go on taking it. Having cashed in the bulk of his share options he had joined the multi-millionaire club, but he was still coming into work every day, like any other wage-slave, to serve as the butt of Taubman's ill-humour. The only self-respecting basis on which he could stay was to run the show himself, so in February 1993 he went to Taubman with a plan. He would organize a management buy-out using some of his own cash, a stock offering, and funds that he had already negotiated in principle with First Boston, the merchant bank. He proposed to pay Taubman $15 for each of his 17.9 million shares — a profit of some $53 million over the current share price — which meant that Taubman would walk away with $268 million.

Taubman asked for the weekend to think about it, though he says today that he made up his mind on the spot. No one was kicking Alfred Taubman out of Sotheby's. He liked the place too much to sell it, and, contrary to what some might think, he did not need to — least of all to Michael Ainslie.

So it was Ainslie who left, announcing his retirement in November 1993 and handing over to his successor the following spring. It was an apparently civilised, phased departure with no public reference to disagreement of any sort. But people guessed at some sort of disharmony, and that was the truth. Alfred Taubman and Michael Ainslie simply could not work together anymore.

23

DEDE BROOKS FIRST CAME TO THE attention of Alfred Taubman when he walked into a meeting where she was the only woman and asked her for a cup of coffee.

"With pleasure," she replied, handing him a sheaf of documents. "And could you photocopy these for me?"

It was 1983, and the thirty-three-year-old Diana D. Brooks was Sotheby's New York treasurer, in charge of the company's finances in America. Recruited from Citibank in 1979, Brooks had scarcely found her feet when she had been swirled up in the financial chaos of Sotheby's in the early eighties, and unlike many of those administering the tough cutbacks, she managed to keep some friendships among the experts. The flamboyant Robert Woolley, a congenital foe of the accounts department, was a particular admirer.

"We'd spent years discussing the feasibility of setting up an outfit to do furniture restoration," he remembered. "Then this new girl appeared and ran her finger down the figures. 'That makes sense,' she said. 'Let's do it.' Dede cut straight to the heart of the matter."

Jerry Patterson remembers her less fondly.

"I came back from lunch one day," he recalls, "and there was this strange woman I'd never seen before sitting at my desk, talking on my telephone at the top of her voice. 'I'm Diana Brooks,' she said. 'And I just borrowed a million dollars for the firm.' She was early for a meeting, and she'd used the firm's line of credit at the bank to extend the overdraft. It was a routine thing, but it was the first thing she said at the meeting — 'I just borrowed a million dollars.'"

Dede Brooks was always an up-front kinda gal. Five foot ten and bustling around Sotheby's with the exuberance of the school lacrosse captain, she would greet her colleagues with a jocular punch to the shoulder and a cry of "Hiya, kiddo!" (moderated to "Hiya, Boss!" in the case of Alfred Taubman). Anthea Gibson, wife of Thomas Gibson, Eton heavyweight boxing star turned London art dealer, went very quiet after she had witnessed the Sotheby's CEO jab her husband heartily in the ribs.

"It's lucky," observed Mrs. Gibson, "that you're such a big fellow, Thomas."

"Green, yellow, purple, orange . . ." a journalist was checking the details of one of the famously striking outfits worn by Brooks to an opening night on York Avenue, when a Sotheby's executive leaned helpfully over his shoulder.

"Why not try," she suggested, "writing down the colours that she's *not* wearing?"

Bold and brash, Diana Dwyer Brooks displayed little doubt as to where she saw herself heading at Sotheby's.

"When she came in," remembers Jerry Patterson, "she was working for Fred Scholtz. Before you knew it, he was gone. Then there was someone else who left. Then Jim Lally walked away. Ten Little Indians — it left Dede as head of the tribe. People either gave up the struggle, or else they got elbowed aside."

"When she made up her mind she was going to do something," remembers Brenda Callaway, who coached Diana Dwyer at school in field hockey, "Diana didn't care who she walked over. I think it's just part of her nature to bulldoze ahead and not think too much about the consequences — and she never liked to pass the ball."

Dede's predecessor as chief executive, Michael Ainslie, saw her aggressiveness as an asset.

"It was why I kept promoting her," he says. "Every time it was a choice between two people, Dede clearly had the edge. She has incredible energy and she has a very real ability, when it comes to money, to manage the costs out of a situation. She is also charismatic, and after my showdown with Alfred, I proposed to him that we should work her in as my successor. But she has a hard time relaxing. It's almost manic. With Dede it's all attack, attack, attack."

When the cultivated and low-key Ainslie stepped down as Sotheby's chief executive officer in the spring of 1994, the auction house secured in Diana Dwyer Brooks a competitive leader who has proved second only to Peter Wilson in her single-minded intensity. The focus of passionate, almost religious loyalty among her acolytes, Dede Brooks could inspire very different feelings among those whom she brushed with the rougher side of her ambition.

"Try cracking these, Dede," said Michael Ainslie one Christmas party, when he presented her with a bag containing a pair of brass balls. "And stop cracking mine."

When reporting to Ainslie, Dede had seldom made much effort to hide her impatience when she thought she knew better. Now she was the boss, and she focussed her ambition on the cut-throat struggle in which the two major auction houses battled for the slim pickings of the 1990s recession. With prices low, sellers would only send goods to auction if they really had to, and the salerooms had to slash their commission charges to get business.

"It was desperation time," remembered Robert Woolley. "What it came down to was how many ways you could find to say 'Zero.'"

Meaning, zero commission. In the struggle for the slim pickings of the slump, both auction houses were prepared actually to forgo their commission charges to the seller, while also adding "loss leader" inducements like guaranteed marketing budgets or world tours of the property on which the vendor might well be invited to travel, as an extra perk, at auction house expense. Profits depended essentially on what the buyer's premium could yield, and Christie's proved remarkably good at this precarious game, clawing back market share from the 60:40 ratio that had applied for much of the eighties.

By 1994, in fact, Christie's was close to a 50:50 split, and was even managing to break some records: the most expensive drawing sold at auction (Michelangelo's *Rest on the Flight into Egypt,* $6.3 million, 1993), the most expensive piece of furniture (the Badminton Cabinet, $15.2 million, 1990), and the most expensive book or manuscript (a Leonardo da Vinci codex, sold in November 1994 to Microsoft's Bill Gates for $30.8 million).

The meaner edge to Christie's business-getting came from their new chief executive, Christopher Davidge, a non-Etonian raised from the ranks in the tradition of Sir Alec Martin — the sergeant-major figure who tussled with Peter Wilson over the Goldschmidt sale and lost. The meticulously dapper Davidge was the first head of Christie's to drop the pretence that he could not give a damn about Sotheby's. Indeed, he made it clear that he wanted his auction house to be number one.

"You can smell it on him," says one of his former colleagues. "Even more than the Old Spice."

Davidge's grandfather had been Christie's chief cashier, his father the company secretary, and his mother personal assistant to one of the partners — all loyal retainers whose careers had been both made and stunted by the "Upstairs, Downstairs" character of the stuffy and hierarchical auction house. Davidge's own rise had been through the unprestigious, catalogue-printing side of the business, organising the production schedules, and he cultivated a tough, bare-knuckle image. He would boast in interviews of his un-Christie's-like youth, working for pocket money on barrows in London's street markets.

Davidge also made no secret of his intention of terrorising his sometimes languid, aristocratic underlings into delivering Christie's the number one spot. He spoke with all the feeling of the clerk who had been told once too often that he would have to wait for his wretched catalogue copy, and he committed the gaffes of a man on the make. Interviewed by the *Financial Times* for its column on the personal spending habits of chief executives, he confided that, when it came to household economies, he could forgo almost any luxury except quilted toilet paper — inspiring his American underlings to nickname him "Mr. Charmin."

Mr. Charmin versus the Queen of the Universe — it was an inversion of the old stereotypes, Christie's under the command of a blow-dried barrow boy, Sotheby's headed by a Connecticut WASP, a graduate of Miss Porter's and Yale. Both Davidge and Brooks, however, were equally outsiders when judged by the old rules of the game, for they were not experts. Each owed his or her rise to command of the calculator, since this was what the auction houses had come to in the nineties, two multi-national corporations slugging it out in a battle in which art, style, and taste were only means to the ultimate goal — the enhancement of shareholder values.

Their battlegrounds were also a sign of changing times — the rarefied offices of Manhattan's blue-ribbon trust lawyers charged with the disposal of their wealthy clients' estates. While Client Advisory buttered up likely buyers, it was the trusts and estates departments of the auction houses that brought in the big properties to sell, wooing the tax experts and attorneys in whose gift lay estates and art collections worth millions.

In the early weeks of January 1995 there were two such prize estates in the hands of Manhattan executors, and it looked as if Christie's had the inside track on both. Christopher Davidge had just had the pleasure of reporting spectacular sales figures for the first half of the 1994–95 auction season. He had been working personally to build up Christie's business in the Far East, where Sotheby's had been the first to establish regional offices but had now been overtaken by their rival. Davidge had also worked hard, Montague Barlow–style, to improve the calibre of Christie's expertise. He had got rid of Christie's dead wood and replaced it with hard-driving young experts, and these changes were paying dividends. With a half-year turnover of $613 million for the final months of 1994, Christie's had nosed ahead of its rival for the first time in forty years. Sotheby's figure for these late-autumn months was only $577 million, and now Mr. Charmin was looking to decisive victory in the forthcoming spring sales.

The star property was the collection of Donald and Jean Stralem, a wealthy Park Avenue couple who had built up a superb array of Impressionist and Modern paintings in the years after World War II. Stralem's masterpiece was Picasso's 1903 portrait of *Angel Fernandez de Soto,* a haunting and sombre canvas from the painter's Blue Period, depicting the twisted features of a friend and fellow roisterer in turn-of-the-century Paris. In the late 1980s, the widowed Mrs. Stralem had plotted with Christie's to take advantage of the art market boom by sending *Angel de Soto* to auction, and an estimate of some $40 million had been discusssed — $1 million more than the estimate on *Irises.*

In the event, Mrs. Stralem had decided not to sell. But it had been agreed that, when the day came, it would be Christie's who handled her collection, and Mrs. Stralem became the object of the five-star, total care campaign which both auction houses lavish on wealthy widows who happen to have classy paintings on their walls.

You can see the auction house experts on any afternoon as they pay their courtesy calls along Park Avenue: smart suits, polished shoes, striped shirts from Jermyn Street, and plump, knotted silk ties — the very pictures of elegance and solicitous attention. Sipping tirelessly on the Lapsang Souchong, they advise on the paintings, on the porcelain, on tasteful presents for the grandchildren, and on the practicalities of transporting the Picassos to winter in Palm Beach. They proffer their services as private confessor, professional advisor, and occasional walker — they are all things to all widows — and, in the case of Christie's and Mrs. Stralem, the auction house kindly agreed, as she grew more infirm, to take her pictures off her hands and to look after them, free of charge, on their own premises. When invited to provide a competitive valuation after Mrs. Stralem's death, Sotheby's picture experts had to make their appointment and show up at Christie's.

As the spring sales got closer, Christie's seemed to have a similar edge on the $30 million worth of paintings and sculpture built up by Mr. and Mrs. Ralph Colin, Sotheby's nemesis since the days of the Parke-Bernet takeover. As founder and moving spirit of the American Art Dealers' Association, Ralph Colin had raised funds and sent them across the Atlantic to help the British dealers in their battle against the buyer's premium. It was his personal preference that his paintings be sold by a dealer, or a consortium of dealers, since he hated both of the London auction houses with a passion — but he had hated Christie's somewhat the less.

Sotheby's seemed clearly disadvantaged when it came to the securing of both the Colin and the Stralem pictures — and early in January 1995 Dede Brooks got a phone call informing her that Christie's had outbid her on a third set of pictures, the only major property where both houses had started equal. Sued by her relatives for some $20 million, Mrs. Pamela Harriman had decided to auction a Picasso, a Renoir, and a Matisse — and Christie's had made her the better offer. It was not inconceivable that Sotheby's would have to go into the forthcoming spring sales without a single property of note, giving their rivals all the market share they needed to become number one for the whole year.

"Dede is immensely cool under pressure," says Diana Phillips, Sotheby's world-wide head of public relations. "She has a steel-trap mind for figures — she doesn't need to write numbers down. And she has a personal warmth and empathy that gives her the ability to read people and to work out what clients really want."

When Peter Wilson pitched for business, he had scribbled figures on the back of an envelope, and he usually negotiated with his clients one-to-one. By the 1990s, the process involved delegations of auction house experts, lawyers, and promotional advisors arriving at executors' offices with mocked-up catalogues and ingenious marketing ideas. In 1994, Christie's had won the battle for the much coveted Rudolf Nureyev sale when they suggested recreating the dancer's fantastic Dakota salon for the auction preview.

But the lawyers who represented the sellers were looking at the bottom line — minimal commission rates, high guarantees, and defined marketing budgets — and as Sotheby's and Christie's put in their offers for the Colin and Stralem collections early in 1995, Christie's were prepared to put more money on the table. Soon after she learned she had been outbid on the three Harriman pictures, Dede Brooks was told she would also lose Colin unless she could improve her offer.

All the corporate negotiating came down to a question of nerve. There was no one to whom Dede Brooks could pass the ball — though her negotiations for all three sets of pictures had been based on daily, and sometimes hourly, discussions with David Nash, the long-serving Impressionist expert who had come to be acknowledged the world leader in his field, and who had an uncannily precise instinct for what any given painting was worth.

"David felt sure," she remembers, "that the Stralem pictures could yield a really good result — especially the Blue Period Picasso. That was what we really wanted. So what should we do about Colin? They were high-quality pictures, and we could easily offer more for them. But I reckoned that if we did get Colin, we would be saying goodbye to Stralem."

Brooks was planning her tactics around another of the new

realities of the auction business — the fiduciary duty of lawyers, particularly under American law, to secure the best possible deal for their clients. In simpler times, a lawyer might blindly have followed the wish of a Mrs. Stralem that her pictures should be sold by the nice young men from Christie's, or, in the case of Ralph Colin, implement his preference that his collection should not go to either auction house, but should be handled by a dealer, or a group of dealers.

But litigious times had made trustees vulnerable to the complaint of any single heir that they had failed to obtain the maximum possible price for the property in their charge. This had inclined lawyers to consign significant estates to auction houses, rather than to dealers, since an auction more obviously delivered an open market price — and when two major properties were likely to be sold in the same season, there was a further wrinkle which inspired Dede Brooks to take a gamble.

Early in February 1995, she decided *not* to increase her bid on the $30 million Colin collection. She would let it go to Christie's, along with the Harriman pictures. Sotheby's would then be left with nothing — and would risk ending the game with nothing. But they would be in a position to argue to the Stralem executors that, whatever the preferences of the late Mrs. Stralem, Christie's now had its hands full, and that Sotheby's was the auction house that could devote most time and energy to the selling of the Stralem treasures and of the Blue Period Picasso.

Brooks had prepared the ground for this argument by emphasising to the executors of both estates that the moment Sotheby's secured one collection, the auction house would renounce its claim to the other. Both collections were so rich and complex, she had explained, that no single auction house could do justice to both of them at the same time.

This had been the first part of a two-pronged ploy, the second part of which was the deliberate surrendering of the Colin collection to Christie's. But Dede Brooks had no idea whether this message had sunk in with the Stralem lawyers — while Christie's, for their part, had made no such offer. Having secured Colin and Harriman, their experts were now using their long-standing connections with the family to stake their claim to the Stralem pictures more fiercely than ever. One dealer has a poignant memory of the emotional calls he received from one of the Stralem heirs, complaining at the pressure being exerted by Christie's. Mr. Charmin wanted the full sweep.

It was not until the middle of February 1995 that Brooks got the final call. As a matter of fiduciary duty, the Stralem executors had decided they had no choice but to put the entire collection, including the Blue Period Picasso, with the auction house that could commit most energy, time, and money to the sale of their client's property — and that was Sotheby's. Dede Brooks had won her poker game.

Three months later, the Stralem pictures went on the block at Sotheby's to raise a total of $65.2 million, which included $29.2 million ($26.5 million hammer price, plus buyer's premium) paid by the composer Andrew Lloyd-Weber for *Angel Fernandez de Soto* — the highest price paid for any painting since 1990, and the tenth highest auction price for any painting ever.

"I haven't felt this good in a long time," said Dede Brooks, making no effort to hide her jubilation.

Before the auction, she revealed, there had been a pool among the executors and some of the auction house staff to bet on how high the Picasso might go.

"I said twenty million, David [Nash] said twenty-five, and the lawyer's secretary said she thought it would go for just over twenty-six. We've offered her a job."

In the May 1995 sales as a whole, Sotheby's outsold Christie's by nearly $14 million, and that won them back the lead for the full auction year. It had been a close run thing, but Sotheby's was still number one.

24

D EDE BROOKS WAS NOT THE ONLY blonde bombshell contributing to the success of Alfred Taubman's reborn Sotheby's. Lucy Mitchell-Innes, a young English art historian who had worked with the sculptor Henry Moore, joined the auction house in 1981 at the age of twenty-six and built up Sotheby's contemporary art department in New York through the eighties so that it matched, and eventually outstripped Christie's. The cavernous warehouse spaces of York Avenue were ideally suited to the stark and often extravagantly sized products of contemporary creativity, and Lucy Mitchell-Innes had a sharp-edged, contemporary style to match. Decorative, super-intelligent, and blessed with the elusive "eye," she was a darling of the New York art scene, a friend of working artists and their patrons. The buyers of contemporary art are purchasing youth, trendiness, excitement — and Lucy Mitchell-Innes had them all.

Until the departure of Michael Ainslie in 1994, Dede Brooks and Lucy Mitchell-Innes were the two rising young stars of

Sotheby's. There was no sense in which the alluring Director of Contemporary Art was heading for the executive authority that clearly awaited Dede Brooks, but there was an inevitable rivalry between the two women. A sparkling auctioneer, a pre-eminent expert in her field, and married to Sotheby's Impressionist supremo David Nash, Mitchell-Innes enjoyed a glamour which Dede, mistress of the cash ledger, could not hope to match, and Dede was not noted for her willingness to share power or glory. People anticipated trouble when Mrs. Brooks took over Ainslie's mantle as CEO, and it was not long in coming.

Mitchell-Innes's understudy was an ambitious young expert, Anthony Grant, whom she had recruited in 1985, but who had come to chafe under the dominance of his sometimes chilly boss. Sensing a shift in the balance of power, and having been offered a job by Arne Glimcher of Pace, one of the leading contemporary dealers, Grant went to Dede Brooks with an ultimatum. He wanted to run his own show, and he said he would leave Sotheby's if he had to go on playing second fiddle to Lucy.

Alfred Taubman had also been complaining about Lucy Mitchell-Innes.

"From the start," remembers a former employee, "Alfred used Sotheby's to get expert advice, and sometimes to off-load his contemporary paintings — and Lucy was always the person who had to tell him, 'This thing is worth $300,000 to $400,000, not the $700,000 you want for it — and the reserve should be $250,000.' So Alfred would bitch and moan about her, and so did his friend Les Wexner [Head of The Limited, the clothes store chain, and a non-executive director of Sotheby's]. Les was even more bull-headed, and he was just becoming a collector. So he was telling Alfred and Dede, 'This woman is rude, and brusque and difficult, and I don't like her.' Added to this, you had Anthony Grant making great friends with Taubman's younger son, Billy. . . ."

Dede Brooks's solution was to promote Grant and to offer to

shift Mitchell-Innes sideways, giving her international responsibility for the often complicated area of private treaty sales, but Mitchell-Innes declined to move. She wanted to stay in charge of the department that she had built up, so it came down to a choice. Dede opted for Grant, and it was Lucy who left the company.

"I'd done the job for thirteen years," says Mitchell-Innes today, declining to comment on what she describes as the "political embroidery" of her departure. "I'd had the best of everything. I'd sold the best paintings in the world — unbelievable paintings. But this was the fate of my life, and now that chapter is closed."

The move actually proved greatly to Lucy Mitchell-Innes's advantage. Within a matter of days, she had been contacted by most of her major Sotheby's clients, and she found herself acting as a private dealer and consultant for many of them. Today she does business with, and for, such giants of contemporary collecting as David Geffen and Si Newhouse. She flourishes as a private dealer — and Sotheby's might have prospered as well, if Anthony Grant had stayed in charge of the contemporary department. But, six months after forcing his way into the job, Grant received an improved offer from Arne Glimcher, and left to join the Pace Wildenstein after all.

"In my entire corporate life," says Michael Ainslie, "I've never seen a personnel matter that was so seriously botched as this one. To lose the best person in the world in her field, and then to promote her number two and not get him to sign a contract tying him down to the job. It was inexcusable."

From having two of the leading experts in the contemporary field, Sotheby's suddenly had none, and there was worse to come — for, after fifteen months of observing his wife's happy and very prosperous activities as a private dealer, David Nash decided he would join her. He had had problems of his own with Dede's elbowing style. So, thirty-five years after he had started work at New Bond Street, and having risen to become the lead-

ing auction house Impressionist expert, David Nash left
Sotheby's as well.

It was in May 1996 that Sotheby's discovered the cost of losing
their three leading paintings experts and earners. It was exactly
a year after the triumph of the *Angel de Soto* sale and Dede
Brooks was in the auction box. Her remedy for the departure of
the charismatic Lucy Mitchell-Innes had been to take the contemporary picture sales herself.

The sight of Dede Brooks, financial executive and novice
auctioneer, attempting to orchestrate one of the most sophisticated and demanding art arenas in the world, summed up for
many the pivotal flaw in her hard-driving stewardship of
Sotheby's. Dede thought she could do everything. When she
started her career at Sotheby's, the auction house was still taking
its tone from the grandeur of Peter Wilson — one of Dede's
first accounting jobs had been to handle Wilson's American
salary and expenses — and now she had made it to CEO she
seemed to envision a similarly grand and imperial role for herself as the Peter Wilson of the nineties.

But Mrs. Brooks had never begun to command Wilson's instinctive style. The finance director who had built her career on
taking good care of the experts had made the mistake of trying
to upstage her stars.

In May 1996, Christie's had held their contemporary art auction the night before Sotheby's, and though they had a relatively
routine selection of lots, they had secured some reasonable
prices. It was generally agreed that Sotheby's had more interesting offerings, notably a de Kooning, *Woman as a Landscape,* being sold by the actor Steve Martin, and an interesting Jasper
Johns, *Gray Painting with Ball.*

But Mrs. Brooks could not bring the room alive. There was
a curious deadness to the atmosphere, and after relatively few

bids the contests on both the de Kooning and the Jasper Johns petered out. Dede had to admit failure and buy both paintings in. On that evening's sale, the buy-in, or failure rate, was a horrifying 45 percent by value.

"The silence in the room was terrifying," remembers one dealer. "Success and failure are very public in the auction room, and Dede died a public death."

Taking auctioneering lessons had been Dede Brooks's own idea soon after she became CEO in 1994. In the course of the following year she had cut her teeth on some of the low-budget "Arcade" sales on the lower floors at York Avenue, and the Jackie sale of April 1996 had been her first significant test. But coaxing bids from hard-boiled dealers and collectors was very different from selling celebrity souvenirs to a saleroom of starstruck novices, and the massive attention attracted by the Kennedy Onassis sale proved to have been counter-productive when it came to art, since Christie's had cleverly seized on the fiduciary duty argument they had lost the previous year, and had turned it against their rivals.

"How can they sell your Renoir properly," Christie's experts had argued to potential sellers in the early months of 1996, "when they're putting all their efforts into Jackie's plastic jewelry?"

Some key Impressionists had been consigned to Christie's rather than Sotheby's in the build-up to the 1996 Spring sales, and, coupled with the failure of Dede's contemporary sale, these made the crucial difference when the figures came to be tallied at the end of the year. Twelve months earlier, Christie's had nearly made it to number one in the battles over Colin and Stralem. Now, with a sales turnover of $1.602 billion, they had outperformed Sotheby's for the first time since 1954.

The margin was narrow. At $1.599 billion, Sotheby's was only a whisker behind their rival, and they had managed to keep down their operating expenses to achieve significantly larger profits. Dede Brooks could argue — and she did — that Sotheby's had actually provided their shareholders with a better deal. Was it cleverer to be number one in sales or to turn in higher profits? Sotheby's had come out the winner in the efficiency stakes.

But it marked an historic moment. For the first time in forty years, Sotheby's could no longer call itself the biggest auction house in the world. The era of supremacy begun by Peter Wilson had come to an end on Dede Brooks's watch — and there was more bad news. On February 6, 1997, the very day that Sotheby's finally released the figures that showed them in second place for the previous year, scandal erupted in Europe. A Sotheby's executive had been caught smuggling.

At the end of March 1996, an attractive young Australian woman entered the offices of Sotheby's in the north Italian city of Milan. She was carrying a picture, *Old Woman with a Cup,* a gloomy eighteenth-century painting which, she told Roeland Kollewijn, Sotheby's Old Masters expert in Milan, she had recently inherited from her Italian grandmother. She said that she was hoping to sell the painting in London.

What Kollewijn did not know as he launched into a conversation that was to end in him agreeing to evade Italian art export regulations and smuggle the painting to London, was that the young woman's story was a fiction. She was carrying a tape-recorder in her handbag, and her brooch contained a tiny, fish-eye camera that was wired to a videotape machine.

"They don't want me to do it, but they want me to do it. . . ." Kollewijn explained, setting out his interpretation of his employers' attitudes towards smuggling. "I'm not telling you this as Sotheby's. . . . I've got strict instructions not to do it."

Three months later, however, *Old Woman with a Cup* was on sale at Sotheby's in London, having evaded Italian customs controls. Kollewijn had not only taken custody of the picture and organised its illegal exportation. He had arranged for it to be photographed, placed in the catalogue, and sold in Sotheby's July 1996 Old Masters sale in New Bond Street.

It was a classic "sting" staged by Peter Watson, a British journalist specialising in exposés of the art business. The story was first screened in Britain in February 1997, on Channel 4's *Despatches* and later on *60 Minutes* in America, and it attracted headlines around the world. It was so satisfying to see a lofty institution like Sotheby's caught redhanded at such an unlofty game.

"If I were a judge, I would bug Sotheby's," Kollewijn had babbled happily into the microphone that was bugging him. "It's happening all the time, and why are we here? . . . We should be bugged immediately. If I were in power, I would arrest the whole lot here."

For Sotheby's man in Milan, the smuggling of Old Master paintings was clearly a matter of everyday routine. The ease and casualness of his law-breaking were quite breathtaking — and there was no suggestion that he was doing this on his own freelance account. Kollewijn arranged the smuggling of *Old Woman with a Cup,* from which he made no personal profit, simply to swell the range of offerings in New Bond Street. He had to meet his targets, and he was flouting Italian law the better to do his job as a company man. As impresario of the sting, the journalist Peter Watson justified the deception of his tactics by arguing that he was demonstrating a "systematic pattern of wrongdoing" inside Sotheby's, and the evidence seemed to bear him out.

Papers uncovered by Watson told of the smuggling of Italian vases and of Indian village gods crudely smashed out of vandalised temples, along with the telling tale of a black Sekhmet figure, a large and heavy version of the fierce lion goddess. Two Sotheby's experts had arranged for a private dealer to smuggle this from Genoa to New York in 1985, but it had turned out on arrival to be a fake. The dealer who arranged the transportation at the request of the experts had asked for his money back, and since he was claiming £63,699 ($90,500), the problem had had to be referred to senior managers, who included Marcus Linell, Julian Thompson, and Dede Brooks, who, in 1985, was Sotheby's executive vice president in charge of New York.

These senior figures investigated the incident thoroughly, but appeared to treat its illegal aspects as a matter of course. The problem was the refunding of the money, not the evading of a foreign government's export regulations. The dealer, who collaborated regularly with Sotheby's on similar projects, was reimbursed the bulk of his expenses, and there was no reprimand to the underlings who both arranged and botched the smuggling. It was on to the next bit of business. The buccaneering spirit of Peter Wilson was clearly still not laid to rest.

The exposure of the whole scandal stemmed from a disgruntled employee, James Hodges, who had worked for ten years as an administrator in New Bond Street's antiquities department under Felicity Nicholson, a protégée of Peter Wilson. Handling the day-to-day details of the department to the instructions of Nicholson, Hodges had had a first-hand view of all the smuggling and shifty paperwork involved in the antiquities trade, and he had practiced some rackets of his own. A few months after the young man left Sotheby's in 1989, various items, including an antique helmet and bowl worth some £50,000, were discovered to be missing.

Questioned by the police, Hodges first denied having the objects, then lost his nerve. Wrapping the bowl and helmet in old copies of the *Racing Post,* he deposited the antiques in a left-luggage locker at Marylebone Station, then placed the locker keys in the offertory plate of the Brompton Oratory near Harrods, with a note asking the priest to pass the keys to West End Central Police Station. This elaborate strategem led the police to the left-luggage locker — and straight back to Hodges.

Questioned for a second time, Hodges produced a note bearing the signature of Felicity Nicholson, apparently giving him permission to take the objects home. But his former boss denied that she had signed such a note, and in the autumn of 1989, the police arrested Hodges on charges of theft and forgery on which he was later convicted and sentenced to nine months in jail.

An unhappy and nervous young man, given to bouts of over-eating, and never popular with his colleagues, James Hodges appeared to have accomplished his own destruction with bizarrely ingenious incompetence. But he had been highly efficient in his tracking and recording of the sharp practices that had swirled around him in the course of his ten-year career at Sotheby's. As an administrator in the department of classical antiquities, he had regularly handled the illegally exported objects that had found their way to New Bond Street, usually by way of Switzerland. Over the years he had stolen and copied the papers that documented the details of this trade, and he had looked further afield to unearth evidence of wrong-doing in other departments.

There was the chain of dealers and fixers who arranged the illegal excavation and smuggling of both Italian and Indian antiquities. Similar processes apparently spirited Old Master paintings, sculptures, and other objects around the export restrictions of a number of countries. Various Sotheby's experts dealt regularly with all these law-breakers, and Hodges purloined documents indicating that executives at the highest level seemed aware of what was going on.

The documents involved no breaking of English or American laws. In the final analysis, they showed Sotheby's operating cynically and successfully in a wicked world, accommodating the requirements of their clients in the Swiss bank manager tradition established by Peter Wilson. But there were embarrassing papers that seemed to show sharp practice — including a 1987 telex from Sotheby's, Zurich, listing the lot numbers of a map collection consigned by "a European Nobleman." Three Swiss employees were organized to "protect" the price of these lots up to the reserve with telephoned versions of the chandelier bid.

Hodges stole more than three thousand documents in his ten years at Sotheby's, and after his arrest, he tried to use the embarrassing material to get Sotheby's to drop the charges. It was only after his blackmail had failed that he contacted Watson, and turned his stolen material over to the journalist. The papers filled three large suitcases, and Hodges became a partner of Watson's, sharing in the royalties of his book, which was published to coincide with the television exposé in February 1997.

Entitled *Sotheby's — Inside Story,* the book provoked headlines, but it did not sell well in England.

"Everybody's been doing it for years," was the reaction of most art world insiders to the revelations, and there was even a sneaking sympathy for Sotheby's, singled out and crucified for sins that many had committed — and which many did not even regard as sins.

To its credit, this was not the stance adopted by the auction house. Dede Brooks flew to London immediately and, while denouncing the entrapment of her staff, announced two major internal investigations of the allegations and of the company's ethical practices. Lawyers were hired and set on the task in London and New York. More than two hundred employees gave evidence to these tribunals, which were supervised on a week-to-week basis by Max Fisher as deputy chairman, and at the end of 1997 the company announced a charge of over $11 million incurred by the legal fees and related expenses of the enquiries, which had to be set against profits.

Over $11 million produced an anticlimax. The enquiry's report of December 1997 dismissed Watson's allegations as referring "mostly to incidents that occurred many years ago," declaring that "the book and the [TV] programs do not reflect a larger present-day problem concerning participation by Sotheby's in the illegal export of works of art." Roeland Kollewijn, it seemed, was a single rotten apple in the barrel — the only employee to be censured and to leave the company.

Sotheby's sources maintained that the full, confidential text of the report had subjected management to a stringent review, but the few sheets released to the outside world were all corporate-speak — pious assertions of good intentions, with much talk of "specific internal guidelines" and the "need for a greater compliance infrastructure." The report lacked specifics, and, like the original exposé, it signally failed to get its teeth into the wider issues.

Those issues were — and are — substantial. Since the dawn of man's interest in things artistic, it has been assumed that the nature of culture itself involved the digging up and circulation of antiquities, along with the unimpeded exchange of works of art in general. Civilisation as we know it is based on such traffic — which has often been unethical. From the Louvre's looted masterpieces to the Elgin Marbles in the British Museum, the great collections of the world contain their share of pillaged treasures, and it is only in the last few decades that countries have sought to prohibit the export of their cultural heritage, in itself a modern concept. It is like the trade in ivory and the wearing of fur coats. Sensibilities have changed dramatically in the era of political correctness, and there was a powerful argument for saying that Sotheby's sin in turning a blind eye to smuggling was less a question of morality, than of being out of date.

Watson's exposé had drawn attention to the way in which vases and other classical artefacts were dug up and smuggled to the worldwide art market in defiance of Italian law. But how reasonable was it for Italy to insist that every single object excavated should stay in the country and join several thousand examples of the same artefact, out of sight and gathering dust in the cellars of the local museum? Further enquiries into the provenance of *Old Woman with a Cup* revealed that the painting had been previously auctioned at Sotheby's in London and had been exported to Italy only months before Watson found it in a Naples art gallery and purchased it for the purposes of his sting. Valued at only a few thousand pounds, the painting fell within a price bracket for which export licenses were routinely granted. So the *Old Woman with a Cup* could actually have been re-exported to London quite legally and did not need to be smuggled.

It was difficult to see how auction houses and dealers could carry on their business if they were expected to act as surrogate customs officials and tax inspectors, cross-questioning clients about the origins of objects they offered for sale. It turned out that the illegally exported Indian artefacts which ended up at Sotheby's had been smuggled to London by an Indian diplomat who was corruptly evading his own country's regulations.

No one, it seemed, was without blame — and Sotheby's was by no means without virtue. Some of the documents which Hodges had stolen, and which Watson quoted to illustrate the apparent perfidy of the auction house, were actually the consequence of Michael Ainslie's researches in the mid-1980s, when he was seeking to set up a code of ethics and had commissioned enquiries into the legality and desirability of practices like "chandelier bidding."

From Sotheby's point of view, this was the nub of the matter. The auction house's entire twentieth-century history, from its modest start beside Waterloo Bridge to its triumphs in New Bond Street, could be seen as an immense, piratical raid upon Christie's — and it was the go-getting, corner-cutting tactics of Peter Wilson that had provided the drive for its greatest success. Was it possible for an auction house to be dynamic in the age of political correctness? Alfred Taubman, Michael Ainslie, and

Dede Brooks had made it their objective to corral the freeboot-
ing Wilson ethic within the confines of a respectable, American
public company. But the Sevso debacle had demonstrated some
of the pitfalls in the process, and now here was the *Old Woman
with a Cup*. How could an auction house *be* an auction house
without some larceny of spirit?

The guiding principle has always been to follow the money —
from Europe to Britain to America, and onwards. New York
supplanted London as the centre of the world's art market in the
course of the 1980s, and the future will see the focus shifting still
further west — until it reaches the East. If present trends continue, the new century will see an increasing proportion of auction house profits coming from countries like Korea, Singapore,
and Malaysia — and from China most of all.

It will be a question of enterprise. Sotheby's was a family
business for less than a century — from 1778 to 1861 — and for
most of those years it slumbered. Its more dynamic periods have
been as a franchise developed by non-family, equity-holding entrepreneurs with a gift for knowing how to spread the brand
name wider without diluting the exclusivity of its appeal. Gucci,
Moet, Hermès, Chanel, and Polo by Ralph Lauren — they all
play the same game. Possessors of perceived poshness, they
promise particularity to those who purchase — and one element
of Sotheby's future will surely lie in the wider franchising of
its name. You can already buy Sotheby's champagne in London
and eat in the elegant, auction house equivalent of the food
court, the Sotheby's café. Peter Wilson stumbled with the Sotheby's cigarette, but there is chocolate, life insurance, art investment, cultural tours, an exclusive clothes range, or even a select
marque of limousine. The possibilities are endless.

The other future for franchising lies within the categories of
goods which Sotheby's promotes and sells at auction. With so
much art, as Peter Wilson predicted, passing into "captivity,"

both auction houses have had to exercise their ingenuity to create new markets, from the selling of old fountain pens to promoting baseball cards and Mick Jagger's sunglasses as "collectibles." In August, 1993 Sotheby's held a sale of used Russian space suits and related paraphernalia, and actually secured a bid of $68,000 on the title deeds to the derelict and abandoned moon rover, Lunar Hod 2, an ungainly bathtub of a vehicle which is still sitting on the moon's surface, and can never be brought back to Earth.

"I started the bidding at $5,000," recalls David Redden, who had the idea for the sale, "and there were twenty hands in the air. It was a conceptual thing, because true collecting is not about the actual possession of objects. With the greatest collectors — who may physically keep their things in bank vaults — the collection exists in their heads."

Here was the ultimate — and some might say the most twisted — refinement of class, paying $68,000 to become the first human being to own something on another heavenly body, though that something could not be physically possessed, touched, or even seen by a high-powered telescope. Sotheby's selling of Lunar Hod 2 was a small pinnacle in the history of auctioneering, but it also had a flavour of desperation about it. What could the auction house, driven by its shareholders to expand every year, find to sell next?

In the same year as its momentous Russian space sale, Sotheby's reached an agreement with the Walt Disney corporation to auction "cels" (or "celluloids') from new Disney movies like *The Little Mermaid*. Once upon a time, cels were the artwork which actually flipped in front of the camera to create the moving image at thirty-two frames per second, and a celluloid from *Snow White* or *Fantasia* was a working component in the movie process.

But modern cartoon films are computer generated, and virtually nothing is drawn on celluloid. So the modern "cels" being auctioned by Sotheby's are handpainted after the event by Disney artists in order to create "limited editions" in the style of the Franklin Mint.

Dede Brooks shrugs her shoulders at criticism of $20,000 bids being solicited for "cels" that were never used in the film.

"It is what it is," she says. "It's a market and we service it."

She is similarly unconcerned with complaints that more than half the property offered at the jewelry sales of Sotheby's (and Christie's) is not antique, or even second-hand, but brand new, modern brooches, necklaces and earrings. This means that Sotheby's (and Christie's) are soliciting people to bid against each other on items which could be duplicated without too much difficulty for a price that is no more than the low estimate.

"I've never understood what that criticism is all about," she says. "We clearly say 'contemporary jewelry.' Contemporary means that it must just have been made. People walk into Tiffany's every day and buy the same pair of earring that hundreds of people buy."

Dealers retort, of course, that Tiffany's is a shop, not an auction house, and that Mrs. Brooks's comparison shows exactly how the auction houses have lost all sense of limits. As dealers view the rise of Sotheby's in this century, it has been a shameless poaching on their once glorious preserve — the switch from wholesale to retail, the provision of credit, the introduction and increase of the buyer's premium, and the expansion of private treaty sales. The 1990s have seen both auction houses actually taking over dealerships and operating them as divisions inside their ever-diversifying corporate networks. Compared to Sotheby's or Christie's today, the traditional, independent dealer is like the high street grocer trying to square up to the supermarkets, and the auction houses' new private dealer divisions add insult to injury. They are the equivalent of the picturesque fresh meat and fish displays behind which the supermarkets station their staff in striped aprons and straw hats — smiling facsimiles of the high street traders they have overwhelmed.

The dealers' fundamental difficulty in a volatile, international market where the big sums are often spent by ignorant newcomers is that the auction houses offer more fun. A dealer has to set a price, and then invite the client into the serious and essentially dispiriting process of haggling the price down. An art gallery is ultimately just a shop, but the auction house is a theme park where no one tells you which ride you have to take. The viewing galleries of an auction house are deliberately set out with a free-access feel, intended to avoid the uncomfortable sensation that a salesman is about to descend.

The same goes for the auction itself, where no one forces you to raise your paddle. If you choose to bid and win, you have earned your stripes in what is now the world-famous arena of Sotheby's, and no matter how extravagant your purchase, you can tell yourself that you have only overpaid by one bid. The underbidder battled with you and was prepared to pay almost as much — and if you turn out to be that underbidder, you can congratulate yourself on your prudence, and enjoy the pleasure of planning for the next sale.

Old hands complain that auctions have lost their magic now that most serious bidding is done via the telephone. Phone battles make sales as sterile as dating on the Internet. But then a vendor consigns a lyrical Picasso or some weathered item of ancient furniture, and the excitement rekindles. The object works its wondrous alchemy, the money hisses through the air, and even if the bids do come by telephone, the room is briefly caught up in the fantasy of owning some unique product of the human hand and spirit, literally anyone's to capture, before it is going, going, gone.

It was recently calculated that some $10 trillion in goods and chattels will go through the process of transfer as the baby boom generation proceeds to the great beyond, and that should yield more than enough goods on which both Sotheby's and Christie's can place their distinctive stamp. At the height of the art boom of the late 1980s, Anne Horton, who had helped build up Sotheby's department of Latin American painting, often flew to visit the clients who had been induced to spend hundreds of thousands of dollars on works by Latin artists like Diego Rivera and Frieda Kahlo. From Bogotá to Mexico City she found the canvases hanging proudly — many with their round, fluorescent Sotheby's peel-off lot number still affixed prominently to the frame, apparently an oversight, but actually a carefully calculated act of display.

The sticker told their friends — and reassured the buyers themselves — that the folly had been worthwhile. It was the sign of inside knowledge and spending power, the entry certificate to an envied and universally defined world of cleverness. "Purchased at Sotheby's." The name on the label mattered as much as the signature on the canvas — perhaps even more. It was the hallmark of class. Samuel Baker might not have approved, but Peter Wilson would surely have contemplated those fluorescent stickers with a smile.

EPILOGUE: ROYAL EFFECTS

WEDNESDAY, FEBRUARY 18, 1998, found Woody Allen prowling the galleries of Sotheby's, Manhattan. Dressed in baggy corduroys and scuffed white tennis sneakers, the owl-like director was peering around a succession of gauze hangings that had been suspended like stage flats from the lofty ceiling. The hangings were artfully spotlit from both sides to serve as dividers to a maze of room settings which had transformed the auction house into something resembling a film set. But Mr. Allen was not visiting Sotheby's in his professional capacity. Hand-in-hand with his new young bride, Soon-Yi Previn, the great New York filmmaker was shopping for sherry glasses.

The happy couple had located an attractive set — palish green, on fine stems, each flamboyantly engraved with the letter "W" surmounted by a coronet — and Mr. Allen scurried over to study the price estimate printed in the catalogue dangling on the wall nearby: six hundred dollars low estimate, eight hundred high. Along with bidders from all fifty American states, and from forty-nine other countries around the world, the newlyweds were checking out the goods of the Duke and Duchess of Windsor.

It was the evening before the opening of Sotheby's largest ever American sale, and two floors of the company's Manhattan headquarters had been turned into a mausoleum to the memory of the couple whose love changed the course of British royal history. The Duchess died in 1986, and Sotheby's auctioned her jewels a year later in Geneva in the mother of all celebrity sales. The couple's more mundane chattels took longer to reach the block, thanks to the intervention of Britain's most famous Egyptian, Mohamed al-Fayed, the controversial owner of Harrods, who purchased the possessions from the Duchess's executors with a view to creating a permanent memorial in the Windsors' villa outside Paris, then tired of the exercise.

The goods were originally catalogued and scheduled to go to auction in September 1997, but the August 31 death of Fayed's son Dodi in the company of Diana, Princess of Wales, caused the sale to be postponed. Now, five months later, Sotheby's were trying again, with the net proceeds of the sale destined for a newly formed fund, the Dodi Fayed International Charitable Foundation, "dedicated to causes supported by Princess Diana and Dodi Fayed in their lifetimes."

"Who would dream of buying this stuff?" asked one scornful viewer, casting a disdainful eye over the serried ranks of engraved and embroidered "W"s. "It's only good for dentists called Wasserman."

But "W" also stands for Woody, Whoopi (who would be turning up to place a few bids), and Walters (Barbara, who later confessed to making a purchase). Buy one of these lots, and no one could have any doubt where it came from. Denied royal identity by an angry and fearful House of Windsor, the former Wallis Warfield Simpson compensated by tattooing her personal possessions with a riot of monograms that defiantly asserted her own identity and that of her exiled husband: ww, we, hrh (this painted on a toothbrush mug), ER (Edward Rex), EP (Edward Principus) — and Prince of Wales's plumes in all directions.

The Duke and Duchess were an auctioneer's dream. Filling their Bois de Boulogne villa with a profusion of banners and badges, they devoted their energy to turning their suburban home into a palace — and that was precisely the ambition of most of the 32,763 eager spirits readying to bid at Sotheby's.

As the auction opened the following evening, attendance was surprisingly light. The auction house staff in their black ties and black dresses seemed to overwhelm the relatively thin crowd of bidders. There were half a dozen empty rows at the back. When it came to auction appeal, it seemed that the Duke and Duchess of Windsor were no Jackie Kennedy.

"Three thousand lots and nine days to go," worried one expert, wondering if there were enough Americans left alive who knew or cared who the Duke and Duchess were. "Yesterday somebody asked me if this was all about Fergie paying off her overdraft."

It had been a bad twelve months for Sotheby's. One year earlier, almost to the day, the company had been rocked on its heels by what came to be described, in-house, as the "*Dispatches* affair," referring to the series title of Peter Watson's television programme, and carefully avoiding the name of Watson himself — or the still more dreaded word, "smuggling."

In September, after months of expensive promotion and with every detail of the exhibition in place, the Windsor sale had had to be postponed. And then, in November, Sotheby's had to endure the spectacle of Christie's notching up a record $206.5 million for the sale of the famed Ganz collection of Picassos and modern art, the largest sum ever raised by an auction house from a single-owner collection. At the end of 1997, Christopher Davidge was able to announce with triumph that Christie's had got to number one again, for the second year running — and by a significant margin: $2.017 billion sales turnover, as compared to Sotheby's total of $1.843 billion, representing a market share of 52:48 in Christie's favour. Mr. Charmin was apparently making a habit of life at the top.

But you would never guess any of this from the assurance with which Sotheby's Chief Executive Officer stepped onto the York Avenue rostrum at 6:35 P.M. Dressed in elegant red satin with a choker of oversized natural pearls, Dede Brooks was radiating confidence and relaxation. One of the lessons she had evidently learned in the two years since the Jackie sale was how to inject energy into a room. Her débâcle in the woebegone contemporary sale of May 1996 was the worse for the visible distress that she telegraphed as the bidding failed to go her way. But this was a very different Dede, composed and smiling, determined to make everything fun.

The first lot was a minute, oval, hand-coloured portrait of the baby Prince Edward in his christening robes, dated 1894, and Mrs. Brooks got the bids going at a compulsive clip. Ten, eleven, twelve, thirteen thousand dollars — switching surefootedly from the list of absentee bids in the book in front of her to the banks of her staff taking telephone bids to right and left, and then out into the room, Dede marshaled the price of the little christening picture efficiently up above the $20,000 level.

"$21,000, $22,000, $23,000. At $24,000 then, fair warning! Are we all done?" And tensing her lips in a brief, sharp grimace, Mrs. Brooks brought down the hammer in her left hand. "Sold!"

At $24,000 — $27,600 with buyer's premium — the christening picture had gone for more than twelve times its low estimate, and though the succeeding lots did not quite match that rate, the sale still span along at a sprightly pace: the Prince's confirmation bible, a present from his mother, Queen Mary, $9,775 (low estimate $2,000); a pair of claret jugs, a present from his grandmother, Queen Alexandra, when the Prince went up to

Oxford, $40,240 (low estimate $2,000); Cecil Beaton's 1937 wedding album of photographs, with further studies of the couple on their first wedding anniversary, $32,200 (low estimate $8,000).

There was applause for the Beaton album, but it was nothing to the reception accorded, two lots later, to a small, white, ribbon-tied box inscribed in the Duchess's handwriting: "A piece of our wedding cake, WE," with the date of their elaborate but lonely wedding in exile, at the Château de Candé, June 3, 1937. The bidding for this lot was lively, and largely among bidders in the room, with the pace set by a neat, young, Asian couple who held up their paddle and kept holding it resolutely until the white box was theirs for $26,000 ($29,900 with buyer's premium). They turned out to be two Americans, Mr. and Mrs. Benjamin Yim, who had seen the cake in the catalogue, and had flown together from San Francisco to purchase it.

"It is so surreal," said Mr. Yim afterwards, revealing that he and his wife, Amanda, were collectors of surrealist art. "Man Ray once exhibited what he called 'An Object Meant to Be Destroyed,' and when we looked at the cake it appealed to us as 'An Object Never Meant to Be Eaten.' Maybe there is nothing in the box. Who knows? We are not going to untie the ribbon. Something like this should remain a mystery."

The Yims' interesting line of thinking was wasted on the thrusting crowd of cameras, lights, and microphones which besieged them at the back of the room.

"Isn't that an obscene amount of money to spend?" called out one voice — which sounded, inevitably, English.

Mr. Yim was unfazed.

"It is a lovely object," he replied. "It's like a time capsule. There are more than 40,000 objects in the sale, and less than ten relate to their wedding day. For us it is a piece of history."

The media evidently agreed. Next day, the $29,900 piece of wedding cake was all over the front pages. The lead item in the

breakfast TV bulletins, the cake would turn out to be the lot
that made the whole sale, fixing the auction in the public imagination. *Seinfeld* rang up to see if they could put it into an
upcoming episode: Jerry would buy a piece of wedding cake
at Sotheby's and leave it in the fridge; then Elaine would come
over late at night and open the fridge door, starving hungry. . . .

"It's like the cigar box in the Jackie sale," said one member of
Client Advisory. "Before that, whenever I phoned somebody
and had to leave my name with a receptionist or the secretary, I
always had to spell 'Sotheby's.' 'Oh,' they'd say, '*That's* how you
spell it.' After the Jackie sale, I never had to spell it again."

Two days later, Dede Brooks was sitting in her small but airy office overlooking York Avenue.

"It's not easy being Queen" read a needlepoint pillow which
she hastened to cover up when a visitor spotted it on her sofa.
Her neatly proportioned desk was purchased from a low-budget
York Avenue Arcade sale for a couple of thousand dollars, and
on the wall behind it hung a handsome Picasso left over from a
previous sale — sold on the night, she hastened to explain, and
not bought in. The new owner was happy for it to hang there,
pending reframing.

Christie's had just disclosed figures showing that its number
one position in sales turnover had, for the second year, been
achieved at the expense of profits. $173 million ahead of
Sotheby's in sales, Christie's should have been $20 million or so
ahead in profit. In fact, they lagged $18 million behind.

Mrs. Brooks avoided detailed comment on her rival's finances.

"I know why *we* are profitable," she said, "but I don't understand why they are not."

Market analysts have been less reticent, pointing to Christie's printing division, which has involved continuous reinvestment to keep abreast of technology, while Sotheby's have shopped their catalogues around to get the best price. Christie's appear to have spent much more on marketing — and then there is the cost of New York real estate. In 1999 Sotheby's will be exercising an option to purchase their York Avenue building outright for $11 million, while Christie's are committed to paying more than that each year for the rent and conversion costs on the new premises to which they will be moving in Rockefeller Center. The People's Palace has turned out to be a bargain.

Since losing the number one ranking in sales, Mrs. Brooks has got in the habit of saying it is profits that matter — and the stock market seems to agree with her. On the opening day of the Windsor sale, the financial pages showed Sotheby's valued by investors at $1.152 billion, as compared to Christie's at approximately $707 million. The valuation is calculated by multiplying the number of shares in each company by the price of each share that day, and the $445 million difference represents the market's judgement on which company is the real number one.

"What matters most to me," said Mrs. Brooks, "is the heart of the business — the people who make it happen. Back in the eighties, John Marion, Jim Lally, and I had to ask several hundred people to leave, and I vowed we would never have to do that again. We have run New York so we have never had to ask good people to leave, even in the toughest days. I am proud of our profits. But I am also proud that our compensation to our staff is significantly higher, on average, than that of Christie's."

On the subject of money, is Mrs. Brooks entirely happy with the salesroom atmosphere that is inducing a large number of novice buyers to pay out far more for celebrity items than they can ever hope to recoup? What chance, for example, do Mr. and Mrs. Yim have of turning a profit on their $29,000 investment in wedding cake?

"Your first reason for buying," said Mrs. Brooks, "must be for the love of the object. That is the advice we always give to our clients. People should be buying to *own*. If they are buying to re-sell, then they should be dealers — and they should take the advice of dealers. Art can certainly be a profitable investment. We demonstrate that regularly with the great collections that we sell. But the successful collector buys with both the heart and the head."

The Duke of Windsor wrote the book on clothes — *A Family Album,* a meticulous catalogue, published in 1960, in which he recorded almost everything he wore in his life and why: "Few of my father's clothes were of any use to me at his death. Not only were they out of fashion, but they did not fit me. I did, how-ever, take . . . a Rothesay Hunting tartan suit, which he used to wear for tea after shooting. I had it altered to fit me, substituting zip flies, which would have horrified my father, for the buttons. It still contains in the pocket a tab bearing my father's name — H.R.H. The Duke of York — and the date, 1897."

In the course of his life, the Duke of Windsor popular-ised tweeds, tartans, co-respondent shoes, flat caps (hitherto a working-class adornment), baggy plus-fours, his own Prince of Wales check, and his own tie-knot — though his wardrobe re-veals that his original version of the bulky Windsor knot was not the product of elaborate twistings and tyings. It came from the specially thick stuffing which he had inserted into all his ties. The Duke had his jackets made in London, but felt that Amer-ican tailors cut a better pair of trousers. So whenever he com-missioned a suit, half the cloth was sent to New York. The Duchess called it "pants across the sea."

In terms of social history, Session 16, The Duke of Windsor's Wardrobe, had a claim to being a high spot in Sotheby's mara-thon sale of February 1998. In terms of privacy invasion, it ranked as something of a low. The opening page of the catalogue listed the Duke's personal statistics, including his inside leg: twenty-nine inches.

"Dressing right or left?" wondered one of the bidders gathered at York Avenue on a grey Manhattan afternoon.

The irreverence seemed the greater for the presence of the clothes themselves, set out on a little army of Duke-sized dummies on the stage to the right of the rostrum. It was costume night in Gatsbyland — a yachting suit, a golfing suit, a safari suit, several evening outfits, a heavy, dark blue overcoat with astrakhan collar, a pair of lederhosen, a grey Tyrolean suit with green velvet trimmings, numerous kilts and sporrans, the morning coat and trousers in which he got married, and the tartan suit worn by two kings, a garish red, white, and green creation with its button flies converted to zippers.

"My father's tartan suit," the Duke wrote proudly in his book, "began to influence fashions. . . . One of our guests mentioned the fact to a friend in the men's fashion trade, who immediately cabled the news to America. Within a few months, tartan had become a popular material for every sort of masculine garment, from dinner jackets and cummerbunds, to swimming trunks and beach shorts."

The ghostly cluster of mannequins waited by the rostrum, listening to the bids that would decide who they would go home with. Rumour had it that Ralph Lauren would be here this afternoon, but if he was buying any of these outfits that helped inspire his style, he must have been doing it by telephone. A British costume museum made a bid for the historic wedding outfit but found itself outgunned by the telephoned bids of a menswear designer from Italy.

"A good suit is so expensive these days," said David Redden from the auction box.

But wait a minute, who is that sitting in the second row, boldly offering bids for the suit of the two kings?

A tall, young, handsome, swarthy fellow, with designer stubble and barrel chest, Jimmy Rodriguez looks like an outfielder for the Yankees, a big hitter if ever there was one. But he is a different sort of star of the Bronx. Jimmy Rodriguez is the Prince of Salsa. He would not dare to call himself King, for there are already two monarchs of that undulating, hip-hugging dance — Tito Nieves and Tito Puente, an immortal pair whose silver satin suits hang proudly on the wall of Jimmy's Bronx Cafe, ten thousand square feet of the jumpingest salsa in the whole of New York.

Jimmy is syndicating his restaurant. He is opening a branch in Harlem, and they want him in Paris, France. He had already bought the lederhosen and the Tyrolean suit. But it was the suit worn by two kings that the Prince of Salsa really wanted, and he managed to secure it as evening closed in, against remarkably little opposition: $7,000 ($8,050 with buyer's premium).

Jimmy could hardly believe his luck.

"I thought I couldn't touch it," he said, "not for $30,000 or $40,000."

Jimmy's Bronx Cafe is scarcely in need of additional attractions. Thousands flock to the nightclub, a former Oldsmobile dealership beside the Major Deegan Expressway, to dance and sweat away the pounds every night. But Jimmy knows exactly what he is doing with his new acquisition.

"It's going on the wall there," he said. "Right in the middle. Where else does it belong? Between the kings of Salsa — the kings of England."

A. Alfred Taubman was in philosophical mood.

"How did Churchill put it?" he asked. " 'We shape our buildings, and thereafter they shape us.' "

The mallmeister was relishing the view from the thirty-eighth floor of his elegant Fifth Avenue office tower, which once seemed a white elephant but had since become spectacularly good.

"This building," he said proudly, "is now the most sought after in New York. If you invest long enough in value, the value will pay off in the end."

Mr. Taubman's focus this morning, however, was on the other side of town, on the former camera depository at York Avenue and Seventy-second, where Sotheby's were still hard at work auctioning the goods of the Duke and Duchess of Windsor, and where major plans for expansion were about to be announced.

"Look at these drawings," he said, laying out a pile of blueprints on his desk. Even as Sotheby's were exercising their option to become the outright owner of their York Avenue headquarters, Al Taubman was drawing up plans to build six new floors on the top of the existing four and create an art merchandise marketplace unlike any other in the world.

"At present," he explained, "we handle each object that passes through Sotheby's a minimum of eight times. When furniture comes in, for example, it is catalogued, then goes up to our warehouse in Harlem — and that is just the start. What happens if an expert wants to show a client something really nice that is coming up in several months' time? How does he display the lots that we have bought in and are offering for private treaty sale? When we have expanded to the full ten floors, all our storage will come into the building, and then each expert will operate surrounded by the entirety of their stock."

At the time of writing the rebuilding is imminent and, if completed on time, the six new storeys will be open before the end of 1999.

Chairman Al ran his finger over the blueprints to point out the high-speed lifts for trucks that will unload directly into the upper floors, and the escalators in the glass-clad front of the building which will take clients up through a succession of "agoras," or forums. Since this is an art auction house, "shopping floor" would be too banal a word. Dede Brooks has plans for ongoing tag sales, where the price on everything will be reduced by, say, 2 percent every day in a running Dutch auction. Snap it up now, or wait till it is cheaper tomorrow — but you may find you have left it too late. . . .

Taubman unrolled the artist's impression of this merry temple of commerce — light and playful, with curved glass surfaces that give the impression of waves.

"We will change the way that auctioneering is done," he said happily, the dyslexic lad from Pontiac bringing the 400,000 square feet of floorspace to life as he described the flow of people, goods, and money across the plan. There will be large auction rooms, small auction rooms, and skyboxes, of course. The private treaty area, the inner sanctum which dealers call "the killing room," will be particularly secluded and luxurious. There will be classrooms for the education programme, and restoration workshops where you can select your own upholstery. The real estate division will move in, so you can pick yourself a house. There will be safe storage for your paintings so you can holiday with a tranquil mind — a staff gym, a staff café, and elegant food and drink facilities dotted everywhere for clients. It brings Sotheby's 253 years of history full circle — from the Exeter Exchange to the York Avenue lifestyle auction-mall.

"People are always asking," said Kevin Bousquette, Dede Brooks's clean-cut number two, "whether Al is planning to sell out — whether he wants to be boss of Sotheby's in the year 2000. I got the answer at the last board meeting. There was the Chairman personally carrying the model of the new building into the room."

It is Session 18 of the Windsor sale — Friday, February 27, 1998. Dede Brooks is knocking down the final lots, and in the buyers' rush to go home with something, the bidding on some items is taking on a tinge of folly. A pair of brass buttons, adapted for use as one cuff link, gets bid up fiercely to $2,587.

"Just the thing," remarks Windsor chronicler Hugo Vickers, "for a one-armed man."

The nine-day sale has been a personal triumph for Dede Brooks. Fears that demand would peter out midway have proved unfounded. In fact, the sale has gained momentum, with fresh bids flooding in every day, and much of the credit for that goes to Mrs. Brooks's performance in the auction box. Britain's Channel Four, which broadcast an hour live from the auction every day, faxed a request that Dede should take extra sales. Every time she was on screen, the viewing figures soared.

A decade and a half after the death of Peter Wilson, Sotheby's "face of the place" has become an assertive, blonde-maned, all-American woman, as different from Wilson as it is possible to imagine. In her first days of power, Dede Brooks was unkindly compared by disconcerted English underlings to Sekhmet, the lion-faced goddess over the door in New Bond Street. But if that comparison is made today, it is made with affection, for Dede has become the company mascot. Though she is sharp and forceful in business, her public manner is deceptively unintimidating. She is the auctioneer for the age of the common bidder, and her solidity through the recent hard years of eroded market share and adverse publicity has earned her staff's respect.

In 1998, in any case, it looks as if the hard years might be coming to an end. After some spectacular successes in the January Old Master sales, the $23.3 million raised by the Windsor auction has already put Sotheby's $49 million ahead of Christie's in the annual turnover race — though the pickings for the May sales look thin.

"No dead collectors," explains Michel Strauss, recently appointed Chairman of Impressionist Art worldwide. "It's been such a warm winter. It's all the fault of El Niño."

The Windsors themselves have fared better than many had feared. Often derided for their superficiality, the Duke and Duchess have come to be seen in a kinder light as three thousand lots, grand and petty, have revealed the plucky determination with which the couple fought to maintain their style. The Windsor auction has proved the ideal farewell party, a more appropriate memorial in its glorious extravagance than confining two brilliantly flawed lifetimes to gather dust in a museum. Nine days of hard selling have displayed the auction process at its most organic, recycling these royal effects to provide their new owners with forty thousand different definitions of class.

Round at the collection counter the successful bidders are collecting their lots. It all came from money, and to money it reverts as the credit cards are handed over and the sales invoices signed.

"I'd like it shipped to California," says Mrs. Susan Graf, who has bought a couple of Wallis's handbags and a pair of velvet-bowed evening shoes to lend tone to her clothes store in Healdsburg, Sonoma County. "But I want to touch and feel it all first."

So the goods are brought out to her before being consigned to the bubble wrap. This is where Jimmy Rodriguez came to claim his suit of the two kings, along with 1,095 other buyers, 907 of them North American, 12 Asian, and 177 "Europeans and other." Of these purchasers, 683 had never bought at Sotheby's before.

The curtain has come down and the building has grown suddenly silent, but there is already another production in the wings. As the buyers leave the collection area, they walk past the glass cases that are set out with the lots for next Saturday's Arcade sale: a French painted panel, oil on coarse canvas; fifty lithographs of fish; two Japanese lacquer boxes; a carved figure of a peacock; a framed photograph of the *Titanic*; an American hooked rug.

The recycling continues. The buyers hug their packages, and head their separate ways into the night.

DATES IN THE HISTORY OF SOTHEBY'S

1734 Samuel Baker issues his first book catalogue

1745 Samuel Baker's first auction

1766 James Christie's first auction in Pall Mall

1767 George Leigh becomes a partner in Baker and Leigh

1778 Samuel Baker dies. John Sotheby becomes a partner in Leigh and Sotheby

1818 John Sotheby's son, Samuel, takes a ninety-nine-year lease on 13 Wellington Street

1823 Sale of Napoleon's books by Samuel Sotheby

1842 Samuel Leigh Sotheby takes full control following the death of his father, Samuel Sotheby

1850 Accountant John Wilkinson becomes a partner in S. Leigh Sotheby and John Wilkinson

1861 Death of Samuel Leigh Sotheby

1864 John Wilkinson and Edward Grose Hodge form Sotheby, Wilkinson and Hodge

1896 Tom Hodge becomes a partner in Sotheby, Wilkinson and Hodge

1909 Montague Barlow, Felix Warre, and Geoffrey Hobson take over Sotheby, Wilkinson and Hodge

1913   Sotheby, Wilkinson and Hodge sell the Barrett-Browning letters

1916   Millicent Sowerby becomes the firm's first female expert

1917   Sotheby, Wilkinson and Hodge move to 34 and 35 New Bond Street

1924   Sotheby, Wilkinson and Hodge reorganised as Sotheby & Co

1929   Montague Barlow retires

1936   Peter Wilson starts work at 34 and 35 New Bond Street

1958   Peter Wilson becomes chairman of Sotheby & Co

1964   Sotheby & Co acquires Parke-Bernet in New York

1973   Christie's goes public in London

1977   The Sotheby Parke Bernet Group Limited goes public in Britain

1983   A. Alfred Taubman and his partners acquire Sotheby Parke Bernet, take the firm private, and change the name to Sotheby's

1984   Death of Peter Wilson

1988   Sotheby's goes public again, in America and Britain

SOURCE NOTES

Prologue: Property of a Lady

As with all modern Sotheby's sales, the contents of the Jacqueline Kennedy Onassis auction were set out in a meticulous illustrated catalogue. This listed the high and low estimated prices of each item, and was complemented by the itemised list of prices published after the sale. These prices include the buyer's premium, thus showing what each purchaser paid — but not, of course, what the seller received. I am grateful to Diana Phillips and the Sotheby's Press Office in New York for their particular help during the sale.

Chapter 1

Neil McKendrick pioneered our understanding of eighteenth-century England as the birthplace of the modern consumer society, and this chapter draws on his work and on the subsequent researches of John Brewer and Roy Porter. The paragraphs on Samuel Baker are based almost entirely on the invaluable official history of Sotheby's by Frank Herrmann, as well as on the microfilms of Baker's early catalogues. My interpretation of James Christie leans heavily on the books by Marillier, Colson, and Cooper, and also on Denys Sutton's article "The King of Epithets," in *Apollo* for November 1966.

Chapter 2

Frank Herrmann is the guide once again. His masterful study of the English as collectors is an invaluable collection of firsthand source material. Sotheby's records were destroyed by a disastrous fire in the middle of the nineteenth century and it was more than a century before Herrmann gathered such material as remained into his official history in the 1970s. My thanks to the Hans Tasiemka Archive for the *Strand Magazine* article describing the late-nineteenth-century auction houses.

Chapters 3–6

Montague Barlow's crucial role in transforming Sotheby's identity has never been fully explored, though Nicholas Faith's book *Sold* added fresh perspective to the pioneering work done by Herrmann. The memoirs of Millicent Sowerby provide a lively firsthand glimpse into life in New Bond Street in the early years of transformation. I am grateful to Anthony Hobson for his memories of his father, Geoffrey, which included the details of the investments made by these partners.

Chapters 7–9

With Peter Wilson, the story enters the realm of modern memory. I am grateful to Wilson's sons, Tom and Philip, for their help and also to John Winter. The rumour that Wilson was a Russian spy has enjoyed undeserved life. It is an over-simple interpretation of a subtle and complex character, and I am grateful to Rupert Allason, the writer Nigel West, for providing solid grounds for dismissing it. He recently re-visited Moscow to continue his researches into the KGB's Department 3 and its work in the British sphere, and I asked him if he had located any information on Wilson. He replied, "Not a sausage." The portrait in these chapters of Carmen Gronau was given happy life by her friends Jocelyn Feilding and Adrian Eeles, and the account of the Goldschmidt sale owes much to the memories of Jesse Wolff, who says that he remembers little, but somehow manages to recall a lot. Sir Edward Ford kindly recalled for me his visit with the Queen to New Bond Street, and Clifford Henderson shed helpful light on the backstage politics of these years.

Chapter 10

Wesley Towner's story of Parke-Bernet, *The Elegant Auctioneers,* is enchantingly lighthearted and, with S. M. Behrman's biography of Duveen, shares the award for providing the most enjoyable reading in the research for this book. Tom Norton's illustrated history of Parke-Bernet is also most original and I am grateful to Mr. Norton for sparing time to talk to me. As is evident from the text, Jerry Patterson was an invaluable source of wise and vivid memories of Parke-Bernet's final years, as was Peregrine Pollen from his different perspective. Anthony Hobson profoundly disagreed with the Parke-Bernet takeover, but recalled the incident for me with dispassionate accuracy.

Chapters 11–12

With the hectic and glorious story of Sotheby's in the sixties, the eyewitnesses multiply. I am grateful to Geraldine Norman for her memories as a most informed outsider, and to the insiders: Richard Came, Elizabeth Chatwin, Neal Davey, Kenelm Digby-Jones, David Ellis-Jones, Fiona Ford, Derek Johns, Lord John Kerr, Marcus Linell, Katherine MacLean, Peter Nahum, David Nash, Patricia and Peregrine Pollen, Howard Ricketts, Rosa and Stephen Somerville, Julian Stock, Michel Strauss, and Nicholas Ward-Jackson.

Chapter 13

The late Robert Woolley kindly granted me several interviews before his death, and I am grateful to Edward Lee Cave for his meticulous memories of

Sotheby Parke Bernet in the 1970s. Peter Spira has written his own memoir of Sotheby's in the years of going public, and he recounted his memories to me with generous effort and hospitality. I am grateful to him for making available the offer document and other material with regard to Sotheby's public flotation, and to Andrew Alers-Hankey for his memories and comments on my account of the years when he had responsibility for the company's financial affairs.

Chapter 14

The takeover period in Sotheby's history has been well covered by two books, Nicholas Faith's *Sold* and Jeffrey Hogrefe's *"Wholly Unacceptable."* I am grateful to both authors for the additional time they made available to help me with my own researches.

Geraldine Norman is the pre-eminent professional on the auction business and on Sotheby's in particular, and she has been most generous with her memories. The late Graham Llewellyn talked frankly about these years, as well as the rest of his career at Sotheby's. My thanks also to Armin Allen, Julian Barran, Anna Maria Edelstein, Simon de Pury, and Julian Thompson.

The portrait of Peter Wilson at Clavary owes much to Christine Chauvin and to Colin Mackay, as well as to Conway Vincent, who kindly showed my friend Nina Drummond around the estate that he has watched over for so many years.

For many general perspectives I am grateful to John Richardson and Brian Sewell, critics and experts extraordinaires.

Chapter 15

I am grateful to Sir Gordon Brunton and to Marshall Cogan, the two principal protagonists in the takeover battle, for sparing time to talk to me. Gordon Brunton kindly allowed me to read and quote from his report of April 1982. Jim Lalley and Julian Thompson, the two chief executives promoted as a consequence of this report, both shared their memories of the tense takeover period. James D. Robinson III told me of the brief involvement of American Express, and I am particularly grateful for the input of Andrew Alers-Hankey who, as financial director following the departure of Peter Spira, executed much of the re-structuring inherited by Alfred Taubman.

My account of the Sevso episode is based on the investigations of Geraldine Norman and Peter Watson, and on my own interviews with Michael Ainslie, Richard Camber, Jo Och, and a number of off-the-record sources.

Chapter 16

In addition to the sources already mentioned, I am grateful to Marjorie Crodell, Ian Dunlop, Michael Heseltine, Anne Horton, Jon King, Belle MacIntyre, David Park, Felix Pryor, Lars Tharp, and Joan Timbers for their memories of Sotheby's in the 1980s.

John Herbert's amusing memories of his years at Christie's contain some very well informed paragraphs on Sotheby's takeover travails in the early eighties, and I am grateful to him for sparing time to supplement these personally.

Chapter 17

I first met Alfred Taubman in 1984, shortly after he had taken over Sotheby's. I was then living in Detroit, and he kindly spared me time to discuss his friend Henry Ford II and the book I was then writing about the Fords, Detroit, and the motor industry. In 1996, he was similarly generous in granting me a long and intensive interview to talk about Sotheby's. My thanks to Christopher Tennyson for his help in arranging both interviews.

I am most grateful to my friend Jim Nicholson and his family for their hospitality during the time I spent in Detroit in the summer of 1995 and would also like to thank for their help: Laura Berman, Billy Chapin, Keith Crain, Charlie and Peggy Davies, Larry Deitch, Paul Dorman, Max Fisher, Charlotte Ford, Jean Guerke, Joseph Hudson III, Harold Kaufman, Robert Larson, Marj Levin, Richard Manoogian, Madeleine Phillips, Sam Sachs III, Allan Schlumberger, Alan E. Schwarz, Peter Spivak, Jack Tarpley, and Stanley Winkelman.

David Metcalfe seems to be an invaluable source on almost every book I write — and particularly so on this one.

Chapter 18–19

In addition to the sources already mentioned I should like to thank Bill Acquavella, Lord Gowrie, Tessa Helfet, Hugh Hildesley, Dr. Stephen Roe, James Stourton, and Paul Whitfield for their memories of the 1980s and early nineties, and Marc Blondeau for his memories of Peter Wilson, particularly of the final years.

Chapter 20

David Nash has been a wry and knowledgeable source on the entire story from the 1960s onwards — and on *Irises,* in particular. My thanks to John Whitney Payson for telling me about his thoughts and experiences when selling the picture, and to Billy Keating and Angela Neville for their account of buying it on behalf of Alan Bond. Calvin Tomkins wrote a lengthy and revealing account of the sale of *Irises* for *The New Yorker,* April 4, 1988.

Chapter 21

For my sources on Sevso, see the notes for Chapter 15.

Chapter 22

It is to the credit of Christopher Tennyson, Vice President in charge of Public Affairs for the Taubman Company, that there are virtually no newspaper or magazine accounts of the financial difficulties of the late eighties and early nineties from which Alfred Taubman has so solidly re-emerged. My thanks to the Detroit sources listed in the notes for Chapter 17 and to a number of informants who prefer to remain off-the-record.

Chapter 23

This chapter is based considerably on an article commissioned by *Vanity Fair* in the summer of 1995, and I am grateful to Condé Nast for permission to re-use the material here. My thanks for their help to Graydon Carter and Wayne Lawson at *Vanity Fair,* and to Tim Bathurst, Desmond Corcoran, Kathy Doyle, Larry Dumouchelle, Wendell Garrett, Thomas Gibson, George Goldner, Richard Gray, Geza von Hapsburg, Johnny van Haeften, James Hill, Rita Hillman, Leslie Hindman, Philip Hook, Cyril Humphris, David McConnell Mason, James Miller, Richard Oldenburg, Rick Wolfe, Henry Wyndham, and William D. Zabel.

With regard to Christie's, my thanks to their official spokespersons Taggarty Patrick in New York and Susan Adams and Victoria Coode in London. All other Christie's sources are off-the-record.

Chapter 24

In addition to the sources mentioned in the notes for previous chapters, my thanks to John Block, Christophe Graf Douglas, Betsy Garrett, Lesley Keno, Fred Leighton, Lucy Mitchell-Innes, David Redden, and Heinrich von Spreti.

The original British edition of Peter Watson's well-documented book, since corrected in its American edition following the legal representations from Sotheby's, is the principal source on his sting and on the documents stolen by James Hodges, together with some off-the-record sources.

Epilogue: Royal Effects

At Sotheby's my thanks to Joseph Friedman, prime mover of the Windsor sale, to Mallory Hathaway, Queen of Client Advisory, and to David Redden, seldom at a loss for a wise word. Kevin Bousquette provided invaluable understanding of the financial realities of the auction business.

For their help in my researching of the complicated history of the Windsor possessions, I am grateful to Michael Bloch, Kenneth Rose, Hugo Vickers, Nicholas Rayner, Michael Cole, and Mohamed al-Fayed. I regret not having room to describe Nicholas Rayner's brilliant handling of the sale of the Windsor jewels in 1987, nor to pay tribute to the achievement of the extraordinary Mr. al-Fayed. He went back on his promises to create a permanent Windsor memorial, but I do not blame him. Before he handed everything over to Sotheby's, he had the entire collection restored, catalogued, and recorded to create an archive of immense value to historians.

My thanks to Richard Turley and Jimmy Rodriguez for their hospitality in the Bronx — and to my mother for taping the long hours of Channel 4 television coverage so I could relive the sale all over again.

The author would also like to express his thanks to Warren Adelson, Philip Astley-Jones, Graham Billington, Tom Bower, Brenda Callaway, Elizabeth Capon, Lou Gartner, Richard Falkiner, Richard Gray, James Hill, Rita Hillman, Geza von Hapsburg, Michael Hooper at Teather and Greenwood, Richard Keresey, Jane McAusland, Duncan MacLaren, Tobias Meyer, David Ober, Brian Pilkington, Dr. Stephen Roe, Hugh Stevenson, James Stourton, Wallace Walden, Jurg Wille, and Rainer Zietz.

ACKNOWLEDGEMENTS

By their own admission, Sotheby's are appallingly deficient in documentary material on their history. Their records were destroyed by fire in the nineteenth century, and it was something of a miracle that Frank Herrmann, their official historian, was able to gather so much material for his book, *Sotheby's: Portrait of an Auction House,* published in 1980. This must stand as the definitive record, and my own contribution is very much a personal impression, taking its starting point from his researches.

The modern Sotheby's has been the principal source of much of my material, including many of the illustrations, and my first thanks must go to Diana Phillips, Senior Vice-President Corporate Affairs, who responded to my request for assistance in 1995 with cautious professionalism and who has since proved to be unfailingly open and honest. Her British colleagues Luke Rittner and Chris Proudlove have taken their lead from her, and I would also like to thank Matthew Weigman and all the other members of the press departments in London and New York. None of their help would have been available without the willingness of Dede Brooks to let me roam and ask questions freely about the work and personalities of the company. Mrs. Brooks may have come to regret her cooperation, but her grace never faltered.

At other auction houses, I am grateful for the help and objective opinions of Nicholas Bonham, Kathy Doyle, Larry Dumouchelle, Leslie Hindman, Christopher Weston, and a number of off-the-record sources at Christie's. I should like to thank Susan Adams, Virginia Coode, Taggarty Patrick, and the other members of Christie's press offices for their prompt and professional help.

Among dealers, it was my friends Barry Cronan and Sandra Cronan who originally encouraged me and opened many doors. My thanks to Susanna Allen and Martin Chopland for their hospitality and many insights, as well as to Billy Beadleston, who suggested enough avenues of enquiry for a dozen books. My thanks also for interviews, help, and advice to the Aletto brothers, John Couper, James Danziger, Edward Herman, David Nash, and Tamara Thomas. William Drummond is the dealer I have known longest of all, and his idiosyncratic observations have been a constant delight.

I spent less time than I would have liked among the fraternity of saleroom correspondents. As hacks go, they make up a civilised and stimulating band, and this hack would like to express particular gratitude to Godfrey Barker, Anne E. Berman, Laura Berman, Dorothy Gelatt, Jeffrey Hogrefe, Neil Letson, Geraldine Norman, Alexandra Peers, Brian Sewell, Laura Stewart, Judd Tully, and Donald Wintersgill.

The Wilson brothers, Philip and Tom, courteously helped me to research the life of their father, and I am particularly grateful to Philip Wilson for his thorough and forthright thoughts. He feels strongly that I have been unfair to his father in several respects, and while I stand by my own verdict, I must make clear that it is by no means his.

I am grateful to Lili Agee for her exuberant and devoted help with the book, and many other aspects of my work in America. Deborah Dalton not only typed the first draft of the manuscript with exemplary efficiency, but strained her hearing for long hours piecing together the transcripts of nearly a hundred interviews, while also travelling to England and making it possible for me to meet some very tight deadlines. My thanks to Eunice Ridenauer for her typing. Such depth and wisdom as the book possesses would not have been possible without Nina Drummond, who gave so generously of her time and thought and contacts in the art world. It was on her recommendation that many of my most informed sources agreed to share their expertise and experiences. My thanks too for their help to my friends Wendy Alexander, Louise Armour, Tom Baldwin, Arthur Braunstein, Joy Briggs, Duncan Scott Campbell, David Cannadine, Danny Danziger, Ralph Destino, Dominick Dunne, Joe Feinberg, Caroline Graham, Gerald Grant, Fergus Greer, Audrey and Martin Gruss, Nicholas Haslam, Kitty Kelley, Earle Mack, Christopher Moorsom, Bonnie Morris, Jean-Jacques Naudet, Jim Nicholson, Robert Perlman, Simon Schama, Piers Secunda, Forrest and Kimberly Smith, Willie Surtees, Edda Tasiemka, Virginia Valentine, Richard Waterman, Ken White, Jacqueline Williams, and Amanda Willis.

Vincent Page has researched and recorded a selection of pictures that has brought the subject to life, and I am grateful to Fred van Deelen for his imaginative map of London. On the editorial side, my thanks to David Coen for his painless copy editing, and particularly to Heather Kilpatrick of Little, Brown, New York, for advice which went far beyond her legal remit. It has been a pleasure to work again with Philippa Harrison, the inspiration of Little, Brown, London, to get to know Alan Samson, and to renew acquaintance with the warmth and wisdom of Michael Shaw at Curtis Brown.

This book was the idea of my wife, Sandi, who first saw the story with typical insight, and has helped me pursue it with unfailing love and support. My thanks, as ever, to Sasha, Scarlett, and Bruno, my three patient children, for their encouragement of my work, and their tolerance of the inconvenience it continues to cause them.

Originally inspired by my wife, this book owes its subsequent existence to the faith and vision of Bill Phillips, who has now edited and fired my best work for more than fifteen years. His energy is unquenchable, his encouragement and loyalty unflagging. His greatest gift is his rigorous instinct for meaning, which is the heart and spirit of good writing. This book is dedicated to him.

Robert Lacey. March 10, 1998.

SELECTED BIBLIOGRAPHY

Books

Alexander, Paul. *Death and Disaster.* New York: Villard Books, 1994.

Alsop, Joseph. *The Rare Art Traditions.* London: Thames & Hudson, 1982.

Behrman, S. N. *Duveen.* New York: Random House, 1952.

Boyford, David, and Jo Kirby and John Leighton and Roy Ashley. *Art in the Making: Impressionism.* London: Yale University Press, 1990.

Brewer, John. *The Pleasures of the Imagination.* London: HarperCollins, 1997.

Brewer, John, and Roy Porter. *Consumption and the World of Goods.* London & New York: Routledge, 1993.

Brigstocke, Hugh. *William Buchanan and the Nineteenth Century Art Trade.* London: Published privately by The Paul Mellon Centre for Studies in British Art, 1982.

Chatwin, Bruce. *What Am I Doing Here.* London: Jonathan Cape, 1989.

Colson, Percy. *A Story of Christie's.* London: Sampson Low, 1950.

Cooper, Jeremy. *Under the Hammer.* London: Constable, 1977.

Faith, Nicholas. *Sold: The Revolution in the Art Market.* London: Hamish Hamilton, 1985.

Haden-Guest, Anthony. *True Colors.* New York: Atlantic Monthly Press, 1996.

Hamilton, Charles. *Auction Madness.* New York: Everest House, 1981.

Havemeyer, Louisine W. *Sixteen to Sixty: Memories of a Collector.* New York: Stein & Tinterow, Ursus Press, 1993.

Herbert, John. *Inside Christie's.* London: Hodder & Stoughton, 1990.

Herrmann, Frank. *Sotheby's: Portrait of an Auction House.* New York: W. W. Norton & Co., 1981.

Herrmann, Frank. *The English as Collectors: A Documented Chrestomathy.* London: Chatto & Windus, 1972.

Hildesley, Hugh. *The Complete Guide to Buying and Selling at Auction.* New York: W. W. Norton, 1997.

Hogrefe, *"Wholly Unacceptable": The Bitter Battle for Sotheby's.* New York: Morrow, 1986

Hughes, Robert. *Nothing If Not Critical.* London & New York: Collin Harvill, 1990.

Hyde, H. Montgomery. *Secret Intelligence Agent.* London: Constable, 1982.

Irving, Clifford. *Fake.* New York: McGraw, 1969.

Keen, Geraldine. *The Sale of Works of Art.* London: Thomas Nelson, 1971.

Lowenthal, David. *The Heritage Crusade and the Spoils of History.* London: Viking, 1997.

Marion, John. *The Best of Everything.* New York: Simon and Schuster, 1989.

Marillier, H. C. *Christie's 1766–1925.* London: Constable, 1926.

McKendrick, Neil. *Birth of a Consumer Society.* Bloomington: Indiana University Press, 1982.

Muensterberger, Werner. *Collecting: An Unruly Passion: Psychological Perspectives.* Princeton, N.J.: Princeton University Press, 1993.

Nicholas, Lyn. *The Rape of Europa.* New York: Knopf, 1994.

Norton, Thomas. *100 Years of Collecting in America: The Story of Sotheby Parke Bernet.* New York: Abrams, 1984.

Porter, Roy. *London: A Social History.* London: Penguin, 1996.

Reitlinger, Gerald. *The Economics of Taste.* London: Barrie & Jenkins, 1960.

Rheims, Maurice. *The Glorious Obsession.* New York: St. Martin's Press, 1980.

Sowerby, Emily Millicent. *Rare People and Rare Books.* London: Constable, 1967.

Spira, Peter. *Ladders and Snakes.* London: Private publication, 1997.

Towner, Wesley. *The Elegant Auctioneers.* New York: Hill & Wang, 1970.

Watson, Peter. *From Manet to Manhattan.* New York: Random House, 1992.

———. *Sotheby's: Inside Story.* London: Bloomsbury, 1997.

————— . *Sotheby's: The Inside Story.* Revised version of London edition, New York: Random House, 1998.

West, Nigel, with Juan Pujol. *Garbo.* London: Weidenfeld & Nicolson, 1985.

Wilson, Barbara. *Dear Youth.* London: Macmillan, 1937.

————. *The House of Memories.* London: William Heinemann, 1929.

Wraight, Robert. *The Art Game.* New York: Simon & Schuster, 1966.

Catalogues

Munby, A. N. L. (General Editor). *Sales Catalogues of Libraries of Eminent Persons (6 volumes).* London: Mansell with Sotheby Parke Bernet Publications, 1972.

Sotheby & Co. *Catalogues of Sales, 1734–1980.* 376 reels, Ann Arbor, Michigan: Xerox University Microfilms, 1972–1980.

Newspapers and Magazines

The showy yet secretive art market does not have a formal structure like the stock market. Its identity is defined by the reporting of the often eccentric and congenitally competitive band of saleroom correspondents who work for the British and American broadsheets and for a number of specialist art magazines. I have relied particularly upon: *Apollo, Art & Antiques, Art & Auction, Art Journal, ARTnews, Artnewsletter, The Art Newspaper, Barrons, Burlington, Connoisseur, Daily Telegraph, Evening Standard, Financial Times, Guardian, Independent, Illustrated London News, International Herald Tribune, Journal of Art, Maine Antiques Digest, The New Yorker, New York Times, Observer, Times* (London), *Vanity Fair, Wall Street Journal, Washington Post.*

INDEX

Lightning Source UK Ltd.
Milton Keynes UK
UKOW05f1533050913

216569UK00001B/4/P

9 780751 523621